Christopher Somerville is the author of *Twelve Literary Walks* and presenter of the associated radio series. He is a contributor to BBC Radio 4's 'Bookshelf' and the author of several other walking books. Formerly a teacher, he is now a full-time writer.

Coastal Walks in England and Wales

CHRISTOPHER SOMERVILLE

With maps specially prepared
by the Ordnance Survey

GRAFTON BOOKS
A Division of the Collins Publishing Group

LONDON GLASGOW
TORONTO SYDNEY AUCKLAND

Grafton Books
A Division of the Collins Publishing Group
8 Grafton Street, London W1X 3LA

Published by Grafton Books 1988

British Library Cataloguing in Publication Data

Somerville, Christopher
    Coastal walks in England and Wales.
    1. Walking—England—Guide-books
    2. Coasts—England—Guide-books
    3. England—Description and travel—
    1971–   —Guide-books
    I. Title
    796.5'1'0942   DA650

ISBN 0-246-13029-6

Printed in Great Britain by
Hartnolls Ltd, Bodmin, Cornwall

Maps reproduced from the Ordnance Survey maps with
the permission of the Controller of Her Majesty's
Stationery Office, Crown copyright reserved.

To my Godchildren – Andrew, Caroline, Cathy, Christian, Dominic, Georgina and Corrina – hoping that they will enjoy walking these coasts one day.

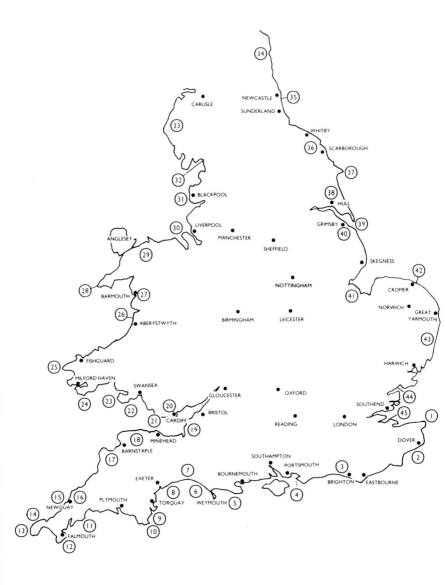

㉞ CARLISLE

NEWCASTLE ㉟
SUNDERLAND

㉝

WHITBY
㉜ ㊱ SCARBOROUGH
㉛ BLACKPOOL ㊲
㉚ LIVERPOOL ㊳ HULL
ANGLESEY MANCHESTER GRIMSBY ㊴
㉙ SHEFFIELD ㊵
SKEGNESS
㉘ BARMOUTH ㉗ NOTTINGHAM ㊷
㉖ ABERYSTWYTH BIRMINGHAM LEICESTER CROMER
NORWICH GREAT
YARMOUTH
㉕ FISHGUARD ㊸
MILFORD HAVEN HARWICH
SWANSEA
㉔ ㉓ ㉒ ㉑ ㉒⁰ GLOUCESTER OXFORD SOUTHEND ㊹
CARDIFF BRISTOL ㊺ ①
㊱⁹ READING LONDON
㊲⁸ MINEHEAD DOVER
BARNSTAPLE ②
㊲⁷ SOUTHAMPTON
⑦ PORTSMOUTH ③
EXETER BOURNEMOUTH BRIGHTON EASTBOURNE
⑮ ⑯ PLYMOUTH ⑧ ⑥ ④
⑭ NEWQUAY TORQUAY WEYMOUTH ⑤
⑬ ⑪ ⑨
FALMOUTH ⑩
⑫

Contents

Preface   ix

Acknowledgements   xi

Note on Using This Book   xii

 1   Margate to Broadstairs   1
 2   Folkestone to Dover   7
 3   Brighton: Palace Pier and the Pavilion to Kemp Town   13
 4   Chichester Harbour: East Head to West Itchenor   20
 5   St Alban's Head and the cliffs of Purbeck   27
 6   Abbotsbury and the shore of Chesil Bank   33
 7   Lyme Regis to the Axe via the Undercliff   40
 8   Sidmouth to Weston Mouth and Salcombe Regis   45
 9   Little Dartmouth Farm to Blackstone Point and   50
      Dartmouth
10   Start Point and Prawle Point   54
11   Portloe and Nare Head   61
12   Around the Lizard   67
13   Sennen to Land's End and Nanjizal   73
14   Zennor and Gurnard's Head   79
15   The lost land of Penhale Sands   84
16   Rock to St Enodoc's and Polzeath   89
17   Clovelly to Mouth Mills and Brownsham Farm   95
18   Lynmouth and Lynton to the Valley of Rocks   101
19   Around Brean Down   107
20   Penarth to Sully Island   112
21   Col-huw Beach to Tresilian and Llantwit Major   117
22   Oxwich to Port-Eynon Point   122
23   Rhosili to Worms Head   126
24   St Govan's Head and the Chapel in the cliffs   130
25   St David's Head   135
26   Aberystwyth to Borth   139
27   Fairbourne to Barmouth   144

28	Above the Gate of Paradise: Braich y Pwll, overlooking Bardsey Island	149
29	Llanfairfechan to Bangor	154
30	Hoylake to New Brighton by Mockbeggar Wharf	159
31	Blackpool's Golden Mile	166
32	Crossing the Sands of Morecambe Bay	172
33	Whitehaven to St Bees	177
34	Craster to Dunstanburgh Castle	184
35	Marsden Bay and Whitburn	189
36	Robin Hood's Bay to Ravenscar	194
37	Flamborough Head	201
38	Skipsea Sands to Barmston Sands	206
39	Spurn Head	210
40	Humberston Fitties to Tetney Lock	215
41	Birds, bombs and big views – the sea-walls of Gedney Drove End	220
42	Cromer to Sidestrand through Poppyland	225
43	Walberswick to Dunwich	232
44	Mersea Island	239
45	Secret Sheppey: Shell Ness and Harty Marshes	246
	Index	253

Preface

We *do* like to be beside the seaside – probably more than anywhere else, given the choice. There's a special magic in the thought of those windy Welsh clifftops with their superb high-level views, the golden crescent of a Cornish beach lined with caves and rock pools, the enormous skies over the lonely East Anglian salt-marshes swirling with clouds of ducks and geese. The appeal of our coastline seems to be ingrained into us from birth – not surprisingly, considering our seafaring history and the fact that the sea is little more than two hours' drive from anywhere in Britain.

I hope this book will tempt you away from the beach and funfair for a few hours to ramble around those cliffs, sands and salt-marshes. You'll discover just why our coastline is reckoned to be one of the most varied in the world, and why the National Trust and other conservation bodies put so much effort and money into protecting it from pollution, erosion and over-usage. Among the 2000 miles of coastline in England and Wales are views that will make your heart sing, while others may shock you. It's a working environment as well as a leisure one, and not all seaside scenes are the stuff of picture postcards.

Most of these walks are 'round' ones, with a chance on the way back to visit historic houses, churches, castles and forgotten corners of the countryside, or just to have a drink in a welcoming pub where the children can play in the garden. Others take you back to your starting point by such diverse transport as miniature railways or a Blackpool tram. The longer walks will give your legs a good challenge, while on the shortest you won't even need to change out of your flip-flops. It's as well to remember, however, that in places many of the cliff-paths run only inches away from an unfenced drop of several hundred feet; so if your children or your dog scorn a straight line, it might be a good idea to leave them on the beach with a kind friend while you go exploring the cliffs; otherwise they may end up in the sea rather more quickly than they bargained for – and you may go with them.

I travelled to many different places along the coastline of England and Wales while walking and writing this book. Each had its own individual flavour, and each left a vivid memory with me. Running an inward eye around the outline of my wanderings and remembering the thrill of crossing the vast saucer of Morecambe Sands against the tide, lazing through the sunny jungle of the Undercliff at Lyme Regis, watching a cormorant on Marsden Rock gobbling a fish with his head thrown back, my only regret is that the adventure had to come to an end.

Reader, have a wonderful time!

Acknowledgements

As usual when writing a book of this kind, I could easily fill another book with the names of all the kind and enthusiastic people who have helped me with their information, notes, personal reminiscences, time and trouble.

I would like particularly to thank J. T. O'Neil, the proprietor of the Study Centre at Hoylake, who sent me a mass of useful information; Bryan Lucas, Wirral's Director of Leisure Services and Tourism, for letting me see a fascinating and very thorough account by John F. Lamb of the sea defences of the North Wirral coast; D. A. Tennant of Long Sutton and Fiona MacNeil of Anglian Water, for information and maps of the sea-walls at Gedney Drove End; Geoff Mallett of the Ramblers' Association (Suffolk Area), who wrote to me about Walberswick and Dunwich; and Betty Corn, who did the same about Aberystwyth.

There's an enormous number of excellent pamphlets, many produced on a shoestring, full of stories and local detail, covering most stretches of the English and Welsh coastline. Those on the Llantwit Major area sent to me by Dennis Watson, the Heritage Coast Warden at Southerndown, and on the South-West Way long-distance footpath sent by Mrs M. Macleod of Kingskerswell in Devon, were especially useful and interesting. The full list of pamphlets I read and learned from numbers several hundred; local libraries will put you on the track of the many associations and rambling groups that produce them. Most can be picked up for a few pence in local bookshops and post offices.

Cedric Robinson, the Morecambe Sands Guide (see Walk No. 32) fired off answers to all my questions while shepherding half a thousand pilgrims safely across the bay – barefoot, too. Philip Holms, the Warden of the Swale National Nature Reserve on the Isle of Sheppey, left his fireside to meet me on the sea-wall in a cutting east wind, and later sent me copious notes of his researches.

I'd also like to thank my wife Jane for taking me to her childhood haunts around West Wittering in Sussex, and Sue and David Pinney and Ursula and Chris Dunne for some rather unusual revelations concerning the effects of visiting Gurnard's Head; also Pat Bray for keeping a cool head while lost in the jungle of my handwriting.

And I mustn't forget the disc-jockey under the helter-skelter on Palace Pier who cheered up a rainy afternoon by asking an easy quiz question and rewarding smartie-boots with a little stick of Brighton rock.

Note on Using This Book

The description of each walk is preceded by the following information: first, the relevant Ordnance Survey map for the walk and, second, the length of the walk. Where the start of a walk is approached by train, the phrase 'railway station to railway station' appears. When a walk ends at a location other than its starting point, and the use of a car has been presumed, the phrase 'one-way journey' is appended. Whenever a walk covers the same ground on its outward and return journeys, the phrase 'there and back' appears; otherwise, for a circular journey covering fresh ground on the return half of the walk, the phrase 'round trip' is used.

1 Margate to Broadstairs

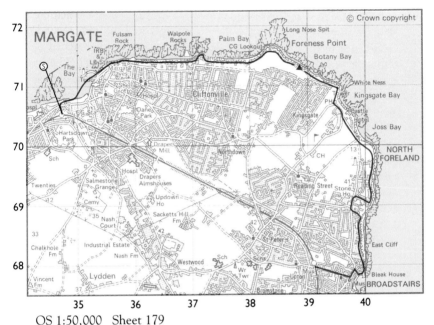

OS 1:50,000   Sheet 179
6 miles, from railway station to railway station

The eastern end of the Isle of Thanet sticks out of North Kent like a bulbous great drinker's nose. Its coastline, warty with bays in the chalk cliffs, commands enormous views all round the flat sea horizon – from Margate, westwards up the estuary of the River Thames and northwards towards the Essex marshes; from the North Foreland, north-east and eastwards into the foot of the North Sea; from Ramsgate, south into the English Channel towards Belgium and France. It was a natural target for day-trippers from London when the railways arrived, but by then the fishing villages around the coast had been catering for visitors for well over a century. When Dr Richard Russell's seawater cure was bringing the first sufferers to Brighthelmstone (later to roar into life as Regency Brighton) in the 1750s, Margate had already become a fashionable place to take a dip from one of the 'bathing machines' recently invented by a Margate man.

1

Before paddle-steamers began plying between London and Margate in 1815, visitors had had to make the journey in sailing hoys, enduring a buffeting from the Thames estuary winds while sheltering under canvas cloaks. It was the steamers and, later on, the railway that brought the trippers to invade the wide curve of sands below the town and pollute Margate's select atmosphere with their coarse manners. Many of the gentry were obliged to remove to Broadstairs.

The seafront at Margate is a minute's walk from the railway station (347705). Standing on the promenade you look out over the Sun Deck Amusement Arcade to the grand and Dutch-looking tall hotels and houses that line the curve of the bay under the cliff. Below them lies the sandy beach, jam-packed on sunny summer days, cradled in the stone arm of the pier that was completed for landing the paddle-steamer passengers in 1815. Turning right, you pass a copper statue of a lifeboat-man in a cork lifebelt and sou'wester gazing out to sea. Margate lifeboat has been working since 1860; her coxswain in 1940 won the DSM for his 'gallantry and determination' in rescuing more than 600 soldiers from Dunkirk while being dive-bombed. The statue is a reminder of the risks that all lifeboatmen volunteer to take, commemorating the disaster in December 1897 that drowned ten members of the crew, including the coxswain and his two sons.

To reach the present lifeboat station you cross the beach below the pier with its splendid blue-and-white clock tower (354713). This building is a replica, put up after the war to replace the Margate Pier and Harbour Company's original of 1812 which was bombed to pieces in 1942. The lifeboat shed stands beyond, looking out to a great box of metal girders stranded several hundred feet out in the water. It's all that remains of a jetty, nearly 400 yards long, whose life from mid-Victorian times was one long saga of storm damage. It had its finest hour during the dark days of the Second World War, when nearly 50,000 Dunkirk soldiers came ashore by way of the jetty. In 1964 the pavilion at the end of what most people by then called the 'pier' was burned down, and in January 1978 a bad storm smashed up the rest and destroyed the lifeboat shed that stood halfway along with a ramp underneath for launching the boat. This metal structure had replaced an earlier wooden one that jutted out into the sea from the end of the stone pier. Built in 1824 to take paddle-steamer passengers, there was a snag in its construction – the

*A cast-iron triton guards the sea-wall above the sands
at Margate, packed with Londoners on summer weekends.*

middle portion sagged so badly that at high tide it was under water. If you
timed your arrival at Margate carelessly, you might end up stranded on
the seaward end of the jetty for several hours, waiting for the tide to go
down, to the infinite amusement of jeering boys on the pier.

The path runs as a concrete promenade just above the sand and
pebbles of the beach and under the low cliffs whose white faces have
fractured into cubes of chalk, each separated from the next by a hairline
crack. Small falls occur almost every day, the white lumps of their rubble
lying on the path. The instability of the cliffs hasn't deterred generations
of holidaymakers from carving their initials into the chalk, or traders
from putting up little cafés, shops and arcades right underneath. You pass
the Winter Gardens with its bars and theatre, and walk below a bridge
over a cleft, beautifully decorated with coloured tiles, to climb steps to
the clifftop path. Here at the seaward edge of Cliftonville stands a row of
fine large red-and-white hotels: the Endcliffe, the Grosvenor Court, the

Grand, the Walpole Bay. The path runs on past the Aquarium and three rusty old cannon pointing out to sea, before making a long curve out on to the chalk promontory of Foreness Point with its new sewage works, a welcome example to the many resorts which still pump their raw waste straight into the sea only a couple of hundred yards from their beaches. Here you can enjoy the view back to the wreck of the jetty off Margate, and on around a wide seascape to the north and east above which swirl spectacular cloud vistas.

The path bends south above Botany Bay to pass a truncated flint tower (395710), built as a folly for the magnificent pile of Kingsgate Castle (397705) which stands in Transylvanian splendour above its bay, the white lantern of the North Foreland lighthouse peeping over the trees beyond. The road dips down past the dignified white Holland House to climb to the castle entrance. Henry Fox, the 1st Lord Holland of Holland House, built Kingsgate Castle in the 1760s, reputedly as his stables. In later years it was bought by Lord Avebury, who extended it and lived there in baronial splendour until his death in 1913. The shaky cliff foundations have been a constant problem throughout the life of the castle; nowadays divided into private residences, it has had to be shored up and underpinned with concrete, and one day will probably end up on the beach below like most of the folly turrets that used to stand on the adjacent headlands.

In January 1857 Kingsgate Bay was the scene of a famous lifeboat rescue. Kingsgate's own lifeboat station had not yet been opened, and when the *Northern Belle* got into difficulties in an easterly gale, the Broadstairs lifeboat, *Mary White*, could not be launched into the teeth of the storm. A team of volunteers dragged the cumbersome *Mary White* up over the cliffs from Broadstairs for two miles into Kingsgate Bay, where there was just enough shelter to get her out to sea to help the stricken ship.

From the castle you walk down the road to a path which runs round the edge of North Foreland, with ploughland the colour of milky coffee running inland up to the lighthouse (399697). The dangers of the Goodwin Sands, a few miles offshore, have necessitated a warning light here since Tudor times, when candles provided the beacon. After a wood-burning replacement had burned down in 1683, the light reverted to a single candle flickering in a lantern at the top of a long pole. This meagre signal lasted ten years, after which coal-fuelled lights took over, burning down and being rebuilt until oil and electricity gave the North Foreland light some permanence.

Large red houses with pinnacles, turrets and steep roofs herald a private estate on the northern outskirts of smug, snug Broadstairs – 'NO parking ... NO picnicking ... NO entry ... NO loitering'. At the end of Cliff Promenade you can loiter inland to turn left along the road (399692), then left again in a couple of hundred yards at a 'Pedestrians Only' sign (398689), down steps through a gully in the cliffs on to East Cliff Promenade just above the beach. Gulls scream along the tideline below the cliffs, whose chalk is lined with thin bands of dark flint. After half a mile, a winding road takes you up on to the clifftop again, with the castellated outline of a historic house just ahead.

The sea had provided Broadstairs people with their living from fishing, shipbuilding and victualling passing ships for centuries before the fine folk began to come here to revitalize their systems with dips in the ocean and blasts of salty air. By far the most famous visitor to the town was Charles Dickens, who regularly spent his holidays at Broadstairs between 1836 and 1850. He took the end house on East Cliff, then surrounded by cornfields and known as The Fort. Nowadays called Bleak House (400680), it contains museums of the smuggling and seafaring history of Broadstairs as well as one documenting Dickens's connection with the town. Here he completed *David Copperfield*, and in various houses around Broadstairs wrote all or part of many other books. Just past Bleak House, Archway House spans the path; here in 1840 he finished *The Old Curiosity Shop*, and *Barnaby Rudge* the following year. Bending inland past the present Old Curiosity Shop you walk up past the Albion Hotel (398679), in Dickens's day plain No. 40, Albion Street, where he wrote *Nicholas Nickleby* in 1839.

Broadstairs is very proud of its adoptive son, and there's a rash of Dickensian names along its narrow roads: Pip's Restaurant, the Barnaby Rudge pub and so on up the main street of the town. So far there has been no move to celebrate another famous attachment in the shape of Edward Heath, the former Prime Minister who kept his boat, *Morning Cloud*, here. It can only be a matter of time, though.

Walk up the street past Bown the Bookmaker (yes! Dickens lived here, too) to reach the railway station (391680) at the top of the town.

2 Folkestone to Dover

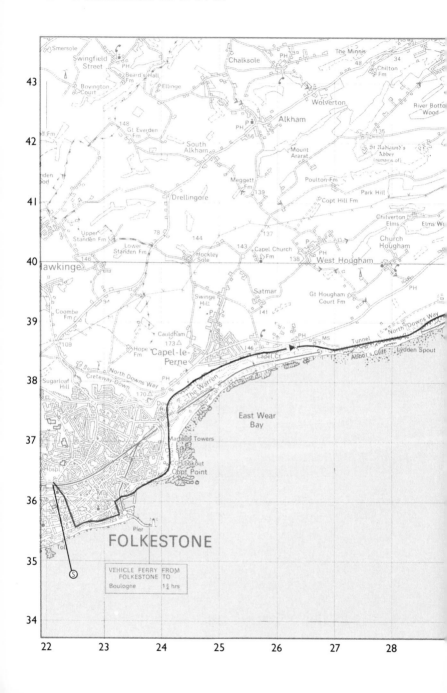

OS 1:50,000   Sheet 179
8 miles, from railway station to
railway station

Folkestone was a fishing and
smuggling village – in about equal
proportions – when the railway
arrived in 1842 to open it up for
tourism. In return for lace, brandy
and tobacco, golden guineas had
found their way over the Channel
during the Napoleonic Wars, to be
gobbled up by a gold-starved
Europe. Now the guineas stayed in
Folkestone, building the clutch of
grand hotels and houses that stand
along its shore. Soon the village
had swelled to fill its valley under
the chalk downs, and prosperity
arrived as the gentry brought their
gold and trippers their coppers to
the seaside here.

The path to Dover is the pro-
duct of a marriage of convenience
between two long-distance footpaths, the Saxon Shore Way and
the North Downs Way, which join
hands to run along the edge of the
great chalk cliffs that link the two
towns. There are wonderful views
from the heights in all directions:
forward to the South Foreland,
back around the sweeping coastline of Romney Marsh, and out
across the Channel to the French
hills.

7

From Folkestone Central railway station (220362) you walk straight down to the seafront, turning left (225355) on to a wide promenade under ornamental lamp standards which slopes down above the roller-coasters of the Rotunda Amusement Park to reach the Sealink terminal (233358) by the sheltering concrete arm of the pier. In the cliff walls are the crumbling remains of wartime shelters, full of chipped sinks, broken steps and rubble, into which the inhabitants of Folkestone dived when the sirens sounded – as they did daily at the height of the Battle of Britain.

By the terminal there's an exciting prospect ahead, over the boats bobbing in the harbour to the black cliffs of Copt Point and beyond to the white chalk ramparts of the cliffs, blotched with dark-green scrub, marching away to the long line of breakwaters off Dover. You round the harbour along a cobbled quay (234361) full of chandlers' shops, fish-mongers and the little stalls – Bob's, Chummy's, Lottie's, Pat's – where you can eat fresh cockles and whelks dipped in vinegar and salt as you look out over the moored Folkestone trawlers with their fishing nets draped over the harbour railings to dry. Then carry on under the cliff to climb steps on to East Cliff by the Pavilion Café. Looking forward here at the cliffs around East Wear Bay, you can see how the unstable chalk has fallen, to such effect that the original base of the cliffs has been left cut off short above the water, while the eroded higher portions have been bitten back several hundred yards inland. The wide ledge thus created has become a tangled undercliff, trapping water to feed a jungle of buck-thorn, elder, willows and gorse. Between the patches of green growth are rushy ponds where youngsters sit with hopeful rod and line, and paths criss-cross each other through the undergrowth. The coast railway line to Dover (by which you will be returning) runs along the ledge, the trains looking just like toys as they rattle into and out of the tunnels through the flanks of the cliffs.

The path continues from the Pavilion Café by way of a cracked and sunken tarmac stretch of road to climb up past a line of three Martello towers, built against the threat of Napoleon's invasion barges, and another knot in a string of reminders along this walk of how vulnerable this coastline has always been to attack from across the Channel. More defence remnants await you after your struggle up the steep, chalky path on to the clifftop above The Warren (241377) – brick-and-concrete gun-emplacements and pillboxes showing the wear and tear of half a century's weather since they were sited here in 1940 to ward off the invasion by Hitler's troops that most people thought inevitable. Up on these heights the coastline of France looks only a shell-shot away – as it proved to be when the German long-range guns began firing over the Channel late in the war. You can pick out individual clumps of trees, fields, patches of chalk and TV masts. It was lucky for Britain that the stars warned Hitler to cancel Operation Sealion.

Down below, all of Folkestone is spread out – the harbour, pier, hotels and houses – behind it, the white circle of the racecourse; beyond, the great curve of Romney Marsh running away to the square superstructure of the nuclear power station at Dungeness in the distance. The clifftop path, grassy and wide, continues above the railway to descend by steps into a hollow below Capel-le-Ferne, created by a landslip, a quiet little ledge out of the wind and out of sight of houses and cars. Up on the far side there's a curiously designed red triangle warning of cliff falls, showing a man respectably dressed in a suit apparently in mid-air, floating calmly seaward, accompanied by chunks of cubist cliff-face.

'North Downs Way' signs point you onwards (treading warily to avoid the leavings of Capel-le-Ferne's canine population) to reach Abbot's Cliff House (267387), a fine square white building claimed by its owner to be the nearest house to France. It was built in 1904 by a merchant banker named Morris as a seaside retreat, and is surrounded by a superbly curving balustrade. Here you join the old Dover high road, declined from the glory of coaching days to a flinty track overgrown with grass. It runs above deep orange splashes of ironstone in the sheer chalk cliff-faces to enter an army firing range; you can avoid this by keeping close to the cliff edge, looking down at the foreshore far below where the sea is stained a milky grey by the chalk rubble in the shallows. You pass more Second World War gun-sites, slits, holes, roof angles and brick walls skulking under bushes and frowning under concrete brows from earth-banks.

From the top of the path there's a really fine view down to the inland valley that rises in a green ramp until it plummets over the edge of Shakespeare Cliff (306397), a backward-tilted right angle of chalk whose edge has been eroded in a series of vast white bites. Beyond the cliff lie the arms of the breakwaters encircling Dover harbour, ferries continually coming and going; above them the outline of Dover Castle

Looking over Folkestone's yacht basin to Copt Point and the white chalk cliffs marching away towards Dover.

on its cliff, and more cliffs – the White Cliffs of Dover – going away under caps of green and yellow to round the south-eastern tip of England at South Foreland. Walking down into the mouth of the valley you look inland over the closely grouped houses of Aycliffe to the red-and-white fortress of the Citadel, a prison since it was built in Napoleonic days and still in business as a Borstal, though now it ramifies behind barbed wire all over its plateau.

The conical brick ventilation-shafts of the railway tunnel beneath your boots run in a straight line across the green back of Shakespeare Cliff, which the path climbs gently to the top. 'Dover Cliff', Shakespeare called it:

> . . . a cliff, whose high and bending head
> Looks fearfully in the confined deep.

Here in *King Lear* he brings Edgar, aware that his blind father, Gloucester, is intending to leap to his death from the cliff and keeping him well away from the edge. Gloucester wonders why the ground is so level and why he can't hear the sea, but Edgar is a competent faker:

> ... the murmuring surge,
> That on the unnumber'd idle pebbles chafes,
> Cannot be heard so high. I'll look no more
> Lest my brain turn, and the deficient sight
> Topple down headlong...

Well fooled, Gloucester takes his jump safely inland of the cliff edge and survives to be roundly cursed by Lear, arriving for a good rant before running away from the 'gentlemen come to detain him'.

The murmuring surge on the idle pebbles comes up clearly from below as you walk over the brow of Shakespeare Cliff among the bright yellow flowers of wild cabbage plants, to come suddenly on a view of the whole of Dover harbour laid out below you: cranes, breakwaters in long grey stripes on the sea, white-hulled ferries and rusty cargo ships tied up, a bunch of railway sidings and marshalling yards, the white Christmas cake of the ferry headquarters building by the Western Docks. William Cobbett, reviewing the scene from up on the old Dover road in 1825, though it 'much more clean, and with less blackguard people in it than I ever observed in any sea-port before. It is a most picturesque place, to be sure.'

Dover has seen more action than most English towns through its long history. The locals were determined enough to beat off the first landing attempt by the Romans in 55 BC, but the invaders weren't kept out for long. They established their port of Dubris, and built the lighthouse that still stands below the castle. This great fortification, dominating the town from its position 465 feet above the sea, was built around the turn of the thirteenth century. The French immediately tried to get in, but were beaten off. Strengthened and re-strengthened against the ever-lengthening roll of England's enemies down the years, it escaped damage during the Civil War when the Dover townsfolk took it over in the name of Parliament, thus preserving it from siege.

Dover had its share of bombing and shelling during the two World Wars, but the network of tunnels under the Citadel on Western Heights made a good refuge for the citizens. Looking down from Shakespeare Cliff at the shipping activity in and out of the docks, it isn't hard to picture the scene in 1940 when the sea was crowded to the horizon with the motley vessels of the Dunkirk rescue fleet, everything from Thames barges to private yachts and oyster smacks, shuttling backwards and forwards across the Channel to bring the exhausted men back to Dover. There was a rather different fleet moored here four years later, though just as remarkable: a great gathering of ships threatening a reverse invasion of the French coast. Every one was a dummy, carefully camouflaged to represent the real thing and designed to distract attention away from the genuine landing-points in Normandy.

Dover has been the scene of other famous cross-Channel events, too. In 1875 Captain Matthew Webb set off from the beach to swim the Channel, the first man to achieve the feat. Then there was the great day in July 1909, when all of Dover turned out in the fields by the castle to see Louis Blériot come puttering overhead for a bumpy landing in his monoplane – another first.

The path drops down the eastern side of Shakespeare Cliff to pass high above the entrance to the railway tunnel and descend beside allotments to reach the road (309401) on the outskirts of Aycliffe. Turn right here to reach a winding road on the left (313402), passing the entrance to the Citadel to arrive at Dover Priory (BR) Station (313415).

Before climbing this road, however, it's worth going down for a drink in one of the dock pubs. The conversation sooner or later turns to the proposed Channel Tunnel and the effect it will have on the livelihoods of Dover people. The posters on the bar walls put in a nutshell local reaction to the latest threat from across the water:

INVEST IN
REAL JOBS

NOT A
HOLE
IN THE
GROUND

3   Brighton: Palace Pier and the Pavilion to Kemp Town

OS 1:50,000   Sheet 198
2½ miles, returning on Volk's
Electric Railway

The best panorama of Brighton seafront is from the top of the candy-striped helter-skelter tower on the seaward end of Palace Pier (313033). On a really clear day it commands a 50-mile sweep of coastline, from the white slice of Beachy Head in the east to Selsey Bill in the west and on across the jaws of the Solent another 20 miles to the Isle of Wight. Brighton itself sits magnificently in the foreground of this huge stretch of coastline, combining its two contrasting characteristics, elegance and raffishness.

Moving from west to east, your gaze passes from the tower blocks of Worthing, over Shoreham's cranes and power station chimneys to Hove's graceful lines of terraces and crescents. In front of these the gaunt and pathetic skeleton of grime-grey, dilapidated West Pier pokes out into the water – built back in 1866, it was closed in 1975 and still awaits a saviour. Salt, wind and water are making short work of the cast-iron decorations of the pier as each year passes. Nearer still are the florid red and cultured white of those two arch-rivals among Brighton's hotels: the functional, efficient Metropole of the conference trade and the luxurious, nostalgic Grand. This latter, a great sugar-cake of a building, leapt into the twentieth century and the headlines in 1984 when a bomb hidden in one of its bedrooms exploded during the Conservative Party Conference, killing several people, injuring others and tearing the hotel's façade from top to bottom like a curtain. The bomb had been aimed at the Prime Minister and members of her Cabinet, many of whom were staying at the Grand; they were lucky to get out alive. Today it's almost impossible to spot the scars, so clever has been the restoration of the Grand.

The few hundred square yards of Brighton just to the west of Palace Pier hold the original heart of the town, for it was here that the fishing settlement of Brighthelmstone grew up in Saxon times. The Lanes, a

13

tightly knit maze of narrow alleys just behind the Brighton rock shops and cafés of the seafront, is largely an eighteenth-century rebuilding of the original area; but a stroll there gives you something of the flavour of that cramped little fishing village. For 1000 years Brighthelmstone remained undisturbed by the outside world, except by French raiders who paid it periodic unwelcome visits, on one occasion in the sixteenth century burning most of the settlement to the ground. The sea took a regular levy of fishermen's flint cottages, and life here was a hard struggle for the inhabitants until Dr Richard Russell of Lewes came along in 1754. Dr Russell's tract on 'The Use of Sea-Water in Affections of the Glands', published in 1750, was the foundation stone of the fashionable seaside health resort which Brighthelmstone soon became. Patients arrived to bathe and to drink seawater mixed with new milk to counteract nausea – it sounds even more nauseating than seawater taken neat. Visitors in full possession of their health soon followed, insisting on better accommodation than the fishermen's shaky cottages. Brighthelmstone became Brighton, an expanding resort waiting for the tides of history to sweep it into the arms of royalty in the corpulent shape of 'Prinny', His Royal Highness George, Prince of Wales, eldest son of King George III.

Looking eastward from Palace Pier, you can see the metamorphosis brought about by the arrival of that figurehead of Regency fun and frolics. The splendid hotels and houses sweep away towards the pride and glory of south coast architecture, the grand symmetrical curves of Kemp Town, begun when Prinny at last became king after decades of waiting, and completed well into the reign of his niece, Victoria. Below Kemp Town lie the cradling arms of Brighton's new and controversial Marina, above it the racecourse grandstand, beyond it to the east the high houses of Woodingdean and the South Downs sloping away above a series of white arches of cliff-face to distant Beachy Head.

From the pierhead you walk landwards along the wooden decking in a cloud of piped pop music, through the central pavilion crammed with flashing and yelling slot-machines, above which circular stained-glass windows from a gentler age show seagulls swooping over rocky bays and windmills on shining chalk clifftops. At the entrance to Palace Pier cheapjacks draw laughter from the crowds as they torment volunteers with demonstrations of trick sneezing powders and laughing bags. To right and left stretch the broad pavements of the seafront promenades with their sea-green-and-cream-painted ornate shelters and superb lamp standards covered in cast-iron leaves and flowers. In 1829 the various segments of shore road were joined up in one continuous line from Kemp Town in the east to Brunswick Terrace in the west, a fashionable route in mid-Victorian times to drive along, nodding to your friends and cutting your enemies dead. Strolling along the prom-prom-prom is still very much the thing to do on a day-trip to Brighton – so is kissing and cuddling in those wind-repelling shelters.

Cross the road here and walk to your left into Old Steine around the corner of the Royal Albion Hotel (312039), a dream in primrose yellow and white of Corinthian foliage on window columns, scallop-shell mouldings and a massive porch topped with a Union Jack. It stands now where in 1754 Dr Russell built himself a house whose garden ran right down to the shore. A few yards further on is Royal York Buildings, now housing various Borough and County Council offices, but built in 1817 as the Royal York Hotel.

Around the curve of the road stand two buildings side by side which between them hold a history of heartache engendered by Prinny. Marlborough House, nowadays the Tourist Information Centre, has its name writ large in gold capitals across its face. Robert Adam rebuilt it in the late 1780s, and here in 1795 came George, Prince of Wales, to stay with his new bride, Princess Caroline of Brunswick. The relationship was a disaster from the moment they met. Podgy George, soured by his long apprenticeship to his increasingly unstable father, spoilt and flattered by a crowd of sycophantic hangers-on, permanently in debt and hopelessly spendthrift, impulsively generous and sentimental, collided head-on with his wilful, independent and lecherous wife, who despised and tormented him throughout their marriage. Yet right on his doorstep he had had his heart's desire, for Steine House just along the road (now Brighton's YMCA) had been built on his orders for the only woman he ever loved, the sweet-tempered and long-suffering widow, Maria Fitzherbert. Ten years before wedding Caroline, George had gone through a morganatic marriage with Mrs Fitzherbert, and his politically desirable but emotionally devastating coupling with Caroline turned out to be only a painful interlude in his long association with Maria. By 1800 the princess had been replaced by the commoner, Steine House contained its rightful occupant and bliss held sway once more – for a few more years.

It's a pity that the subterranean passage connecting Steine House with Brighton Pavilion exists only in mythical form – it's nice to think of Maria hastening underground in response to a royal summons from the Pavilion. A short stroll north brings you to this fabulous fruitcake of an Oriental palace (313044), condemned by William Cobbett as 'a box crowned with turnips and tulip bulbs', and by Hazlitt as 'a collection of stone pumpkins and pepper-boxes'. Harsh words for George's temple to extravagance and self-glorification, grafted in 1815 by John Nash on to a Palladian villa built for the Prince of Wales at the same time as the rebuilding of Marlborough House. The minarets and onion domes of the exterior, fantastic in themselves, are easily outdone by the dragons, monsters and other overblown trappings inside, which live side by side with (and over and under) delicate and tasteful furniture and decorations. Nearly a million visitors a year give themselves over to an hour's tour through this Regency Disneyland.

Walking back to the seafront by the Royal Albion, you can sympathize with the fishermen of Brighton who once used the open spaces of the Steine as a drying ground for their nets. Visiting strollers here were forever catching their elegant heels in the nets; their complaints led to the Steine being railed off in 1822 and the permanent loss of the fishermen's drying area. Nowadays cars surge in nose-to-tail lines around the central green, and crossing to the far side of Marine Parade is a dangerous business. Once safely across, you look down on to the flat terrace on top of the Aquarium (315038), built in 1872 and a perennial attraction with its enormous range of fish on display and its energetic dolphins who have been trained to squeal 'Happy Birthday to You' while skittering upright across their pool. In the 1930s the Aquarium terrace held a cricket scoreboard which provided ball-by-ball updating on the contemporary Ashes series for the holidaymakers. In 1964 it was the scene of a notorious Whitsun Bank Holiday incident when 3000 onlookers watched the Mods and Rockers battling it out. 'Outnumbered by 10 to 1', reported the *Brighton Gazette*, 'Rockers were cornered at the Aquarium by hordes of Mods. They escaped by jumping 20 feet from the terrace into the arms of the police.'

From the Aquarium, turn east and walk up the easy slope of Marine Parade, popular with roller-skaters coasting down to Palace Pier. The

007 makes a splash at Brighton under Palace Pier's criss-cross forest of legs.

Hungry Years Gathering Place, an eating, drinking and dancing emporium, fills the space between Manchester Street and Charles Street once occupied by Tuppen & Walker's subscription library, one of a number of such libraries which visitors in the Age of Elegance would visit as soon as they arrived in Brighton to register their names and see who else was in town for them to acknowledge or ignore. Gently rising streets run inland from Marine Parade: Madeira Place, Margaret Street, New Steine. The seafront hotels gradually give way to large individual houses and terraces, many divided into flats and some showing those signs of dilapidation peculiar to seaside buildings: scabby peeling of paint around salt-encrusted stonework, rusting balconies and railings, salt-streaked windows that remain uncleaned. Their decay indicates the gulf that lies between those two queens of Regency architecture, Brighton and Bath: Brighton's split personality – of architectural splendour on the one hand and holiday superficiality on the other – allows the kind of neglect that Bath would never allow to go unchecked.

17

Royal Crescent, however – built between 1799 and 1807, and one of the earliest Regency developments along these cliffs – is in good repair, white windows and awnings standing out sharply against the black brick of the houses. Marine Square and Portland Place, put up about 20 years later, cut inland in deep, open-faced squares of houses, all slightly different from one another in the size and shape of their balconies, awnings, columns and window sizes. They stand above the funfair by Brighton's nudist beach – hence the number of giggling young persons who line the green-painted railings of Marine Parade hereabouts. Don't let the delights of voyeurism exhaust you, however, for a few hundred yards further on stands the finest monument to Regency dreams, albeit a late-flowering one, on the south coast.

Thomas Read Kemp was MP for Lewes in the 1820s, a noted figure in local society, with a wild youth and a squandered inheritance behind him. Kemp Town (332035) was his grand design, a project both to fix his name in Brighton's memory for ever and to recoup his debts. In 1823 work began on land belonging to Kemp, under the direction of Brighton's top architectural firm of Busby and Wilds. The plan was for a great and glorious housing estate of terraces and crescents, Regency in inspiration if not in date, leading inland to a central square fronted by a seaward-facing garden, the whole township dominating Brighton's eastern clifftops. From the west, the gaze of the onlooker would pass Chichester Terrace and move inland around the curve of Lewes Crescent and the three straight sides of Sussex Square before descending the opposite arc of Lewes Crescent, to run out east along Arundel Terrace. The façades were put up first, followed by the interiors of the houses which were each custom-built to the requirements of purchasers. By the 1850s, Kemp Town was as complete as it would ever be (it was planned to be twice its eventual size, but the money ran out), and Kemp himself was dead, bankrupt and discredited. His masterpiece was the social centre of Brighton for decades, playing host to such famous names as Palmerston, Gladstone and Sir Robert Peel, Landseer, Thackeray and Vita Sackville-West. King William IV and Queen Adelaide, Queen Victoria, both as a girl with her parents and as an adult with Prince Albert, King Edward VII in boyhood and manhood, all perambulated these pavements and sat, strolled or played in the gardens of Kemp Town.

No. 14 Chichester Terrace and No. 1 Lewes Crescent (two faces of the same residence) belonged to the Duke of Devonshire for 30 years between 1829 and 1858; here took place the grandest and most glittering of the early Kemp Town's balls, dinners and parties. King Edward VII stayed in the house in February 1908. At the top of Sussex Square, Nos. 19 and 20, forming the angle of the left-hand corner, were the temporary refuge in April 1856 of Louis-Philippe, the exiled King of France – he had been lent the houses by the Marquess of Bristol as a generous gesture from one noble gentleman to another. No. 22 was Thomas Read Kemp's own house, a suitably focal position for the King of Kemp Town. He lived here from 1827 until fleeing abroad ten years later with £100,000 of debts at his heels. Elegant and exclusive as his monument still is, there are signs of financial belt-tightening and a changing economic climate all round Kemp Town's charmed circle. These curlicued balconies and ornate mouldings are not as immaculately maintained as they once were, and more than one of the gorgeous houses is in use (1987) as a squat.

Leaving Kemp Town, you can see where Brighton's money is now circulating, by crossing the road and looking over the cliff wall. Great curving arms of concrete loop out into the sea, encircling the Marina (335032), built under the cliffs of Black Rock. Opened in July 1978, to the fury of conservationists headed by Sir John Betjeman, the Marina holds scores of yachts. At present it's being converted into a self-sufficient village at sea level, with a supermarket, cinema and flats. Fabulously expensive penthouses rise from the cliffs above the Marina, beyond which stands the red-roofed scholastic barracks of Roedean School.

Below Kemp Town you descend the cliff stairways to reach the toffee-and-cream-painted Marina Station (331033) of Magnus Volk's Electric Railway, opened in 1883 from the Aquarium to the Palace Pier's forerunner, the Chain Pier. Later extended to Black Rock, the rackety little railway is another attraction you just have to have a go on if you want to enjoy a day in Brighton to the full. The tiny, glassed-in wooden carriages trundle along the seafront back to the Palace Pier every few minutes. Under the ornate cast-iron arcade opposite the terminus is Volk's Tavern, a rowdy beer-cellar usually open for an extra hour or two on weekend afternoons in summer; but just up the cliff steps are many quieter pubs and tearooms in the streets and lanes of 'old Ocean's Bauble, glittering Brighton'.

19

4 Chichester Harbour: East Head to West Itchenor

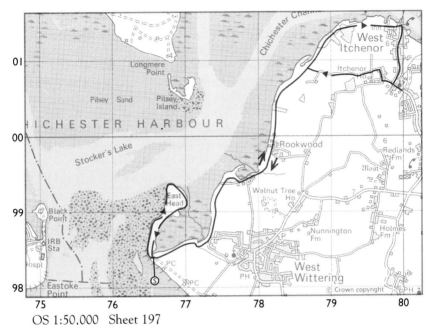

OS 1:50,000   Sheet 197

9 miles, starting and finishing at West Wittering car park

A thick-necked peninsula, shaped in rough outline like an arrow-head, stretches south and west from a line drawn between Chichester and Bognor Regis. The former fishing village of East Wittering has grown sideways along its southern shore, joining hands with Bracklesham to create one of those typical south coast ribbons of houses, small hotels and beach shops, nearly three miles from end to end. Most recent development has been confined to this coastal strip, however, leaving the western part of the peninsula much as it has been since medieval times: isolated farms and small settlements of red brick and flint standing by themselves in a quiet landscape of woods and flat fields running down to a fringe of salt-marshes at the edge of the sheltered waters of Chichester Harbour. These 11 square miles of creeks, mud-flats, saltings and tideways ramify outwards and upwards from the narrow entrance between Hayling Island and East Head like a four-fingered hand: Emsworth

Channel and Thorney Channel gripping Thorney Island between them, Bosham Channel running north to the sailors' haven of Bosham village, and Chichester Channel wriggling north-east past the low shores of the harbour's little peninsulas on its eight-mile journey to the sumptuous palace of the Romano-British governor Cogidubnus at Fishbourne, just south of Chichester.

The Atrebates, an Iron Age tribe sympathetic to the Roman invaders, held this low-lying sea-girt land whose atmosphere is still rather other-worldly, remote both geographically and in flavour from the rest of the tourist-bedevilled Sussex coastline. The Romans' settlement of Noviomagus grew into the flourishing medieval wool port of Chichester. The harbour, declining along with the wool trade, revived in the eighteenth century when corn became big business; but the railways finally put the cap on its profitable days 100 years later. Nowadays the sailing fraternity make use of the protection of its land-guarded water-ways and go shopping in the snug red-brick streets of the city.

Just inland of the south-western tip of the peninsula stands the village of West Wittering, largely passed over by the sideways expansion of neighbouring East Wittering. Our walk along the eastern shore of Chichester Harbour begins at the car park to the south of the village, where a road runs west beside a tamarisk hedge to the parking bay (765984) at the foot of East Head. This club-shaped spit of sand dunes and pebbles is well worth exploring as an entrée to the main walk. Since the National Trust took it over in 1966 its shifting dunes have been stabilized by sand-catching fences and the planting of sea couch grass and long-rooted marram grass, but its previous history had been one of constant movement as the strong tides flowing through the constricted harbour entrance pushed and ate away at the spit. In the 1830s it lay across the harbour mouth at right angles to its present north–south station, breached by a gap 300 yards across, through which all traffic had to pass.

From the top of the shingle bank below East Head there is a tremen-dous view across the outer waters of the Solent to the humpy back of the Isle of Wight, the sharp white cliffs of the Foreland at Bembridge as a foreground to the taller ridge arching down into the Channel at Vent-nor. The eye moves inland over Hayling Island's dark wind-blown trees and bare forest of yacht masts to the long swell of the South Downs, the

21

white scar of a chalk quarry on the west and the run of wooded uplands continuing in an unbroken line right round the arc of Chichester Harbour. As you walk north up the western side of East Head, this grand panorama opens more and more widely over the brick and concrete RAF architecture squatting lumpishly above the shore of Thorney Island, and moving eastward to Cobnor Point and the throat of the Chichester Channel on its way inland to Fishbourne and the cathedral city. Along this channel passed the ships loaded with luxuries for Governor Cogidubnus, and with the marble and glass and the craftsmen for the building of his splendid palace with its many intricate mosaic floors. These days the boats are almost all for pleasure: white, red and yellow yacht sails make tall strips of colour against the dark green of the shoreline trees and the paler green of the Downs beyond. The harbour waters, in spite of the protection of the surrounding land, can get very choppy when a stiff sea-breeze raises white horses' heads around the wildly pitching yachts.

The central spine of East Head is a stretch of dunes of yellow sand showing through the tufts of marram grass in bald patches. These yellow dunes are newcomers; they have been growing since 1963 when a storm smashed a hole right through the waist of East Head. A shingle bank on your right soon gives way to a broad skirt of sand, turning from yellow to grey as you approach the older part of the spit at its tip. Sprigs of marram grass poke up out of the beach, each one trapping its tithe of sand and contributing to the slow process of dune-building. Tiny pimples of sand, raised by the wind, throw their needle-like shadows all in the same direction, like a close-up photograph of the moon's surface, and a fine veil of sand powder constantly brushes across the beach. Outside noises die away here under the murmur of waves and wind, though the larks over the dunes manage to make themselves heard as usual.

Above the broad, sandy brow of East Head many dozens of flowering plant species grow in the sheltered hollows of the dunes, which are carpeted with soft patches of shaggy green moss. Bright yellow heads of lady's bedstraw and the fat red-green leaves of lyme grass, rather like an elongated artichoke, put colour into the drab browns and greys of the old dunes which, in spite of the conservation planting, are still imperceptibly shifting position. From here you look straight across the water over the low strip of Pilsey Island to the RAF settlements on Thorney Island.

The South Downs make a green backdrop to Chichester Harbour and the scrubby sand dunes of East Head.

One wonders what the Vietnamese boat people, filled with all the anxieties of stateless refugees from the moment they were pulled aboard tankers and merchantmen on the other side of the world, can have made of those grim and windy barracks when they were billeted on Thorney Island as a temporary refuge.

The eastern flank of East Head is another world; here the sheltering dunes have kept the harbour waters in a state of sluggish tranquillity, allowing a broad band of salt-marsh to develop out from the spit. Salt-crusted grey mats of sea purslane hold the marsh together, and a green algal slime coats the shoreline below a strip of firm sand, out of the wind and speckled with slipper limpet, scallop, oyster and crab shells – perfect for toddlers. Here the air is full of the pipings and whistlings of waders: turnstones, dunlin, plovers and red-billed oystercatchers in their smart black-and-white dinner jackets. Shelduck float on the calm fleets of water that intersect the marsh, and in winter there are visits by members of the 3000-strong flock of dark-bellied brent geese – a tenth of the entire world population – that come to Chichester Harbour for its lurid green enteromorpha seaweed.

Back at the car park, a wooden footpath fingerpost adorned with a pessimistic-looking curlew points the way on to the path around the harbour. Well sheltered by thorn hedges and grassy underfoot (though muddy after rain), the path runs steadily round the curving shoreline where tiny pebbly beaches lie between the bank and the marsh. At low tide the marshes and mud-flats extend well out into the harbour, and a strong smell of salt and mud wafts across the path. On the landward side, you look over the flat meadows of the peninsula to the tall, thin tower of Cakeham Manor (pronounced 'Cackam'). The house dates back in part to medieval times, and still contains portions of its original undercroft and hall. In the sixteenth century it belonged to the Bishops of Chichester who used it as a glorified bed and breakfast place while carrying out their episcopal duties down here. Bishop Sherburne built the red-brick tower (784976) which lifts two fingers to the wind. The path, fringed by gnarled old gorse bushes and spotted in spring with celandines, daisies and daffodils, squeezes between the marsh and the large houses of West Wittering in their grounds of tamarisk and pine trees. Beyond West Wittering, the heavy grey ploughland comes right down to the harbour edge, where stoats scuttle after rabbits among the bushes.

South of Rookwood House, a new hooked spit is being formed by the tide (777996), a miniature version of East Head with only rudimentary dunes and little vegetation. Its landward side encloses another completely sheltered salt-marsh where flocks of shelduck stand warily inspecting intruders with their heads stretched up well above the sea purslane. The path passes tiny groves of oak and holly trees with grassy floors overlooking the harbour, to reach the magnificent early eighteenth-century red-brick Rookwood House (782998) with its corner porticos and large semi-elliptical central window commanding a peerless view out over the water. The path dodges between the gardens of houses built in what were once the grounds of Rookwood House and runs on along the bank and above another embryo hooked spit (786010) to enter the shade of woods of beech, oak and alder. Here grow bushes of butcher's broom, rather a remarkable plant; at first sight, it looks like a drab-green, prickly bush with sharp little spear-blade-shaped leaves, brightened by red berries or tiny white flowers in due season. However, closer inspection reveals an oddity: flowers and berries grow from the surfaces of the leaves themselves, something no self-respecting bush does. The explanation is that the spiky little leaves are not actually leaves at all but branches which, during the course of the plant's evolution, have become flattened out into leaf shape.

Emerging from the woods, there is a final view back over Chichester Harbour's broad expanse of green water, green islands and green downland, before you reach Northshore Yacht Yard (798015) at the edge of the waterside village of West Itchenor. Here the calls of curlew, oyster-catcher and gull give way to that monotonous chinking of halyards against metal masts so characteristic of yachting havens on windy days, combined with a discordant howling whistle caused by the wind vibrating hundreds of runs of standing rigging, each of a slightly different size and tension. To the layman, the idea of working with that noise in your ears all day seems unbearably nerve-racking, but the yacht owners don't even appear to notice it as they go about their rubbing, scrubbing, sanding, greasing and painting. The yard is a flourishing concern, turning out 60 sleek fibreglass yachts a year for those lucky enough to afford them, as well as servicing boats and providing their winter quarters. The path runs right across the yard below the construction shed, passing new boats in every state of creation: windowless hulks, hulls wrapped in tight-fitting plastic jackets of polythene sheeting, boats with masts and rigging up.

A couple of hundred yards along the shore is Haines's boatyard, a complete contrast to the smooth operation over the fence. Here they service small sailing craft and build just a couple of wooden clinker-built boats a year – old-fashioned things that most sailing nuts would give their bollards to own.

The path continues along the shore, to turn inland just past the sailing club's little garden and reach the village street. This road of brick and flint and colour-washed houses simply stops when it reaches the shore and dangles its toe in the water. From here in the spring and summer you can catch a ferry across the channel to the yacht moorings at Bosham Quay. Itchenor's present-day boatyards are reviving an ancient craft which flourished in the village from before Tudor times until it collapsed in the nineteenth century. Itchenor also plays host to three bodies that do not always entirely see eye to eye with sailors: the Customs, the marine police and Chichester Harbour Conservancy. The Ship Inn in the main street serves good food and draught beer, welcomes children and is usually not too crowded with yachtsmen, thanks to the proximity of the sailing club with its own galley and bar.

Half a mile down the road stands the small and modest church (799006) dedicated to St Nicholas, the patron saint of sailors. It was built in about 1200, the Norman influence showing in its round-headed door and a later one in the tall, narrow lancet windows. The modern stained glass in these windows is the glory of this church: a Swordfish biplane flies under the feet of St Christopher in the south wall window, a memorial to the Fleet Air Arm pilot Malise Graham who went missing over the Mediterranean in 1942. The three east windows are given over to a wonderful illustration of the *Benedicite*, the Lord being praised by such examples of His works as a cock, sheep, dogs, a squirrel, an owl, a fox prowling over a snowfield, two children skating, a cloaked man battling through wind and rain, and the bright sails of yachts on the waters of Chichester Harbour.

From St Nicholas's you can make your way back to the East Head car park by a number of footpaths and lanes that criss-cross the interior of the peninsula. By far the most attractive return route, however, is to go back a few yards towards the village from the church, turn left and walk down the lane past Itchenor House and on for the best part of a mile to where the lane bends sharp left (788008). A short stretch of footpath here brings you back to the path beside Chichester Harbour, with its wide and windy views over salt-marsh, sail-dotted green water, wooded islands and sand-spits to the splendid backdrop of the Sussex Downs.

5 St Alban's Head and the cliffs of Purbeck

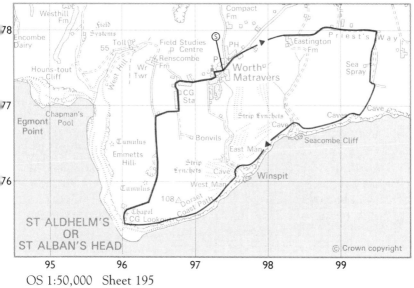

OS 1:50,000 Sheet 195
6½ miles, the round trip

It is hard to imagine a prettier village than Worth Matravers. There are even snow-white ducks around the pond on the village green, behind which the honey and cream-coloured cottages under stone-tiled roofs climb the street to where the little peaked hat of the church tower peeps over the treetops. Isolated down the centuries at the end of their narrow lane on this southernmost tip of the Isle of Purbeck, the villagers of Worth have had to look to those livelihoods whose raw materials are at hand: quarrying, lobster fishing and agriculture. Worth was famed in the past for the insularity of its inhabitants, but nowadays the true strain is well diluted with commuters and retired people.

The church of St Nicholas of Myra (972755) makes a worthy centre-piece for the village. St Nicholas, a fifth-century saint from Asia Minor, stilled a storm in the manner of his Master and thereby became the patron saint of sailors. Children were also under his protection – and, curiously, pawnbrokers. There's a fine dog's-tooth chevron Norman doorway into the church, above which is all that Roundhead enthusiasts

Worth Matravers: once a bustling quarry town, but these days the very picture of rural tranquillity.

left of a tympanum showing the coronation of Mary, flanked by angels. Inside the church is its chief treasure, a wonderful three-tier Norman chevron arch between nave and chancel.

It's good to see how well the church is used today. The pride the local people feel for St Nicholas's breathes from the display of photos of round-the-year festivals, the seasonal flower arrangements and the individually worked kneelers, one of which carries the lines:

> Books ships and horses
> The country and the sea
> These are the few things
> That mean the most to me.
> Brave things! Glad things!
> The green country and blue sea!

Just north of the church lies the grave of local farmer Benjamin Jesty, next to that of his wife Elizabeth. Jesty's epitaph records how he was first off the mark in the inoculation race, beating the much more celebrated and scholarly Edward Jenner by some 20 years. His tombstone speaks of

'. . . an upright honest Man: particularly noted for having been the first Person [known] that *introduced* the *Cow Pox* by *Inoculation*, and who from his great *strength of mind* made the *Experiment from* the (*Cow*) on his Wife and two Sons in the year 1774'. One is tempted to wonder to whom that *strength of mind* really belonged!

From the church, walk down the village street past the Tea Shop (home-made fruit pies, ice-creams) and post office to the pond, beyond which you look over a wide cleft opening to the south between East and West Man, its sides ridged up to the top with the strip lynchets of primitive farming. Climb the lane and bear right under the Square and Compass pub (bar food and local Purbeck bar games) to the top of the hill, where you go right over two stiles (977777) on to the Priest's Way. This old highway runs as a stony field-path for three miles between Worth Matravers and Swanage. To contemplate its history is to be reminded of how communities' fortunes can wax and wane; for this was the route by which the pre-Reformation priests would travel from the mother church at the prosperous quarrying and fishing centre of Worth to say Mass in the chapel-of-ease at the tiny fishing settlement of Swanwich.

The Priest's Way crosses drystone field-walls over stiles, running through the sheep pastures where strong winds blow off the sea. The bright stone walls of farms and barns gleam against the green slopes of the round-shouldered valleys that drop away southwards to the edge of the cliffs. Eastington Farm's dove-grey buildings (983779) squat low behind sheltering walls and sparse trees, typical of Purbeck's wind-blown farms. The Priest's Way, well signposted, runs on through a landscape which might easily be part of the Cotswolds if it were not for the many small quarries which have bitten holes down into the plateau. Purbeck stone has gone to build fine structures in many places, and for at least 1000 years has given local people a means of employment and a source of pride. These quarries, however, aren't beautiful. Blocks of unweathered yellow stone lie in heaps around still-operating quarries, mounds of rain-tempered grey stuff around the disused ones. Working quarries tend to accumulate a peculiarly twentieth-century detritus: runs of conveyor belt beside dusty tracks, rusting corrugated-iron sheds housing tractors and diggers. There are tall crane-jibs mounted on the backs of ancient creaky lorries with great square snouts and divided windscreens that should have been pensioned off 30 years ago. The desolate little quarrying settlement of Acton is bleak enough to take its place in some northern industrial landscape. But far beyond the tin shacks and dusty machinery rises the long back of Nine Barrow Down, running east into Ballard Down: a superb upland view, ending in the seaward plunge of Ballard Down into the bay beyond the compact curve of Swanage around the shoreline. These are the eastern outliers of the Purbeck Hills that make a natural barrier right across the Isle.

A stone marked 'Footpath to Dancing Ledge' (995780) soon points you on to a path that runs due south towards the sea. Along this track have raced generations of boys from the Old Malthouse School in Langton Matravers to swim in the pool blasted out of the rocky shore at Dancing Ledge. On your left as you walk are the stone buildings of Spyway Barn (999777), a suitable name for a one-time smugglers' haven where the 'gentlemen' would set a fierce bull free in the barn to keep the excisemen away. The path drops down the fields past quarry delvings, some less than ten yards square, to another waymarking stone. Bear left here to descend the slope to Dancing Ledge, right to continue the walk between gorse bushes, where a fine coast view opens up ahead of the long finger of St Alban's Head pointing out into the waves.

The path runs west along the hillside, over boggy streams and through grass tussocks, to meet the Dorset Coast Path at the foot of a wide green gully above Hedbury Quarry (991768), where a cannon from Napoleonic times lies pointing out to sea from a green apron of grass. Quarrying was a tough job on this exposed coast – after hacking out the stone, the quarrymen lowered it on ropes to ships, anchored at the foot of the cliff, which took the dusty cargo round Durlston Head into the more sheltered waters of Swanage Bay. There were frequent falls of stone and lungfuls of dust to threaten the life of a Purbeck quarryman: but if you were not a fisherman or farmer there was no other way of earning a living. Quarrymen stuck together, refusing to allow outsiders to work with them and making their own laws in the manner of the Dartmoor tin miners' stannary courts. The Ancient Order of Purbeck Marblers and Stonecutters has existed since Tudor times, one of the oldest trade unions in Britain.

The Coast Path, a broad green carpet of grass, leads on above the cliffs where black-backed gulls and jackdaws wheel to another old quarry on

Seacombe Cliff (984766). Here you descend among the greened-over mounds of quarry-spoil beneath the stone faces cut out of the cliffs, gradually weathering from creamy white to dull grey streaked with black. The path turns briefly inland along a track up which, one wild January night in 1786, staggered the cook and quartermaster of the East-Indiaman *Halsewell* which had piled up on the cliffs. The two crew members somehow managed to struggle inland as far as Eastington Farm, where they roused the occupants. The local quarrymen were soon out of their beds and down on the cliff, lowering ropes to haul up the victims of the disaster. Some 82 people were saved from the wreck, but 168 lost their lives. A mirror salvaged from the *Halsewell* now hangs above the door of St Nicholas's church in Worth Matravers.

At a stone marked 'Winspit ¾', turn to your left up steps to the path along the clifftop. Above you on the hillside of East Man are the shallow green steps of the strip lynchets, perhaps pre-dating the Romans, ploughed out of the slopes by subsistence farmers who had to take what they could get, poor soil only a few inches thick that with luck might yield another year's crops. Here the victims of the *Halsewell* disaster are reputed to be buried, which may account for the name of the hill (East Man = East Indiaman).

Foxholes dive into the ground beside the path which curves over the cliff and down again into the cleft above Winspit Quarry (977761), the oldest in Purbeck, which worked up until the end of the Second World War. Square black mouths of quarry levels yawn out from the stone faces above the spoil heaps and ruins of old buildings. Climbing upwards towards West Man, the path is fringed by the bright yellow flowers of wild cabbage. More dizzying cliff drops lead out to the rounded nose of St Alban's Head, a jungly undercliff running down to a mass of jagged rocks off the tip – a well-known sailors' death-trap.

Here on top of the Head, between a row of coastguard cottages and the coastguard lookout, stands the square little Norman chapel of St Aldhelm (961755). For centuries a landmark for sailors in lieu of a lighthouse above the dangerous tide races off St Alban's Head, the chapel has turned its thick stone walls and massive buttresses to eight centuries of wind and weather. A plain round-arched doorway leads into the dark interior, dimly lit by the narrow slit window. Sitting in one of the mouldering, bird-splashed pews amid smells of damp earth and stone, it takes time to appreciate the unique design of the chapel. Four square compartments are joined by arched vaulting to a solid central pillar, its stone carrying graffiti from at least the last three centuries. Superstitions have always clung to the chapel: one says that it was built as a warning to seafarers by a distraught father who had watched his newly wedded daughter and her husband drown off the Head; another that during a period of disuse in the seventeenth century Black Masses were celebrated here. Until quite recently, local girls would drop a pin into one of the holes in the central pillar and wish for a lover. Nowadays there is evidence of local affection for the chapel in the vases of flowers left on the altar steps. Dawn Communion on Easter Day is celebrated in St Aldhelm's – the saint, installed in 705 as the first Bishop of Sherborne, would be pleased to learn that his latterday successor in that post was the celebrant in 1985.

From the chapel you can enjoy the superb view westwards over miles of cliffs and coastline before taking the stony white road inland from the coastguard cottages towards Worth Matravers, seen ahead on the top of the next ridge. At a stone waymarker inscribed 'Worth $\frac{3}{4}$' (964769), turn right by a barn to meet another lane (968770) which leads to a farmyard on the road down to the village.

6 Abbotsbury and the shore of Chesil Bank

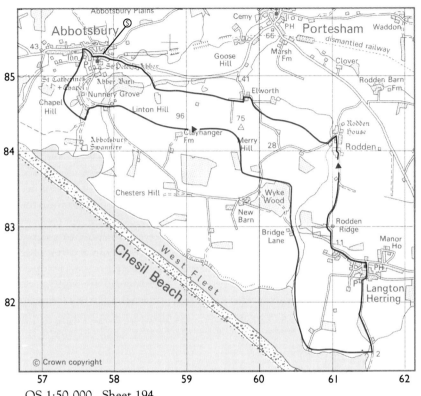

OS 1:50,000 Sheet 194
9½ miles, the round trip

Sweet St Catherine –
A husband, St Catherine –
Handsome, St Catherine –
Rich, St Catherine –
Soon, St Catherine!

So prayed the spinsters of Abbotsbury to their patron saint as they climbed up to her chapel on top of the hill outside their village. 'Arn-a-one's better than narn-a-one,' added the more practical if their petitions didn't look like being granted. From this high viewpoint the hopeful

33

maidens could at least spy any likely victims approaching ten miles off, by land or sea.

The snug little village of Abbotsbury, all cream-coloured stone and thatched roofs, lies in a sheltered crevice on the Dorset coast, its back to a great ridge of downland and its face to the sea. The rise of ground in front spreads a blanket of fields and woodland before you as you stand in the churchyard of St Nicholas's, but it denies you a view, for the moment, on to Chesil Bank, the long, thin bar of pebbles that shields this indented coastline from the sea for eight ruler-straight miles from Abbotsbury to the Isle of Portland. Chesil Bank has been the death of many a fisherman and sailor, wrecked there in the storms that often blow across Lyme Bay, but it protects the coast villages from the worst effects of those storms. Not always, though; East Fleet, a few miles east of Abbotsbury, was overwhelmed by the sea in 1824 and lost all but six of its houses and the chancel of its church. In cutting off the settlements along these eight miles of coastline from the open sea, Chesil Bank has also preserved them from the fate of so many West Country seaside villages. No boom times of hotel building, piers, promenades and amusement arcades came to Langton Herring, Fleet or Chickerell. They remain today much as they always were, small agricultural places between the downs and the sea, where the locals outnumber the tourists for all but the high summer season.

The holidaymakers do come to Abbotsbury, though – it's the prettiest of the Chesil villages, and makes a good thing out of the tourists with its swannery, sub-tropical gardens, antique shops, pottery, craft workshops and the impressive remains of the Abbey of St Peter, all within the space of a mile or so. The fourteenth-century church of St Nicholas stands beside the car park at the eastern edge of the village (578852). Weathered gargoyles gape from the walls, while inside the tall arches of the nave lead to a fine barrel roof in moulded plaster over the chancel, decorated with six-winged angels. In 1644, Colonel Strangways, the local landowner, was holding out for the king in his manor house just across the road, and had posted 13 of his men inside the church. When a trumpeter arrived from Sir Ashley Cooper, the Roundhead general, demanding surrender, the colonel sent him away with a flea in his ear; whereupon the Parliamentarians attacked the church and captured it and its defenders after a brisk exchange of shots among the arcades. The canopy of the baroque pulpit still carries bullet-holes as a reminder of the skirmish, and two bullets were found embedded in a beam above the north aisle when the roof was being restored in 1930.

The view from the south wall of the churchyard encompasses most of the remains of Abbotsbury Abbey. One wall of the abbot's house still stands to the south-east of the church, a gateway on the west corner frames St Catherine's chapel on its hilltop; and between the two, you look down on to Abbey Farm, behind which is the great thatched Tithe Barn, the largest one in Britain. Other fragments of the fourteenth-century abbey buildings stand or lie nearby, and more have been built into a garden wall of the manor house to the west of the church. The abbey was founded in 1026 by one Ore, a member of the household of King Canute, and in its day it controlled a large part of the surrounding land and the bodies and souls of the people who lived and worked on it.

The outlines of their narrow field-strips can be seen in green ribs on the side of Chapel Hill, which you reach from the church by turning left up the village street past the Ilchester Arms inn and the post office. Chapel Lane on the left (575854) leads to the foot of the hill, up which a path climbs over the humps of the strip lynchets to reach St Catherine's chapel perched on the summit (572848). The chapel is a massive building with thick and heavily buttressed walls and a bare, echoing interior. The tall east window still holds its much-eroded stone tracery, through which only the sky is visible. St Catherine's stands alone above village, fields and hills. It was allowed to remain as a landmark for sailors while its sister buildings in the valley below were being pulled to pieces after the Dissolution. The view from the hill is superb – to the north you look over Abbotsbury and the abbey ruins, the tower of St Nicholas rising at the far end of the long line of houses, and the downs sweeping up to the skyline behind. To the east are fold upon fold of downland running away to the long, low wedge of the Isle of Portland sloping away from the mainland into the sea. Westward is a sandy strip of Chesil Beach and the trees around the sub-tropical gardens; while to the south, the coastal swell of fields still hides the bar of Chesil Bank and looks straight on to Lyme Bay. As you run your eye eastwards along the coastal fields, green gives way to grey as the long pebble bar emerges into view and curves gradually away to meet the neck of the Isle of Portland. Between bank and mainland there is a glint of the flat waters of the Fleet, the narrow

35

lagoon trapped against the shoreline by Chesil Bank that runs with it all the way from Abbotsbury to Portland.

Go over a stile on the south side of the chapel and follow a wooden fingerpost marked 'Swannery' down over the strip hummocks on Chapel Hill, making for the seaward end of a little wood. More stiles take you down to a lane at the foot of the hill, where you can turn right if you want to visit Abbotsbury Swannery (575841).

Monks may have had tough sinews and souls, but they also had discriminating taste-buds – especially when roast swan was on the menu. When the abbey was being built, the abbot of the day wanted his own supply of swans near at hand for the monastery kitchens, and established the swannery at the tip of the Fleet below the village. For 200 years it kept St Peter's supplied with roasts, and after King Henry VIII's Thunderbolt from Heaven had put paid to abbot, monks, abbey and monastery, Sir Giles Strangways bought and preserved it for the use of his family (who still own it today). Nowadays there are more than 500 swans at the swannery, still fattening on the eel-grass in the Fleet – though not for the table.

From the swannery lane, turn up past the car park and bear right on to the road (577846). At the first right-hand bend a fingerpost points you up to the left (579846) on to the Dorset Coast Path, one link in the chain of that great long-distance coastal path which runs for 500 miles right round the West Country peninsula, from Minehead in the north, by Somerset, Devon, Cornwall and Dorset to Poole, near the Hampshire border. The waymarking of yellow arrows and black acorn symbols is excellent, and fingerposts and stiles are just where you need them – a fine example to those responsible for some of the country's less carefully maintained footpaths. 'Follow ridge' says the notice on the stile; good advice, as by scrambling up the spine of Linton Hill you can enjoy a mile of high-level walking with Portland in front, the downs to your left and the sea to your right. The sea-breezes bring a fragrant combination of smells up to this ridge: turf, warm vegetation, salt and dung. This is mixed countryside of cattle- and sheep-grazing and cornfields, where the farms lie between hills and sea, sheltered by the rise of their coastal fields and by windbreak copses. Lines of seagulls follow the tractors, settling one by one to squabble over what the plough has turned up.

You continue above the thatched roof of Clayhanger Farm (589842),

St Catherine's chapel and strip lynchets at Abbotsbury,
framed in a gateway of the ruined Benedictine abbey.

looking forward towards the grey stone houses of Langton Herring descending their hill in a narrowing curve. Soon the path leaves the ridge (596843), following the fingerposts, to run down the slope and skirt around Wyke Wood and Bridge Lane Farm (604829). From here it drops further down the valley, to swing to the left along the shore of the Fleet.

This is a world which man has left entirely to nature – it has been that way for the last 600 years, since the Abbot of St Peter's declared the Fleet an inviolable preserve. In places you can see the remains of previous attempts to drain and reclaim the Fleet, in the shape of tumbledown stone walls running into the water – they all came to nothing. The long lagoon is cut off completely from the sea, except at its extreme eastern end where the tides in Portland Harbour wash into it through the narrow entrance of Small Mouth. Salty at that eastern end, the water in the Fleet becomes progressively less brackish as it runs west and feels the influence of freshwater streams flowing into it from the downs. The plants in and around the Fleet, and the wildlife that feeds on them, change as the water does, producing a series of different environments that shade continuously one into the next. It is a biologist's dream, infinitely varied and giving the opportunity to study how different species adapt and change as their surroundings do. No sailing or motor boats disturb these waters, and the Coast Path you have been walking this far has been deliberately routed well inland to leave the swans, the snipe, the little terns, the redshanks and all the other birds of the Fleet in peace. Over on the pebbles of Chesil Bank, closed to the public during the breeding season – and in any case not the most comfortable of walking – many of these birds nest and breed. Little terns, now in decline all over Britain, have reared broods successfully on the bank, though foxes have recently found their way over the Fleet and have caused havoc among the eggs and the fledglings. Better foxes than egg-collectors, though.

The path runs along the mainland shore of the Fleet through clumps of yellow hawkweed and sea mayweed, purple michaelmas daisies and mats of bindweed. You can also see the pale pink bell-like flowers of marshmallow, whose leaves feel just like velvet. Flocks of waders stab their beaks into the muddy foreshore, and out on the water the gulls and swans rock in the ripples raised by the wind. It's a wonderfully peaceful scene, though noisy enough with bird calls, grasshoppers buzzing and the sawing sounds of swans' wings as they take off and land. The Fleet was a rather different place in the smuggling days of the eighteenth century, when cargoes were landed on Chesil Bank and rowed across the lagoon to the packhorses waiting under the trees. John Meade Faulkner set his smuggling novel *Moonfleet* (1898) round the hamlets of East and West Fleet a couple of miles to the east, and the yarn he spun was not all out of his imagination. The path passes a block of coastguard cottages (607816), built to try and keep an eye on the free traders, and still used by the coastguard today. It runs on below the cornfields and woods to meet a stony lane (615813), up which you turn to the left to climb up for a long mile into the small village of Langton Herring, the 'long village of the Harang family'.

Langton Herring lies along and down a ridge of ground, not stretched out prettily like Abbotsbury to delight visitors. It lies off the main roads, too, a place which you have to be aiming for to arrive at. The Elm Tree Inn is a busy and popular pub with good food and beer and a sunken garden; but that's the only attraction for outsiders. Its little church with a stumpy tower stands just behind the pub (615825) – a small, plain building with Norman arches, some old memorial flagstones and a quirky drawing hanging in the vestry of 'Langton Herring Old Church, with Mr N. Sparks, brother of Mr Isaac Sparks, by the gate'. Mr N. Sparks wears a Georgian long coat, breeches and hat, and an extremely inflexible expression. Stone walls, old stone houses, narrow twisting lanes and some fine tall trees are the sum of this quiet village, and it's a pleasure to wander through it and drink a pint in the garden of the Elm Tree.

The lane northwards from Langton Herring runs for over a mile up to the hamlet of Rodden, perhaps named after the last Abbot of St Peter's, Roger Roddon, who had five years in the saddle before King Henry VIII unseated him and all his kind. Turn left opposite the square-built Georgian Rodden House (611842), following a sign marked 'Abbotsbury Swannery', and after a curve in the lane go right, through a gate (610842) to climb up on to the top of the ridge. This is a windy, high and exhilarating walk along the sheep-nibbled turf, looking forward to Abbotsbury and on either side to the downs and the sea. The path meets a lane (600845) which leads off the ridge and down to the right into Elworth, another hamlet of farms. Opposite the thatched Old Farm House you turn left into a muddy lane (598847) that ends in the fields – carry straight on to meet the end of a track which brings you out on the B3157 road (583851) half a mile short of Abbotsbury. Walking into the village, you look over the abbey ruins and the tower of St Nicholas's to the ridged green mound of Chapel Hill, crowned by the golden stone walls and buttresses of St Catherine's chapel – a landmark for walkers as well as for seafarers.

7 Lyme Regis to the Axe via the Undercliff

OS 1:50,000 Sheet 193
7 miles, the one-way journey

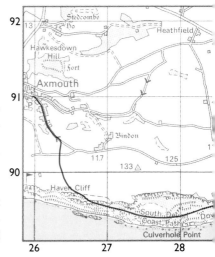

CONDITIONS:
*A strenuous walk which can be slip-
pery after rain. Path climbs and falls a
good deal. No escape routes. Return
transport by bus or taxi. Only try this
one if you are feeling fit and are well-
shod and waterproof.*

Through the Undercliff! Most
naturalists and geologists would
give their eye-teeth to be coming
with you on this seven-mile walk.
The surroundings are unique: a
long, straggling belt of clifftop woodland running west from Lyme Regis
for about five miles which has quite simply been left to itself for a century
or more. There is a good reason for this isolation: the cliffs east and west
of Lyme Regis are tumbling and skidding into the sea faster than anywhere else in England.

If you think of the cliffs as a sandwich, the top layer of bread is made of
chalk and Upper Greensand, both of which can be penetrated by
rainwater. The bottom slice is of Blue Lias, Rhaetic White Lias and
Keuper Marls – bewitching names – and they keep the whole sandwich
relatively stable, but they slope towards the sea at an angle of about five
degrees. It is this incline, together with the 'jam' in the middle of the
sandwich – slippery black gault, a kind of clay – which causes the trouble.
Trapping the seeping rainwater, the softened gault acts as a skating rink
for the clifftops. Great falls occur at long intervals, minor ones often, as
the whole sandwich totters seawards year by year. There were several
dwellings, even a small farm or two, on the Undercliff until the
nineteenth century, but the ground kept disappearing from under them.
Cottages, fields and sheds cracked, crumbled and went over the edge into
the sea, and eventually the whole strip of coast was abandoned by man.
Birds, animals and plants lived on in undisturbed seclusion. In 1955 the

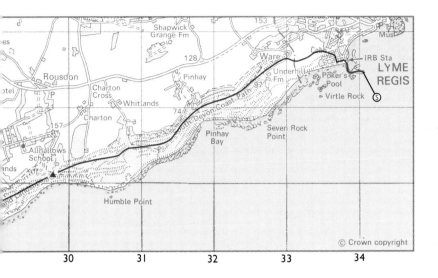

© Crown copyright

| 30 | 31 | 32 | 33 | 34 |

whole Undercliff was declared a National Nature Reserve. A glance at the lists of occupants tells you why: 130 species of birds (nuthatches, flycatchers, nightingales, buzzards, kestrels, owls, kingfishers, herons, jackdaws, long-tailed tits, tree creepers, lesser whitethroats, willow warblers, goldcrests, rock pipits) ... mammals (foxes, badgers, stoats, weasels, wood mice, harvest mice, dormice, shrews, hedgehogs, bats) ... reptiles and amphibians (lizards, slow-worms, three species of newt, toads and frogs) ... insects (more than 30 species of butterfly, 200 species of moth, grasshoppers, dragonflies, beetles, hover-flies) ... plants (400 different species, including 11 species of orchid, Viper's Bugloss, Yellow Rockrose, Hairy Violet, Horseshoe Vetch, Ploughman's Spikenard, Cathartic Flax – ah, those names!) ... and that doesn't include the ferns, the mosses, the liverworts, the fungi ...

Man is the intruder here, and he is suitably confined to the narrow, slippery, up-and-down jungly path. It is a long five-mile hike through the Undercliff, especially tricky and tiring after rain, and there are no escape or return routes – so be prepared. This is not shorts-and-sandals territory. There are other paths leading off into the interior or down towards the sea, but they are strictly forbidden to all but serious botanists and naturalists who apply to the Nature Conservancy Council for the neces-

41

Bird song, sunshine and silence deep in the tangled heart of the Undercliff near Lyme Regis.

sary permission. Once off the track and among the thickly tangled undergrowth, you can easily fall into a crevice and probably won't be found.

The entrance to the Undercliff reserve is about a mile west of the Cobb (338915), Lyme's famous fossil-studded stone pincer of a breakwater, often drenched by storms but still serving as a shield for the town against

42

wave and wind. Jane Austen in *Persuasion* caused Louisa Musgrove to knock herself unconscious after a fall from Granny's Teeth, a jagged set of stone steps on the Cobb; and Sarah Woodruff, the enigmatic Scarlet Woman of Lyme, first met and enmeshed Charles Smithson at the seaward end of the breakwater in John Fowles's *The French Lieutenant's Woman.*

From the Cobb you turn left down Ozone Terrace, then climb up a flight of steps above Lyme Regis Bowling Club (337917) to a clifftop path that runs west under the hamlet of Ware, climbing over fields cracked and seamed by landslips, to a road (331917). Here you turn left to reach the entrance to the Undercliff. Just down the slope to the left stands Underhill Farm (327915), where John Fowles was living when he wrote *The French Lieutenant's Woman.* The walls of the house gape with cracks, and the garden beyond is already beginning its long slide into the sea.

As you enter the Undercliff all sounds of the outside world fade away, and you walk accompanied by birdsong, rustling leaves, trickling streams, the crack of twigs, squelch of boots in mud and the muted surge of waves on the shingle far below. The sunlight falls in spots among the clearings and lights up the mossy, sodden carcasses of fallen tree-trunks where fungi and ferns sprout. Sections of flint wall run along by the path, or cross it at right angles – they were built in the 1840s by John Ames of Pinhay, who tried to deny access to the inhabitants of Lyme. They defeated him in the House of Lords, whereupon he built these long flint corridors to keep the peasants in their appointed place. The shady bowers and grassy banks of the Undercliff were notorious trysting places for the lads and lasses of Lyme, and their secret pleasures went on despite Mr Ames and his walls.

After about a mile the track joins a tarmac road coming down from Pinhay (317908), which slopes steeply downhill between privet bushes and great ilex trees – Ames was one of a number of local landowners who planted rare and exotic species in the Undercliff. Between Pinhay Bay and Humble Point is a little corrugated-iron water-pumping station (312904) humming away to itself, the first and last man-made sound in the whole five miles of virgin woodland. From here the path climbs uphill and forks left by a splendid ilex tree, to pass the ruins of a cottage, one of the dwellings forcibly evacuated by nature. On your right are the tall white inland cliffs formed when the land on which you are walking slipped downwards. Their cracks and crevices make sheltered roosting places for gulls, pigeons and jackdaws. The path climbs to a wooden seat with a rare sea view (298902) below Allhallows School, whose students have contributed a large part of the information about the natural history of the reserve on their forays into the interior. Steep wooden steps lead down to another tarmac road, a kind of dilapidated carriage-drive fringed by Victorian garden plants: rhododendron, box, privet and yew. Soon mud and chalk take over underfoot and the slippery path passes between ash trees, a rare example of a naturally seeded and regenerating ash wood (281895).

Beyond the wood is Goat Island (275895), a flat-topped 15-acre table of chalk and greensand now smothered in vegetation which was isolated in the middle of a great chasm on Christmas Eve 1839, during the greatest landslip ever recorded on this coast. About 20 acres of land in all, weighing some eight million tons, detached itself from its neighbouring cliff and rumbled downwards for about 200 feet. The chasm created by the foundering chunk of land measured half a mile from north to south and 400 feet across. The following year, the crops on the top of Goat Island were harvested, and local people flocked to the chasm to celebrate the occasion with flags, bands and a fête.

Views over the sea are few and far between in the enclosed world of the Undercliff, but they begin to open out as the path leaves the trees through a belt of thick scrub, to mount wooden steps to a stile (271895). The houses of Seaton around the mouth of the River Axe appear to the left, and can be reached by crossing the fields to a lane (263902) and turning left over the golf course. Alternatively you can carry on through two more fields to the lane that leads steeply down into Axmouth. There has been no railway link between Seaton and Lyme Regis since the closure of their branch lines in the 1960s, and the return journey must be made by taxi, bus or obliging chauffeur – or, if your legs and lungs have plenty in reserve, by plunging back among the well-preserved secrets of the Undercliff.

8   Sidmouth to Weston Mouth
and Salcombe Regis

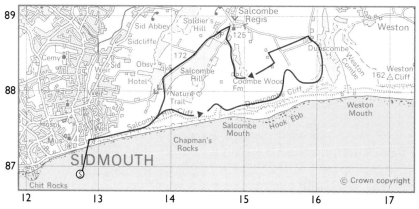

OS 1:50,000   Sheet 192
5 miles, the round trip

The Sidmouth where Jane Austen lost her heart to that handsome, charming and intelligent (but, alas, nameless) young man is still there, not buried very far beneath the modern face of the little Devon seaside town. Splendid Regency crescents look out in white-faced dignity over the floral gardens and seafront promenades where clergymen and their families still go for an evening chat and stroll – nowadays alongside day-trippers, coachloads of pensioners and, in summer, the folk-music fans who throng Sidmouth during its far-famed Folk Festival.

Miss Austen's mysterious admirer, whom she met during a holiday here in the summer of 1801, has always been a shadowy figure, the object of much fruitless speculation by her biographers. He may have been a clergyman himself; he certainly had to leave Sidmouth on business after a few rosy weeks in Jane's company, giving her the strong impression that he would soon be back to talk turkey. She waited in vain, for a letter from the gentleman's brother soon arrived announcing the death of her friend. Historians search unavailingly for any other clues to the one man who seems to have arrowed straight through to Jane's heart.

Looking along the coastline from the car park at the eastern edge of Sidmouth's seafront (128873), you see the characteristic deep red sandstone of these East Devon cliffs in steeply falling shanks running down,

45

*Dunscombe Cliff sweeps up to the skyline from
the wooded cleft of Salcombe Mouth.*

one behind another, into Lyme Bay. The sandstone forms a base for a
topping of chalk and greensand, a stone soft in name but hard in nature,
much in demand for medieval church-building. The sea extracts a good
toll from the cliffs along this coast, stroking away at their feet with each
tide until a fall brings anything from a thin trickle to a roaring cascade
tumbling down on to the beach. Before Sidmouth's sea-wall was built in
1835, the houses closest to the shore were in constant danger during
storms and high tides. At Chit Rocks, off the western part of the town, a
whole headland was swept away. Sidney Smith invented an inhabitant
of this outpost, Dame Partington, who would repel the floods from her
house with a broom.

From the car park you cross the footbridge over the River Sid and
climb up steps in the side of the cliff to a grassy area whose benches
command a fine view over the town to the cliffs by Budleigh Salterton,
and on for miles in clear weather down the coastline south of Exmouth.
A concrete path runs between the neat gardens of neat houses and the
cliff edge, only a couple of feet away in places, to emerge at the side of the
fields high above Sidmouth. Here it climbs gently through a grove of

hawthorns, then more steeply by steps through a wood of ivy-smothered, lichened, stunted sycamores whose undergrowth is a haze of bluebells in spring. Clearly marked throughout the walk, the path reaches the top of Salcombe Hill at a grassy mound on which stands a circular viewing map naming the various points you can see from here in clear conditions: Scabbacombe Head in South Devon (26½ miles), the Hardy Monument in Dorset to the east (29 miles), and parts of Dartmoor 33 miles away in the dim blue west.

Continue over the shoulder of Salcombe Hill, where violets grow under the gorse bushes, to look down into the deep cleft of Salcombe Mouth. Coombe Wood Farm's thatched white house and old stone barn (149882) stand well up on the far side of the valley under the cap of woods that crowns the straight back of Dunscombe Cliff. The sheer face of the cliff drops to the cream-coloured pebbles on the beach far below, splashed red with the rubble of rock falls. The peaceful beauty of the scene may be marred for you in contemplation of the steepness of your descent into the cleft and the corresponding climb up the other side: 193 steps down (I counted them all in) and about 400 sweating paces up (I counted them all out), bridged at the bottom by marked field-paths and a footbridge.

Arriving at the top on Higher Dunscombe, you can regain your breath by strolling along the side of a wide, dandelion-dotted meadow and looking over the edge at the chalky strata above their sandstone footing. These cliffs have been extensively quarried in the past. The chalk covering was removed and burned for the lime that was the only available fertilizer before modern chemicals came along. The 'rubble knapps' or piles of flints that were left behind after burning still lie in swaths beside the path. The underlying greensand was destined for higher things: it was originally quarried here to be used in the building of Exeter Cathedral almost 1000 years ago. There were two ways of getting the stuff to Exeter in those days, both euphonically named: the great rafts that made the journey round by sea were called 'bagatae'; the land transport went under the apt name of 'truckamucks'.

The path continues over the short green turf of Dunscombe Cliff, turning inland on a wide, level curve into the valley of Weston Combe. Here the scene is almost the same as at Salcombe Mouth, another deep wooded cleft rising to a long-backed cliff. Below you on the beach at

Weston Mouth stands the Watch House (165880), a lonely position for a lonely function; this was the lookout station for the coastguard in their bitterly fought battle with the local smugglers. You turn up the valley through the middle of a discreetly camouflaged township of mobile homes among the trees, all painted green or brown in a not wholly successful attempt to blend into their surroundings. At the thatched old Dunscombe Manor farmhouse (159886) you turn left along the lane, then immediately left again at a wooden 'public footpath' fingerpost, along a stony lane where pink campion and white stitchwort give colour to the banks. The path goes over a crossroads of lanes (154885) and dog-legs around barns (153885 and 153883) as it makes for a stile (150881) leading into the woods above Coombe Wood Farm. Bear left here on to a descending track, which hairpins back on itself at an open view over the sea and cliffs at Salcombe Mouth, to pass between the farm buildings and reach a lane climbing up to the quiet hamlet of Salcombe Regis.

The prosperity of this isolated cluster of houses came in the past from panning salt from the River Sid, though tradition says it depends on the well-being of the ancient thorn tree that still flourishes at Thorn Farm (148891) up the hill. The church of St Mary and St Peter (148888) has a curious barn-like building attached to its tower, the home of the priest in medieval times and a pretty cramped one at that. Later on it did duty as the village school before settling down to its present-day status as the church's vestry. Inside the church are two short, square aisles flanking a short, square nave, like three small boxes side by side. The lectern is a rare treasure, a great black chough that dates from the middle of the fourteenth century. Parts of the original Norman building still remain, including the solid pier of the north arcade and, outside in the south wall of the chancel, the outline of a tall, narrow doorway, some of whose blocking stones carry medieval masons' marks. The churchyard makes a lovely sight in springtime, pink and white with cherry and apple blossom. Just up the lane to the right of the church is the old village school, its doorway inscribed 'Jesus said Suffer Little Children . . .'. I just bet they did!

From the church, follow the lane signposted 'Sidmouth' up the hill to meet the road by the War Memorial (145887). Seven men from Salcombe Regis died in the First World War, a more than heartbreaking sacrifice for such a tiny place; however, unlike most other villages throughout the country, the later additions on the other side of the memorial's plinth show an even greater loss during the Second World War – nine more lives.

The old high road to Sidmouth runs straight between its hedge-banks to pass the observatory on Salcombe Hill (139883), founded in 1912 by the discoverer of helium, Sir Norman Lockyer, who lies buried in Salcombe churchyard. Three observation domes rise out of the gorse on the right of the road, looking like the crested metallic heads of alien monsters working hard at not being seen. The observatory is run these days by the University of Exeter, and you can look round its various wonders if you are organized enough to phone them well in advance of your visit.

Opposite the observatory a fingerpost points down the drive to South-down (139880), beyond which the coast-path leads you back to Sid-mouth with stunning views in front of you all the way down the hill.

9   Little Dartmouth Farm to Blackstone Point and Dartmouth

OS 1:50,000   Sheet 202
3½ miles, the round trip

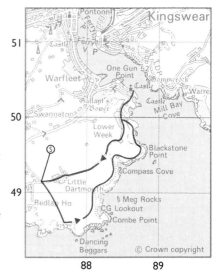

© Crown copyright

Like a slowly unfolding secret, this walk gradually prises open the tightly squeezed mouth of the River Dart, leading you from views over the English Channel through cliff prospects to the dramatic sight of the houses of Dartmouth packed along their river shore. It's a walk of sharp contrasts, its keynote the effect that the enclosed estuary of the Dart has had on the defence and development of the little naval town, sited well inland but drawing all its flavour from the sea.

The National Trust owns the segment of cliffs to the south of the estuary, and you start the walk into Dartmouth at the car park just below Little Dartmouth Farm (873491). At the southern end of the car park a wooden fingerpost marked 'Coast Path – Dartmouth 2¾ m.' points over a stile to a track that runs down to the clifftop path on Warren Point (877486). Turn left when you reach the cliffs above the Dancing Beggars rocks and walk round the top of the great banks of bracken and grass that slope down to the dark rocks and little coves at their feet. Warren Point, as its name suggests, was a free-range rabbit farm in former days, supplying fur and meat to the local community courtesy of the nets, dogs and ferrets of the warreners.

The cliffs curve northwards around the crooked finger of Combe Point (883486) which encloses a tiny bay of calm water. Out beyond the shelter of the Point the sea tears at the sides of Meg Rocks (884489) whose gleaming black surfaces are splashed white with the droppings of cormorants. On sunny days the birds squat in rows, stretching their necks up to digest the latest catch and holding their wings out to relieve the aching weight of fish in their crops. Rounding Compass Cove, you look forward across the mouth of the River Dart to the craggy fin of the

Mew Stone (910494) standing offshore from Inner Froward Point on the other side of the estuary. High above on the crest of the hill rises the Day mark, an 80-foot tower looking like the stump of an old windmill; it was put up about 100 years ago as a navigation mark for ships approaching the sharp turn into the Dart estuary. Compass Cove was the site of an early experiment in 1860, when a telegraph cable was laid under the sea from the cove out to Guernsey. The path passes a peeling old post topped with a wooden lozenge that still bears the label 'Telegraph Cable', a marker for ships passing over the wires on the sea bed.

Under a row of coastguard cottages (884495) the path drops steeply down to run close above the water. Side streams are spanned by wooden footbridges, the handiwork of cadets from Dartmouth's Royal Naval College. These days they don't just absorb a stern diet of trigonometry and naval history, but are encouraged to make practical contributions to the local scene. The tide surges under the footbridges to wash round the caves under the cliffs, making grunting, snorting and heavy breathing sounds as it sucks and echoes inside the caverns. Listening to these animal noises, you can well understand how superstitious folk believed that sea monsters inhabited these dark nether regions.

In the seventeenth century Blackstone Point (887495) carried a battery of heavy guns to guard the mouth of the river; nowadays there's just a small lookout hut below a signal mast, and a rough path bordered by clumps of wild cabbage. From the Point you look ahead into the narrow jaws of the Dart estuary, with Kingswear Castle (891503) low down among the trees across the water. The castle was built at the turn of the sixteenth century as a supplementary defence to Dartmouth Castle which stands on the opposite bank. Between the two of them, any attackers infiltrating the estuary could be raked from both flanks long before they came within range of the town beyond.

The path climbs up into the woods, then drops downhill between bushes of blue and pink hydrangea to reach Dartmouth Castle (886503) on its bluff above the river. Not much remains of Kingswear Castle's older brother: a couple of angles of wall, a few beam-holes and stone steps. The crenellations of the square light-tower below (now a shop) look far more warlike. Dartmouth Castle was built in 1481 on the site of a fort 100 years older, and was a pioneer in its use of angled gunports to give a wide field of fire. The cannon in the castle were known as 'murderers':

shakily constructed of short lengths of iron welded together and bound with hoops, they were liable to murder friends as well as foes. The castle garrison, not content with their twin forts, made assurance doubly sure by stretching a great chain each night from Dartmouth Castle across the water to an anchoring point around a rock beside Kingswear Castle. 'A cheyne sufficient in length and strength to streche and be laid over-thwarte or a travers the mouth of the haven of Dartmouth', the chain soon gained the nickname of Jawbones.

Below the castle stands St Petrox church, overlooking the estuary. Its nave is flanked by high, graceful arches, and under the tower is a sad little display of memorials to dead servicemen, painted on portions of the dismantled west gallery. The lonely deaths in war and peace of those Dartmouth men and boys are vividly captured in the short inscriptions: 'Died from exposure . . . killed in action . . . died from wounds, disease . . . died at sea . . . missing'.

Beyond the church there is a fine view upriver to the promontory village of Kingswear on the far bank and, beyond it, the long stretch of Dartmouth's waterfront, crammed with old inns, wharves, warehouses and the steep streets of the town rising one above another. Dartmouth was brought into being during the twelfth century to service the depart-ing ships and men-at-arms of the Crusades of 1147 and 1190. Once established in its sheltered position, the town grew and prospered as trade with the continent expanded, and it got a further boost when the Newfoundland fisheries opened up. Dartmouth vessels went away to the frozen north-west and returned with their holds full; when Newfound-land's rich fishing grounds had been worked out, the Admiralty revived the town by sending its hopeful young men here for training. The predecessors of today's builders of footbridges led a hard life of bad food and harsh discipline aboard hulks moored in the river, following the Royal Navy's age-old principle, proved during the Napoleonic Wars, that the harder the training the better the officer. In 1905 the Royal Naval College was established just north of the town, and the cadets slept a little easier – but only a little. Nowadays the college is still one of Dartmouth's mainstays, and further business comes to the town from the yachtsmen who have made it a major sailing centre, taking advantage of its favoured position away from sea-winds and waves, and its long frontage of sheltered river.

St Petrox church looks out over the Dart estuary to a glimpse
of the piled houses of Kingswear on the far bank.

The path back to Little Dartmouth Farm follows the route you have
walked, up into the woods as far as a fingerpost beside a cottage at the top
of the rise. Keep straight ahead here into a stony lane which runs above
and parallel with the coast-path for a mile and a half, back to the car park
below the farm, with long sea-views to your left all the way.

10   Start Point and Prawle Point

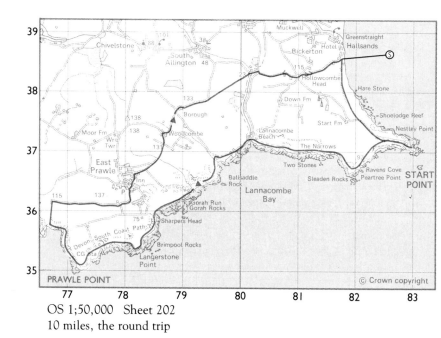

OS 1;50,000   Sheet 202
10 miles, the round trip

Hallsands, the village that was but is no more, lies tucked away on the east-facing sweep of Devon's southern coastline that faces out into Start Bay. Finding the place is quite a job in itself; once you have threaded your way down the narrow lanes from Kingsbridge or Dartmouth, however, you reach a lovely spot where few people other than bird-watchers or walkers bother to come outside the summer high season. Here the downland of the South Hams runs in billowing swells down to the sea, and there are few sounds outside nature. This cliff walk between the two headlands of Start Point and Prawle Point is strangely unfrequented even by coast walkers – perhaps it owes its serenity to the steepness and narrowness of those lanes. Yet there are several tiny sandy beaches, superb rock scenery, sea-birds and steep downland fields, all redolent of that Devon of the old railway company posters which today's tourists would give an arm and a leg to discover.

Nothing remains now of the Hallsands village which Walter White, writing in 1854, described as 'a dozen rude little cottages, some close to the shingle, others raised a few feet on a shelf of rock, others on ledges and recesses of the cliff'. White, who was walking to Land's End, slept on four chairs under a blanket at the London Inn in Hallsands before striding on, early the following morning. Rude little cottages they may have been (in fact there were 37 of them), but they continued to shelter the village's fishermen until the end of the century, when an ill-considered dredging operation condemned Hallsands to a watery grave.

From the small car park above the Trouts Holiday Flats building (817385), walk down the lane and follow the sign 'To the Old Village' down a steep path to a long ledge of rock between cliffs and sea. There is a short view south to the lighthouse at the tip of rugged Start Point, and a long one north around the gradual curve of Start Bay to Combe Point at the entrance to the Dart estuary. The face of the cliffs is open to all weathers and the storm waves, but here on the rock shelf the fishermen built their houses for easy access to their boats on the beach. The few crumbling doorways and walls that remain are crammed together under the cliff. They rise from every available flat surface, some built into the cliffs themselves.

Out below the waves lies a bank of shingle which protected the little village by breaking up the force of the tides and maintaining the beach at a level not far below the rock ledge. In 1897, with the new Devonport docks being built near Plymouth, the authorities decided to use this shingle for the works. In four years they had taken half a million tons from the Hallsands bank, and in doing so had lowered the level of the beach by 15 feet. Now the seas broke with tremendous force against the beach, the ledge and the cliffs.

In February 1903 a row of cottages on the beach was washed away. A sea-wall was hastily built, but in January 1917 it was overwhelmed in a terrific storm. The haven in the cliffs turned out to be a trap as mountainous seas raced inshore and thundered among the fishermen's cottages. The foundations beneath the houses were washed away, the dwellings began to collapse into the waves and those villagers who were hardy enough climbed up the sheer cliff-faces to safety. Those who couldn't climb had to wait, terrified, for the storm to abate and rescue boats to be launched, in pitch darkness and with each succeeding roller threatening to sweep them away. After that awful night, Hallsands was

55

abandoned and the broken cottages and inn left to slip gradually into the sea.

You can buy a booklet with the full story of the Hallsands tragedy in the tearoom at the holiday flats building. From here you follow the yellow arrow waymarks along the cliff-path, a narrow but well-surfaced track that runs across the bracken-covered slopes. Toadflax, buttercups and the yellow buttons of tansy grow in the rich purple earth by the path, which climbs past stunted trees thrashed by the wind into flattened, inland-pointing mats of foliage. Soon you are above the lighthouse on Start Point (829371), which is reached by crossing a stone stile and walking down a rough road under the jagged spine of the promontory.

The light-tower and buildings stand over the last few grassy yards of mainland, with the waves breaking around the tooth of the Black Stone, marooned offshore. The lighthouse, whose beam can be seen 20 miles out at sea, was built in 1836 to warn ships off this dangerous turning-point; but the sea went on claiming ships and men. The Black Stone, often hidden by waves and spray, was a hazard on which many vessels came to grief – in March 1891 the Colombian *Marana* ran on to the rock and went down with all but three of her crew of 28. Start Point was the scene of more premeditated deaths, too: pirates were hanged here in chains in Elizabethan days *pour encourager les autres.* The whole headland sticks out into the water like the spiky tail of a sea monster, which gave the Saxons inspiration for its name, 'Steort' meaning a tail. Walter White fortified himself at the lighthouse for his journey to Land's End with an early breakfast of coffee and mutton chops.

From Start Point you continue around the rocky arc of Ravens Cove to Peartree Point (I didn't spot any ravens or pear trees here) and come out to a wide view around the sweep of Lannacombe Bay. Below you lie Great Mattiscombe Sands (817369), the name almost bigger than the tiny beach of silvery-gold sand surrounded by a jumble of boulders and weedy rocks against which the waves cream. Two horns of rock like West Country termites' nests rise from the broken segments of cliff on the shore, the remnants of a wave-cut arch. A more complete version stands clear of Prawle Point at the far end of the bay, a grey glint of sea visible through its central slit.

The grassy coast-path skirts the long shoreline of Lannacombe Bay, unfrequented thanks to a lack of roads leading to it from inland – only

*Peace and seclusion: the old lime-burner's house, mill store
and lime-kiln on the shore at Lannacombe Beach.*

one in the three miles of its curve. Here you can see ravens, and buzzards as well, sitting on the rock outcrops on the brow of the cliffs or wheeling overhead. The beaks of the ravens are so massive that their heads can be seen turning from side to side as they assess your threat potential from 500 feet up. The cliffs here fall to a ledge 20 or 30 yards wide on which the path runs above the beach – evidence of the way that sea levels have changed over millions of years, for beach, ledge and clifftops have all at one time or another formed the floor of a sea. Land, of whatever shape and size, is a valuable thing. At Hallsands that narrow rock platform held a complete community; here farmers have skilfully converted the few available yards of ledge between cliffs and beach into long, narrow fields.

Lannacombe Beach is another slim strip of sand, its depth twice its length. The one road in the bay reaches the beach here and attracts holidaymakers for three months of the year. During the other nine, the occupant of the old mill store and lime-burner's quarters lives the peaceful life he loves, pottering in his garden and on the beach or making wine, a lucky man. His tall white house stands alone at the head of the beach (802372), attached to the old stone-built lime-kiln with its boat-shaped porch whose operator lived above the hoarded grain on the top floor of the store. Just below on the beach was the corn mill and its large waterwheel, placed down here to allow the water in its leat to gather maximum power as it raced down the steep valley from Lanna-combe Green.

The path climbs up from the beach towards the spiky neck of headland above Ballsaddle Rock (797365), favourite haunt of cormorants. It runs in a tangle of buddleia, brambles, bindweed, scabious and yarrow, past tarry sheds, crab-pots and boats and the scatter of large houses that overlook the bay from the ends of their own private tracks. In a hard winter you'd certainly need to get on with your neighbours down here in the nethermost corner of Devon – either that, or be a card-carrying hermit.

Keep close under the cliffs as you walk on round the spires, spikes and spines of the sharp rock outcrops on Langerstone Point, below which grow thick colonies of purple cranesbill. The view ahead swings round to the white coastguard buildings on Prawle Point (773351), Devon's most southerly point, the Anglo-Saxon 'lookout hill' stronghold with an unimpeded view all round. The sea-worn arch angles out from the Point and down into the water like a black spider's leg. It is a clear and uncompromising death-trap for ships, and has had its full share of wrecks. One, the clipper *Lallah Rhookh*, came aground in 1873 with 1300 tons of tea which formed a great bank ten feet high along the beach and provided the housewives of East Prawle with months of salty cuppas. The locals were great plunderers of wrecks, with a reputation for practicality – cargo first, lives a long second. Legend tells of a parson at East Portle-mouth, four miles to the west, who received news of a wreck on Prawle Point while preaching a sermon in church. Realizing that he and his informant were the only ones present who knew what had happened, the crafty clergyman finished his address and then dashed to the church door, guaranteeing himself first place in the race as he yelled over his shoulder: 'Wreck! Wreck aground at Prawle! Now we'll all start fair!'

The path continues from Prawle Point around the cliffs overlooking Maceley Cove, another steep half-circle of rocks and waves. The far side of the cove turns sharply to run out to the needles of rock on Gammon Head (765355), with the tall whaleback of Bolt Head rising beyond. The coast-path climbs by stone steps over the neck of Gammon Head to run on towards the mouth of Salcombe Harbour – but don't go as far as the steps. Instead, turn steeply up to your right before reaching Gammon Head and climb a path under a stack of rock (766357). This soon turns into a walled lane which bends to the right at the top of the slope (767361) for a delightful mile of sea glimpses and flowery hedges into East Prawle. This old field lane contains a store of wild flowers and plants to gladden the heart of any amateur botanist. In fact, I have to admit there were far too many for me to cope with. So here's a suggestion: if any keen botanist will send me a complete list of what's growing in that beautiful lane, I'll include it in the second edition of this book – and my kind informant will feature in the acknowledgements section.

East Prawle is a couple of twisting streets of houses, near death a few years ago from lack of young couples and children, but recently revived a little. The shop closes during the winter, though the baker, butcher, milkman and fishlady do come regularly down the winding lanes, and usually bring some extra necessities (fruit, butter, canned food) with them in their vans. The parish church is a couple of miles inland at Chivelstone, though there is a Methodist Chapel; the nearest entertainment is three miles and a ferry trip away in Salcombe. With the aid of cars, freezers and the occasional bus, the villagers of East Prawle just about keep going from one brief tourist harvest to the next. The village has one warm and lively nerve-centre, however: the Pig's Nose pub, a hooting, cheerful place where you can swap jokes over the bar, eat sandwiches of locally caught crab and drink strong bitter from the hand pump. The pub's walls are covered in notices and advertisements for local events, many of which begin and end with a drink in the Pig's Nose. On one wall hangs a large-scale map of 1904/5, showing the line of houses and the London Inn at Hallsands that were already under sentence of death. The pub manages to combine the functions of church, surgery, confessional, village hall, marriage guidance bureau, advice centre and all-purpose stores under one roof – and the beer's excellent, too.

Walk down the lane from the Pig's Nose and take the first turning on the right which climbs past Town Farm to the telephone box. Turn right here (782367) into a rough lane between hedges, following blue arrow waymarks and fingerposts. The lane dips and climbs to Woodcombe Farm (787372), dips and climbs again above Borough, then runs along the fields to a gate (794379) where it follows the top of the ridge, with a forward view into the combe running down to South Allington and up beyond to a great shoulder of downland patched with the purple of ploughed earth, yellow cornfields and green pasture. Follow the blue arrows down the slope to the lane in the valley bottom, where you turn right to pass the old mill, its leat and the stream at Lannacombe Green (801383). Bear right where three lanes meet at a little island of grass, to climb stiffly uphill to the crossroads at Hollowcombe Head. This rising lane is barely wide enough to take one car, let alone two-way traffic. Grass grows in the tarmac, potholes line its margins, a stream trickles down its slope, the hedges hem it in, hart's tongue ferns and bracken cascade down its banks, slugs crawl across it unthreatened by sudden death, thrushes warble from its bushes. In short, it's a lane to linger in.

On the far side of the crossroads (810383), with the sea in full view cupped in a deep valley of downland, another narrow lane leads even more steeply down to the car park at Hallsands.

11   Portloe and Nare Head

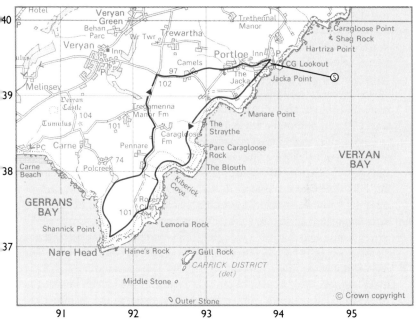

OS 1:50,000   Sheet 204
5 miles, the round trip

In 1910 Portloe was described as 'a poor fishing village in a primitive state, absolutely untouched by pleasure seekers'. These days the touch of the pleasure-seekers is pretty absolute, in the summer season anyway, but there are still fishing boats winning a living from the sea. The white-washed, grey-roofed houses of this Cornish village look as if they have been gently slid into position down a green ramp, coming to rest one behind another above the tiny inlet in the western side of Veryan Bay. Portloe is a tidily kept place: plenty of discreetly sited, recently built houses with swimming pools in their immaculate gardens, as well as the old fishermen's cottages near the harbour.

The Lugger Hotel sits squarely above the slipway with its winch shed, chains; boat trolleys and piles of crab-pots. Nowadays fishing out of Portloe is mostly for crab and a few lobsters. The modern plastic-and-metal pots are baited with mackerel, bought elsewhere and kept ready in salt tubs on the slipway. Another delicacy appreciated by the crabs is the heads of monkfish – a useful taste as far as the fishermen are concerned, because the tails are a gourmet's delight; while these go off to market, the heads are hung up on the harbour wall to go off in their own sweet way. These ghastly, stinking death-masks, gape-mouthed and gape-eyed, their severed necks gluily melting down the wall, are a never-failing source of admiration for visiting children.

Above the Lugger Hotel is the stone-built All Saints' church, topped with a green bell-tower. The church was built in 1870 as a lifeboat shed, housing a ten-oared boat which proved extremely difficult to manoeuvre around the tight curve leading down to the slipway. In 1877 the lifeboat smashed into a shop during a practice launch; this accident led to a new shed being built at the foot of the slipway and the religious conversion of the old building. In 1887, however, the Portloe lifeboat station was closed, the boat having never made a rescue in her 17 years. The narrowness of the inlet – less than 30 yards across – and the dangers of the rocky sides of the cove made it virtually impossible to launch her into an east wind. Things are no different nowadays; even at the height of the summer crabbing season, the Lugger Hotel and the Ship Inn have to take the crab salads and sandwiches off their menus when easterlies are blowing in from Veryan Bay.

Turn right at the head of the slipway (939395) and climb up on to the coast-path past the public lavatory. Alexanders, like a thick yellow cow-parsley, grow here along with pink clumps of thrift and carpets of fleshy stonecrop. Portloe means 'harbour of the inlet', and looking back from these cliffs you can see just how narrow and difficult is the sea approach to the village. 'Huers' (lookouts) stood up here in the autumns of years gone by, gazing down into the waters of Veryan Bay for the tell-tale shapes beneath the waves – a shadowy square changing to a rectangle 500 yards long, then balling into a great reddish sphere – that betrayed the passing shoals of pilchards.

> When the corn is in the shock
> Then the fish are on the rock

ran an old rhyme, for autumn brought the great pilchard shoals that sustained the village through the unworkable winter months. On sight-ing their prey, the 'huers' would shout, 'Hevva! Hevva!' (Cornish for a school of fish), wave wooden clubs or a sprig of leaves, or blow a triumphant blast down a special five-foot trumpet. Watchers in the harbour, receiving the signal, scrambled to launch their boats to round up the shoal with seine nets 500 feet long and 200 feet wide. Once surrounded, the pilchards were guided into the shallows, where short 'tucking nets' were dipped in among the frantic captives and hauled out full. The fish were piled up, salted and left in underground cellars for several weeks in enormous grey-and-pink heaps known as 'bulks'. Then they were squeezed dry of their oil and packed into hogsheads for transportation to market. Italy was an important customer for the catch, which probably explains the toast roared out in Portloe pubs after a successful pilchard haul:

> Here's a health to the Pope! may he live to repent,
> And add just six months to the term of his Lent,
> And tell all his vassals from Rome to the poles
> There's nothing like pilchards for saving their souls!

It wasn't only the pilchards that brought the Portloe villagers running, however; in December 1862 a terrible shrieking echoing round the inlet emptied every cottage and tavern. Thinking the noise was steam escaping from the ruptured boilers of a wrecked steamer, the villagers arrived panting on the shore ready for rescue (and, since this is Cornwall, probably for plunder as well) to find a 42-foot whale beached on the rocks and complaining by way of his blow-hole.

The cliffs don't plummet sheer into the water on this stretch of coast; they slope from green, stone-walled sheep pasture and cornfields to a tangle of bracken and gorse that drops steeply to the gleaming black rocks at the foot of the cliffs. The jagged shape of Gull Rock (927369) stands out of the water off Nare Head, with a view beyond to Dodman Point, four miles away across Veryan Bay. The flowers bordering the narrow grassy path add to the beauties of the walk, especially in springtime. Sea campion hangs its white bells of flowers in dense mats over the bushes of may; bluebells, primroses, stitchwort, red campion, daffodils and violets grow profusely among the gorse bushes. Framed between yellow gorse and white may, Portloe above its inlet and the sharp nose of Caragloose ('Grey Rock') Point make a memorable picture.

*Portloe's houses slope down the cliffs to
the narrow, rocky inlet of the harbour.*

Above the little square bay at The Straythe you look down on to grey rocks veined with white streaks of quartz, chunks of which line the field edges. The path runs below a fine white house through a grove of pines and shrubs and passes an old quarry, to turn left and descend a long flight of narrow steps close above the rock pools trapped in clefts of the rocks on the beach. Unfortunately it's axiomatic in coastal walking, particularly in Cornwall, that he who goes down has sooner or later to come up again; so there's a sharp climb to face on the far side of the bay, rising to a view from the headland of Gull Rock looking ever more spiky, the surf breaking in white spurts over its attendant hazards of the Middle and Outer Stones. Crabbing boats from Portloe chug backwards and forwards across the water below the cliffs.

Kiberick Cove, the next inlet, is even smaller and squarer than the last. There is no access for cars to its tiny rocky beach, so the worst of the summertime tourist invasion passes it by. Above it undulates the green plateau of the Slip Field (924381), named after the landslip in the early nineteenth century that caused the field to drop by 30 feet. As you descend the path, rich in shiny black slugs after rain, you can see the scars above the field marking the route of its slip.

The course of the path around Kiberick Cove is trenchantly described on metal National Trust notices. 'Footpath runs round head of valley to gap in hedge on far side' brings you to a gap in a thicket 20 feet high – if you keep well below the rim of the valley – followed by 'Footpath runs uphill to fence and thence to Nare Head'. The lamentations of cormorants, shags, guillemots, razorbills, kittiwakes and herring gulls reverberate from Gull Rock below you. A perfect nesting retreat in its isolated position, the bare sides of Gull Rock are splashed white with the droppings of its inhabitants who circle in twos and threes over the water. It has its dangers too: the Middle and Outer Stones, and a submerged reef known as The Whelps. In February 1914 the 2000-ton German barque *Hera* tore herself open on The Whelps and sank in just ten minutes. Falmouth lifeboat took off some survivors, but seven men decided to stay with the wreck. That decision cost them their lives, along with 12 others who had been drowned or swept away as the *Hera* went down.

On the top of the cliffs again, you enjoy the first stretch of level ground on the walk, running straight ahead to a spectacular view south and west from the smooth green neck of the 331-foot Nare Head (916371), one of the least visited pieces of National Trust land in Cornwall. A well-sited bench makes a good place to sit and stare out over the march of the cliffs round Gerrans Bay down to the white lines of Portscatho's houses and, away beyond them, a distant glimpse on a clear day of Black Head on the Lizard promontory, 15 miles away. Down to your left, the famous bathing beach of Pendower curves round the bay, the stately colonnades of the Pendower House Hotel (903383) standing above it. Behind the hotel the fields run inland up to a clump of trees on the skyline. They conceal an enormous tumulus, 370 feet around (912386), which when excavated in 1855 revealed the remains of a Bronze Age cremation. Romantic stories have gathered around the contents of that tumulus on Carne Beacon, however; for local legend says that two mighty heroes rolled into one man lie buried here.

Sir Geraint, noble knight of the Round Table, may perhaps have existed as one of the subordinates of that Celtic chieftain, Arthur Pendragon, who saw off the Saxons as the last of the red-cloaked legions marched away from these misty shores. Arthur Pendragon was one of the corner-stones from which grew the legend of King Arthur; and Cornish story-tellers shaded in some of the exploits of his henchman Geraint when they came to recount the life and death of their saintly King Gerennius, who ruled Cornwall 200 years after Arthur's last battle. He, too, was a mighty smiter of Saxons, defeating them in at least one great sea-battle, and by all accounts was as kingly in death as in life.

The story goes that St Teilo, Bishop of Llandaff, met Gerennius while on his way through Cornwall to Brittany in flight from the yellow plague. The encounter between the two saints went so well that St Teilo agreed to come to Cornwall to administer the last rites to Gerennius whenever Death should knock at his door. At the end of the bishop's seven-year exile over the sea, Gerennius appeared to him in a dream with the news that he was dying. St Teilo leapt into a boat, lashing to its bows a stone coffin for his friend which helpfully floated all the way back to Cornwall. After the last rites had been given, the body of the king was placed in the coffin and rowed reverently across Gerrans Bay in a golden boat equipped with silver oars. From Pendower Beach a team of oxen with silver harness pulled the stone coffin up the hillside to the top of Carne Beacon, where Gerennius, King of Cornwall, was laid to rest. His name lives on in Gerrans Bay and in Dingerein Castle ('Dinas Geraint', Geraint's Castle), a mile south-west of Pendower Beach.

From Nare Head you drop down to the footbridge over the stream in Paradoe Cove (915376). If you want to explore the sands of Pendower Beach, carry on up out of the cove and over the next headland. Our walk, however, turns inland at a yellow arrow waymark by the bridge and ascends the valley through a little wood of aspens, elders, sallows, birch, beech and stumpy oaks, their branches heavy with bushy lichens. Stiles lead to the National Trust car park above Kiberick Cove, where you turn left along a flowery lane over whose banks are far views across the two bays: Gerrans on your left, Veryan on your right. You pass the slate-hung house of Pennare Wartha, and bear left at the next fork in the lane (923386) to meet a road. Follow this, in preference to the rather uncertain field-paths, to Camels (928393), where the encouraging sign 'Sunny Corner' points you down over stiles of granite bars through fields whose stone walls have been repaired in herringbone patterns. A final stile (933394) leads into the high-banked lane which drops down into Portloe, passing the Ship Inn on the left (bar meals and good draught beer, brewed in St Austell) and its tiny terraced beer-garden down a steep slope on the other side of the road.

12   Around the Lizard

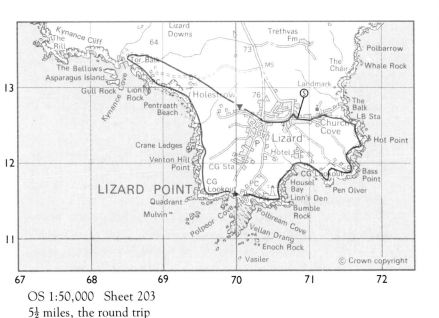

OS 1:50,000   Sheet 203
5½ miles, the round trip

Sir John Killigrew was a bit of a rogue, however you view him. When he built his lighthouse on The Lizard in 1619 it was only piracy under a different name, a trade his family had specialized in for centuries. Sir John was hoping that his coal-burning light-tower would bring him enough loot, in the form of a halfpenny-per-ton levy on passing ships, to allow him to put his feet up and retire from buccaneering on the high seas. He was canny enough to realize the money-making potential of a warning beacon on this deadly stretch of coastline; but he had forgotten that passing ships are not the easiest of targets to extract tolls from: for one thing, they tended not to stop in their passage around the reefs and rocks waiting just offshore to send them to the bottom. Soon the cost of providing coal for the light was outweighing the income from such ships as he managed to track down; and Sir John went back to more direct and forceful ways of making a living.

The hidden rocks off Lizard Point, reaching out a good half-mile from land, have claimed more lives than almost any other hazards around the coastline of Britain. Nowadays they have a 15-million-candlepower light, visible 20 miles away, perched on their cliffs, but they still continue to claw down men and ships in foul weather. They are the wave-torn stumps of offshore islands separated from the mainland by wave erosion; and larger versions of them stand singly or in clusters beyond the edges of the cliffs all round the south-western coast of Cornwall. They give this walk around the southern tip of the Lizard peninsula a striking drama; as you look down on their jagged shapes, they remind you of the ease with which ships are drawn to their doom in the rocky coves of The Lizard during fog or storm.

Walter White, walking through Cornwall to Land's End in 1854, found Lizard Town 'a poor scattered village', though it had probably come up in the world since Elizabethan times, when many of its houses were built from the timbers of wrecked ships. It stands at the end of the road from Helston, isolated and windy in a lonely corner of Cornwall. Looking seaward today over the houses of Lizard Town from the car park at the bottom of the Helston road (703125), there are no foretastes of the wonderful beauty of the coastline that lies south of the town, just stone-walled fields in a flat, treeless landscape. Bear right across the car park into the lane below Rocklands guest-house, and in 100 yards mount a flight of rough stone steps at a blue public footpath sign on the right (702127), which leads on to a path running along the top of a field-wall towards the sea. This is the only direct route between Kynance Cove and Lizard Town, and must have seen many a moonlight cargo passing along on the broad backs of local smugglers.

Arriving at the toll road to Kynance Cove, the path joins the road for a short way before striking off to the right (693132) across a wide heath of heather and gorse which brings you to the car park above the cove (685134). Looking down into this narrow little inlet, almost blocked off from the sea by large stacks of rock, you can see what a perfect haven for smuggling it must have been: well guarded by cliffs from unwelcome visitors inland, the rocky islets in its mouth hiding activities in the cove from the telescopes of Excise cutters at sea, a good path up the gully on to the deserted moorland track down to Lizard Town and its hiding place for barrels and bales. There were good hides in the cove itself, too, among the arches and caves burrowed in the cliffs by the sea. You can scramble down the steep path into Kynance Cove to enjoy the rocky beach with its

A chain of serpentine rocks guards the entrance to Kynance
Cove, whose caves could tell a smuggling story or two.

little white-painted café perched above, and explore the rocks and stacks
at low tide. Smuggling stories are not the only ones attaching to this
famous cove: Prince Albert, away from his Victoria with the children for
a day, landed here from a boat; and, three centuries before, watchers on
the cliffs to the west were the first to spy the approaching Armada and
send the hot message that would interrupt that celebrated game of bowls
at Plymouth.

   The cliffs here are mostly of serpentine, a soft stone shot through with
snake-like veins of green, red or black that glows warmly when polished.
Lizard Town makes a good thing out of its serpentine in the shape of
ashtrays, vases, lamp standards and model lighthouses, turned out by the

69

locally owned and run works and sold to tourists. The cliffs themselves, though extensively dug for serpentine in the past, yield stone of an inferior quality to the quarries on the inland heath. The coast-path runs over outcrops of the brightly coloured rock, scratched and dented by the boots of walkers.

From Kynance Cove climb back up the path towards the car park and take a flight of steps on the right which lead to another high-level view over the shark's-fin shape of Lion Rock (688130), nearly 200 feet high, jutting up from the waves over the dark mouths of caves in the cliffs round Pentreath Beach. The path passes the old teashop on top of the cliffs and runs round the lip of the next cove towards the outreaching arm of Lizard Point which slopes down into the sea from the long line of the houses of Lizard Town. The treacherous rocks offshore show just a couple of their outer teeth, the majority of them lying hidden under the surface of the water. You look down on the screeching gulls that chase in twos and threes after intruding jackdaws, and below them to the wrinkled sea creaming against the rocks. The coastal path is clearly marked ahead of you, a strenuous series of dips and climbs into and out of the stream gullies that run down into a succession of little coves.

With grasshoppers sawing away in the long grass, you round Lizard Point to look down into Polpeor Cove. The now disused lifeboat house and slipway (701115) stand at the foot of the brown, green and orange cliffs on top of which gleams the bright white Trinity House township around the short, squat lighthouse. The purple, daisy-like flowers of sea aster grow by the path as it reaches the little cluster of buildings below the lighthouse: the old lifeboat station, a couple of hotels, 'The Most Southerly Café', a serpentine works and shop. The lifeboat station was shut down in 1961 when the new one in Church Cove replaced it, but the proud record of service is still on display by the cliff-path. The Lizard lifeboat had its greatest moments during a thick fog on the night of 17/18 March 1907, when the White Star liner *Suevic* ran on to the Maenheere Reef. Four boats – those from The Lizard, Cadgwith, Coverack and Porthleven – worked without stopping to bring the 524 people on board the *Suevic* safely to shore; and the Lizard lifeboat was responsible for saving 167 of them during six dangerous trips into the blanketing fog.

The path climbs beneath the huge twin black-painted foghorns of the Lizard lighthouse (705116), whose short octagonal tower stands behind the lighthouse crew's large house, painted in shining white picked out in dark green. Beyond the lighthouse lies the rocky Housel Bay, and away beyond that is the headland of Pen Olver, where a white castellated tower stands on the cliff. This gothic creation was taken over by the coastguard in 1969; it started life as a signal station belonging to Lloyd's, the London-based maritime insurance company, who demanded that all ships registered with them should make a visual signal to their station on the cliffs. In murky weather this meant ships coming dangerously close inshore, sometimes spearing themselves on the concealed rocks. To reach the old signal station, you skirt around the cliffs above Housel Bay where a few houses stand in the shadow of the splendid Housel Bay Hotel. Down in the bay lies the Lion's Den, a black outlier of rock which was a cave in the cliffs before collapsing in 1847 to become a finger pierced by a square block arch. Shags stand gulping skyward on the rocks in the bay, their favourite perching place keel-shaped and splashed white with their droppings.

The piping calls of gulls echo around the cliffs along which the path goes, to pass between the old signal station (714120) and the present small and efficient coastguard lookout. Once the corners of Bass Point and Hot Point have been turned, you are rewarded with a fine view down into Kilcobben or Church Cove, where fishing boats ride in the sheltered water. In a narrow channel of the cliffs is the Lizard–Cadgwith lifeboat station (716125), which amalgamated those two former stations (1000 lives saved between them) when it was opened in 1961. The shed at the top of the cleft has a little platform which can take men and equipment via a funicular railway down the cliff to the lifeboat hut below. Among the 'services rendered' recorded on plaques by the upper shed is a sombre reminder of a recent lifeboat disaster that was splashed across the front pages of the newspapers:

Dec 20 1981 – Penlee lifeboat *Solomon Browne*:
recovered wreckage.

Climb the steps above the shed to walk up the tarmac track to the lane running up through the hamlet of Landewednack. Just up the road stands the church of St Wynwallow or Winwalaus, England's most southerly church (711127). It was built by the Normans in 1120 with a tower chequered in alternate black and pink blocks of serpentine and granite. In the churchyard stands the touching memorial gravestone of a child:

Let
learn
Parents ∧ to be con-
tent when God re-
quires that is but lent
in Youth or child-
hood put no trust for
all must Dye that
come from dust

A beautiful Norman doorway decorated with dog-tooth carving and circular symbols leads into the cool interior whose curved roof is supported on slim arches of granite. An ancient bell standing by the west wall probably dates back to the thirteenth century, like its two sisters that still ring parishioners to worship. The walls of the church carry many brass plaques recording deaths at home and abroad by drowning and war, reminders that the sea has taken more folk from Cornwall to distant parts of the world than from any other county in England.

Walk up the lane from the church to join the road (708126), where you turn left for Lizard Town. On the right of the junction stands an old cross head and shaft, its carvings weathered away to smoothness, where open-air preachers dispensed the Word to anyone who would stop and listen. Around the base of the cross is a carefully planted flower garden, watered, weeded and tended by some anonymous hand.

13 Sennen to Land's End and Nanjizal

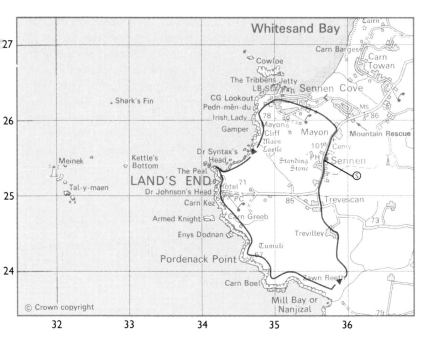

Whitesand Bay

Cairn
Carn Barges
Carn Towan
Cowloe
The Tribbens Jetty
LB Sta   Sennen Cove
Shark's Fin
CG Lookout
Pedn-mên-du
Irish Lady
78
Mayon
Cliff Mayon
Mountain Rescue
Gamper
Maen
Castle
101
Cemy
Meinek
Kettle's
Bottom
Dr Syntax's
Head
Standing
Stone
PH
Sennen
LAND'S END
The Peal
Tal-y-maen
Dr Johnson's Head
Hotel
71
PC
85
Trevescan
Carn Kez
Armed Knight
Carn Greeb
Carn
Trevilley
Enys Dodnan
Tumuli
67
Pordenack Point
73
Carn Boel
Zawn Reeth
© Crown copyright
Mill Bay or
Nanjizal
79

32   33   34   35   36

OS 1:50,000   Sheet 203
4½ miles, the round trip

CONDITIONS:
*It's a good idea to do this walk outside the high tourist season – even though the
visitors who crowd Land's End in July and August are not as noisy and messy
as some writers would have you believe. If you are walking around Land's End
in the summer holidays, the best times are early in the morning before the
coaches get there or in the late afternoon when most of them have gone away.*

*The rocks at the tip of Land's End are not dangerous, if visitors stick to the
basic safety rules – and that's a big 'if'. Sea surges here can be unexpectedly
high and powerful, capable of sweeping you off the rocks at water level; but you
can clamber among the stacks and pinnacles quite safely if you keep to the
higher ground. There have been several tragedies here, so do be aware of the
safety rule that any local person will ram home: stay high and dry.*

In this flat, windy tip of Britain, the yellow-lichened tower of St Sennen church (357255) in the village of Sennen is the main landmark above the stone walls and small fields. A great arc of sea encloses the plain little village, which is strung out along the A30 and divided all day by streams of cars and coaches on their way from Penzance to Land's End. They crawl through Sennen, where King Arthur and his knights once feasted after giving thanks in the church for a great victory over the Viking invaders. So much Norse blood was spilt that day that the wheel of Sennen mill was driven not by water but by a river of gore. The interior of the church has several attractions: beautifully carved angels play medieval musical instruments on the ends of the choir stalls, and behind the altar is a series of little gilt pictures showing aspects of local life: seagulls, ships, fishermen making lobster- and crab-pots and bagging the catch; ploughing, launching the lifeboat, a fish in a net. There is also a wall tablet to a 'lovely accomplished wife', and a great board recording the gratitude of King Charles II to the inhabitants of the County of Cornwall for backing his cause in the difficult days of the Common-wealth, and for their 'wonderful Succefs . . . by many strange Victories over their & our enemies, in difpite of all human probabilities & all Imaginable difadvantages'.

Sennen church underwent a fierce short-back-and-sides of a restora-tion in Victorian times, having become so decayed that grass grew in the pews and the vestments had mouldered away to rags. Services there must have been lively, though, as the barrel-organ had a mind of its own and refused to stop playing when the hymn ended. It had to be picked up and carried out of the church, still blaring tunes, so that the vicar could get on with his sermon.

From the church, turn right up the A30 past the Methodist chapel and the First and Last Store – plenty of Firsts and Lasts hereabouts – to cross the stone wall on the left of the road at a green public footpath sign marked 'Sennen Cove $\frac{1}{2}$' (358259). The view from the tarmac path stretches over the long crescent of Whitesand Bay and the white houses of Sunny Corner on the cliffs, out to The Brisons rearing out of the sea off Cape Cornwall. You descend between flowering hedges to look over the lichen-stained wall on to the curved breakwater at Sennen Cove (351264), built after a disaster in February 1905, when the *Khyber* was wrecked off Land's End with the loss of 23 lives. The Sennen lifeboat couldn't put out in the face of a stiff onshore wind, and the crew had to wait in their boathouse while the victims were drowning just round the corner of the cliffs. Now the lifeboat, with nearly 400 lives saved since it was established in 1853, can put out in all weathers to pull stranded holidaymakers, sick sailors and capsized fishermen to safety, thanks to the shelter of the breakwater.

Beyond the lifeboat station a creaky old winch pulls the fishing boats up their slipway and the slope of the beach, the fishermen in yellow oilskins and high sea-boots piling their catch into red plastic trays for transportation to market. Grey mullet were the main winter prize 100 years ago; a huge shoal came each year into the bay, and every fisherman spread seine nets to harvest it. Those who couldn't take part in the actual fishing would take care to be on the beach when the shoal came in, since any male villager on the shore at the time the catch was made was entitled to his share.

From up on the path, the houses of the fishing hamlet crouch back against the cliff, white blobs of seagulls wheeling above their grey roofs. The path drops down into Sennen Cove, where you turn left above the breakwater to climb up again on to the headland (348262). The ground plunges away in front as you come over the top of the rise, several rocking stones balancing on the very edge of the cliffs. From here, there is a tremendous view over the deeply gashed snout of Land's End, small rock stacks bristling at its very tip, running down into the sea from the white hotel standing at the top of the rise. The spine of the promontory is usually bristling with tourists, too. The crevices in the sides of Land's End are black with shadow, their mouths a mass of fallen boulders. A couple of miles offshore lie the low, bare rocks of Carn Brâs, the 'Great Rock', from which rises the salt-stained tower of the Longships light-house, suitably grim and steadfast-looking. These rocks have claimed hundreds of ships and thousands of lives down the years, and are given the widest possible berth by the vessels that round the tip of Cornwall. Out beyond the Longships, 28 miles across the Atlantic, on a clear day you can see the flat humps of the Scilly Isles, and to the south-west stands the lonely lighthouse on Wolf Rock, nine miles away.

Somewhere between Land's End and the Scilly Isles, the bells of Lyonesse toll under the waves. This Cornish Atlantis has no proven place in history, but legends say that Tristan, brave knight and tragic

The Longships lighthouse lifts a warning finger
off the rock pinnacles of Land's End.

lover of Iseult, was born in a boat bringing his mother across the water from the fair land. Another story tells how one Trevilian, more alert than his fellow countrymen on the eve of the final disaster, leapt on to his horse as the sea came crashing through the defences of Lyonesse and raced the tidal wave to land, beating it by a short head.

The path runs on around the cove past rocks hairy with long green lichens and glinting with quartz. Down in the curve of the bay stands the sharp-edged stack known as the Irish Lady (347261), gazing out towards her homeland complete with creased cloak and little yellow cap. Many other faces, animals and birds can be imagined in the weather-eaten shelves and stacks of granite that slope up out of the heather, bracken, clover and grass. As you walk further round, a crack opens up running clean through the Land's End promontory to a gleam of blue sea on the far side; one day it will reach the top of the rock, and England will be 50 feet shorter.

The outermost point of mainland Britain is made up of a whole tribe of totem-like heads of rock, a well-beaten path winding among them. The National Trust tried to buy Land's End in 1981, but couldn't compete with the highest bids of more than £2 million. In 1987 Land's End changed hands again, for nearly three times that sum. Now, for better or worse, it's commercially run and commercially orientated. There are knick-knacks, gewgaws, kickshaws and fripperies at the 'First and Last House' on the clifftop, but the final blade of land still somehow retains its dignity.

John Skinner, sitting here as a young curate in 1797 on his holiday from Somerset, enjoyed the view, especially over the lighthouse on which his eye 'reposed with pleasure'. That other curate diarist, Francis Kilvert of Clyro, fulfilled a dream by standing on the tip of Land's End on 27 July 1870; but he had to put up with a whole gang of tourists who 'went rushing down the rocks towards the Land's End as if they meant to break their necks, and no great loss either'. This crowd of 'insufferable snobs' even went so far as to insult the ladies of Kilvert's party, upon which the gallant and larky Capt. Parker 'suggested that a kicking might tend to mind their manners'. The Captain had a good day, keeping the wag-gonette in a roar by taking the mickey out of their long-suffering driver, Edward Noy, and ripping open an adder with his knife to find three young mice inside.

Below the Land's End Hotel a hard-working photographer shuffles the alphabet to make up a signpost showing the miles to your home town. The hotel itself is large and busy, offering its own brand of draught beer and just about every other kind of tourist facility. From the hotel the path continues above the cliffs and coves along the edge of the moor, over which peeps the tower of St Sennen. The Armed Knight (341247) stands below Land's End, and beyond him Enys Dodnan, a great slab of cut-off cliffs pierced with a slanting 50-foot arch. You walk around Pordenack Point to another splendid view down into the clear green water in Nanjizal Bay. Its southern arm is gashed with two narrow gullies running far back into the headland, and the breast of the promontory ends in a mass of rock pinnacles that for sharpness and height outdo anything seen so far on this walk. As you clamber along the path halfway up the steep slope above the bay, take a breather to look back on the deep caves eaten by the sea into the cliffs, some separated by central pillars of granite. No wonder that smuggling stories cling so thickly to this lovely, secluded bay.

The track up the hillside and back to Sennen is only faintly marked – it leaves the coastal path just before the footbridge over the stream that cascades down into the bay, and directly opposite a line of stone blocks beside the path (358238). The track climbs through gorse and heather up to the top of the hill, where it forks – bear left here to a stone wall and a series of gates between the cornfields to Trevilley Farm (358245). The barns and outbuildings are made of such massive slabs of granite that they seem to have been quarried complete rather than built. Bear left here to take the field-path to the road below Sennen (357248). The 'First Inn in England' serves food and draught beer, and has a small garden and a children's room.

14 Zennor and Gurnard's Head

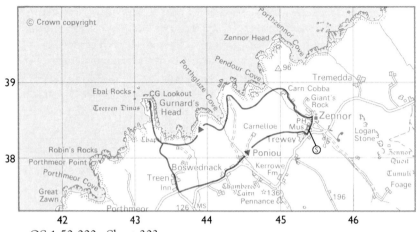

OS 1:50,000   Sheet 203
4½ miles, the round trip

When, during the First World War, D. H. Lawrence was living with Frieda at Tregerthen, a mile east of Zennor on this wild strip of western Cornish coastline, the locals couldn't stomach their bohemian way of life and her German accent. The odd couple were obviously spies, and the Zennor folk made life so uncomfortable for them that they had to pack up and leave.

The insularity of its inhabitants is the chief characteristic noted by past visitors to the outermost tip of Britain: their suspicion of outsiders, and their habits bred by a hard life in hard surroundings. Nowadays local attitudes have softened as the visitors have multiplied, but you can still hear stories of life in Zennor village as it was when no intruders came to this land of Neolithic burial chambers, bleak moors, cliffs and coves. Legends tell how winter got so severe that a cow ate the plaited straw bell-rope in Zennor church; how the villagers built a hedge round a cuckoo so that spring would stay in Zennor; and especially how a beautiful mermaid came to the church, disguising her fish's tail in a long dress, to hear the golden singing of Matthew Trewhella. She enticed him away to Porthzennor Cove and to bliss under the sea; but their duets can still be heard on calm summer nights.

The mermaid – or at least an ancient wood-carving of her – lives in the church at Zennor; but before visiting her it is worth spending half an hour in the Wayside Museum, just down the lane, to catch the flavour of traditional life around the village before it was transformed by roads, railways and radios. Here are exhibitions of the craft and hard labour of the wheelwright, the granite quarryman, the tin miner, the blacksmith, the miller and the subsistence farmer – and cut-away models showing how they lived at home.

St Senara's church along the lane (455385) stands over the village on the side of its valley, a twelfth-century building in origin with the weathered heads of old crosses in its churchyard that pre-date the Normans. There is a plaque outside the porch commemorating John Davey who died in 1891, the very last person to speak Cornish as his only tongue. Services in Cornish are held every so often in Zennor church for the benefit of Cornish men and women who don't intend to let their native tongue die. Inside the building, the nave is flanked by low granite arches and the pews contain beautifully worked kneelers showing local subjects: a tractor, fishes, the village in spring sunshine and under winter snow. The mermaid, perhaps as much as 600 years old, occupies the end of a little stool made from old bench-ends when the church was being restored in 1890; she lacks a nose, but has a pair of piercing eyes, long wet hair, a superb figure and a tail that looks as if she's slipped it on for a fancy-dress party.

Mermaids' reputations suffered more than most from that *angst* about sexual feelings that the missionaries engendered among their converts. Gradually those delicious denizens of the deep became sirens, luring men's hearts and bodies away into the waves and carrying a comb and mirror as symbols of vanity and heartlessness. Before guilt had been stirred in men's souls, the mermaid had been an altogether nicer being, an offshoot of the goddess Aphrodite, the round shape in her hand not the mirror of selfishness but the apple of love. The mermaid of Zennor looks very much as if she belongs to that older and warmer tradition.

Opposite the church, a narrow lane (no cars allowed) winds down past a farm, descending towards a triangle of sea between the slopes of the cliffs. Furze and bracken grow in the small fields, little changed from medieval times and separated from each other by lumps of stone piled together, rather than the neatly executed walls of less weather-beaten districts. The lane ends by the gate of the coastguard houses above Pendour Cove, whose right-hand wall rises to the outcrops on Zennor Head. You continue down a narrow, walled path to turn left at a waymarked stone (450390) and drop down to Pendour Cove by rough steps – watch your feet all the way down, as the steps are uneven. At the bottom, the path crosses a fast-rushing stream tumbling down a cleft, then climbs round the next cove and corresponding headland. Badgers have dug deep sets into the bank supporting the wall that guards the small fields from the cliff edge. Purple bell heather, yellow toadflax and the striking broad white flowerheads of yarrow streak the bracken with colour as you round the headland to a memorable view forward. The dragon's head and neck of Gurnard's Head poke far out into the sea from the green shoulders of the mainland, with a cap of tall, jumbled rocks at its seaward end. From here you can hear the waves sighing on the western side of the Head. Beside the path stands a 20-foot rock stack like a cathedral, but it makes little impact on the eye or mind with that great knuckle of greenstone in view out in the water ahead.

The path passes a couple of white-painted houses on the cliff inland of the Head, and descends to a stream. Above the track stands the gaunt ruin of the Treen copper mine (abandoned in the 1850s), and below lie the gale-battered walls of Chapel Jane (434382) on the cliff edge, being slowly eaten away by the rain and wind. Chapel Jane dates from the twelfth century, and perhaps earlier, and measures a tiny ten feet by eight feet. It has no connection with any Jane, but takes its name appropriately from the Cornish word for bleak and cold, 'Yeyn'. Its position on a clifftop plateau is very reminiscent of the church of St Mary above Bardsey Island, at the western tip of the Lleyn Peninsula in Wales; it, too, has a holy well: the spring which falls down a cliff gully just to the south of the building.

Above the one-time smuggling haven of Treen Cove the path edges round the cliffs to a crossroads of paths; turn right here to descend the slope and reach the track running along the eastern flank of Gurnard's Head. The pile of rocks on the crown of the Head is worth climbing for the far-reaching view west to Pendeen Watch (another outstanding head of rock) and east up the great arc of North Cornwall's coastline to St Agnes Head and beyond. The sea thumps into the crevices on the western side, surging, crashing and crackling with an all-pervading noise

It must have been the melon! Francis Kilvert's 'corner and end of the world, desolate, solitary, bare, dreary': Zennor village basks in late evening sunlight.

of water that outdoes every other sound except the thin cry of the gulls. This knobbly club of land has a pre-Christian fort on its western edge, Trereen Dinas, an easily defended camp for Iron Age settlers. Something magical and other-worldly clings to these points and tongues of rock sticking out into the waves around the coasts of Britain – half in the sea and half on the land, only accessible on foot and with some effort, remote, loud with water and wind, giving their occupants the sensation partly of flying and partly of floating. The atmosphere of Gurnard's Head takes visitors in different ways: some run up and down the rocks shouting their heads off, some cling fearfully to reassuring handholds, others stand and gaze at the coves and headlands on each side, or gleefully embrace their companions.

Francis Kilvert, coming here on an expedition with friends in 1870, left the rest of the party larking up in the rocks and, like any sensitive young curate, 'wandered round the cliffs to the broken rocks at the furthest point of the Head, and sat alone amongst the wilderness of broken shattered tumbled cliffs, listening to the booming and breaking of the waves below and watching the flying skirts of the showers of spray. Perfect solitude.'

From the Head, a straightforward path leads back up the slope of the hill to the Gurnard's Head Hotel (435375), where Kilvert enjoyed 'a capital dinner indoors . . . and I actually ate and liked a slice of melon and like Oliver Twist asked for "more". Memorable day.'

Our path back to Zennor lies across the fields on the route taken by the curate of Clyro and the other gentlemen of his party on their way from Zennor to Gurnard's Head. Opposite the hotel the path crosses the field-wall to run parallel with and below the B3306 road, cutting out one of its many zig-zags. The gaps in these stone walls between the fields are bridged with three or four thick bars of granite sunk lengthways in the ground – a very effective local version of a cattle-grid, though the Zennor pigs are reputed to learn quickly how to skip across. You rejoin the road (439376) for half a mile of more or less pleasant walking, depending on the volume of traffic grinding towards Land's End, before leaving it again where it bends sharply right (445379). Here a lane runs briefly towards Zennor before turning left for Carnelloe, but a footpath sign shows the way across the fields, by way of a succession of Cornish grids, to reach the top of the road down into Zennor. The low top of St Senara's church appears first, its pinnacles poking up out of the valley – then the rest of the church hauls itself up into sight, followed by the roofs and walls of the village below the stony nape of its hill. Writing his diary that Friday evening of 29 July 1870, Francis Kilvert remembered Zennor as 'a corner and end of the world, desolate, solitary, bare, dreary'. Perhaps that melon didn't agree with him after all.

15   The lost land of Penhale Sands

OS 1:50,000   Sheet 200
4 miles, there and back

CONDITIONS:
*This is a low-tide walk, taking advan-
tage of the broad expanse of Perran
Beach, along which you can walk well
away from the cliffs and dunes.
Check tide times locally before you set
out.*

This walk is all about sand: sand
lying as firm and flat as a board for
nearly three glorious miles; sand
blown by storm winds, packed and
moulded into a great range of
peaks and hollows rising 200 feet above the shore. Starting along the
superb Perran Beach that runs north from Perranporth to Ligger Point,
you climb into an utterly different world of spiky grass, yellow clumps of
ragwort shivering in the breeze and faint sand-tracks that climb up and
down the dunes. The one is packed with surfers, bathers and sand-yacht
racers on sunny summer days; the other is almost deserted, a high and
lonely wasteland with a fabled city buried deep in its heart.

Perranporth was just one of the tiny fishing villages of the North
Cornwall coast until the railway arrived. In 1820 it was becoming known
for its 'fine sandy beach frequented as a bathing place by the neighbouring gentry, who procure lodgings in the cottages on the beach', but it was
the railway that changed the village from a haunt of local people into a
busy resort, accessible to holidaymakers from London and the Midlands.
Nowadays in the season it is a maze of loud and brightly lit pubs,
chip-shops and amusement arcades, its streets uncomfortably full,
stretching and rising in a long arc around Droskyn Point and the
southern corner of its beach. Those three miles of dead-level, dull-gold
sand, however, are still big enough to absorb all comers.

There is a fine view over the whole length of the beach from the
clifftop car park above Droskyn Point (754544). The long surfing waves

84

cream over in crests of foam that gradually run together and mingle in a single line of white as they approach the beach, usually dotted with the brightly coloured wetsuits of surfers. At high tide the sands are divided into two stretches by the blunt nose of Cotty's Point, but as the water ebbs they join again into a single shining bar at whose edge black-backed and herring gulls bicker over the sea's leavings. Seen from up here in the early morning, holding only a couple of tiny figures taking a pre-breakfast stroll in all their length, backed and enclosed by the craggy black cliffs, the sands look like a Victorian railway company advertisement.

Steps lead down the cliff-face below the car park to a group of stacks that form a complex of caves, crannies and sea-cut arches: one has been hollowed out and a room built inside, with a rusty iron door and tiny window. Turn up the beach to your right at the bottom of the steps to ford (by stepping-stones) the river flowing down the sands. Far in the distance beyond Ligger Point, the hump of Gull Rock rises out of the water off Penhale Point, and away in the middle of the sea to the south-west are the jagged cones of Bawden Rocks (known locally as 'Man and his man'), more like icebergs in the Antarctic than anything characteristic of an English scene.

Seen from close up, the golden sands turn out to be streaked with black grit, evidence of the mineral wealth locked into the rocks hereabouts. Cotty's Point (757551) is made of this grey-black, iridescent stuff, formed of wafer-thin layers squeezed together under tremendous pressures hundreds of millions of years ago, then buckled and bent into horseshoes and knots. The rocks are burrowed with caves, some 50 feet high and running back more than 30 yards into the cliff. Their peaked roofs hold lumps of white and rose-pink quartz, seamed and wrinkled like brains; and veins of quartz streak the grey sides of the caves. Tin and copper were won from these rocks until expensive labour and cheaper competitors closed the mines one by one. The miners were hard men in a hard business, and had as their patron saint a suitably energetic, lively and human man who founded the fortunes of Cornish miners by accident one cold night.

St Piran had already had a pretty adventurous life before he arrived in Cornwall, some time during the sixth century. Back in his native Ireland he had a reputation as a miracle-worker, on one occasion feeding ten kings and their respective armies for ten days with three mangy cows as his only source of supply. The pettier the king, however, the greater the pride; and when the holy man took King Angus of Munster to task for making a bigamous marriage, the king had him thrown over a cliff with a millstone tied round his neck. But God had other plans for Piran and caused the millstone to float across the sea, carrying the saint to Perran Beach and the savage Cornishmen. The night being cold, Piran took up lodgings in one of the caves behind the beach and built a fireplace of the black stones that were lying around. The driftwood fire grew hotter and hotter and, to the saint's amazement, a trickle of shining liquid began to flow from between the fire stones. In the morning it had dried and turned into strange grey bars, harder than anything Piran had seen before. When the locals arrived, the saint lost no time in showing them the trick – and the tinning industry was born. Saint and sinners, according to the legend, then broached a couple of casks of mead and metheglin and got roaring drunk around the fires.

Much the same story is told of the discovery of copper, another important industry in these harsh North Cornish moors. By all accounts, St Piran was a practical saint and a sociable man, as much interested in the improvement of his converts' living conditions as in their souls, and not averse to a glass or three of the local brew. Saints need refreshment for spirit as well as body, however; so Piran built himself a tiny oratory or praying cell high on the windy dunes of Penhale Sands.

To reach the site of St Piran's Oratory you walk on along the beach from Cotty's Point, passing a flight of steps up the cliff that climb to the holiday camp above. A few hundred yards beyond the steps, a path mounts diagonally up the face of the dunes (760562) – a difficult climb on the sliding surface of sand. At the top are the yellow and blue chalets of the holiday camp, all neat, all well serviced and all exactly the same. Bear left here over the grassy dunes, on which grow thick carpets of moss and colonies of bright yellow ragwort, and make for the top of the nearest dune. You look across a barren sea of wind-sculptured sand-hills to a tall concrete cross which towers above the site of the oratory.

A wedge of granite stands on a mound in a hollow below the cross, under which lie the remains of St Piran's cell (768564). For 1300 years it stood here, for most of that time under a coat of sand, the wind occasionally blowing enough of the covering away to expose an angle of the walls. Local people knew of the site and its sacred history; they built a

Below Droskyn Point at Perranporth, the sea has not yet reached
up quite far enough to break this natural rock bridge.

fine church just to the north in the thirteenth century, and erected a
cross nearby. By 1803 the church had been half buried in sand, and was
rebuilt on safer ground, three miles to the south, at Perranzabuloe. The
old cross was left to weather away, as was the oratory in its waterlogged
hollow. In 1835 St Piran's cell was properly excavated, perfectly preserved from its centuries under the sand. Inside were the skeletons of
three men, their severed heads lying on their breasts; one of them, buried
beneath the altar slab in the tradition of martyred saints, was of a man
seven feet six inches tall. St Piran was evidently big in stature as well as in
heart.

Within three days, treasure-hunters had stolen all the carved
stonework from the oratory, but the little building remained open to the
wind and rain. Soon it was crumbling away. In 1909 it was covered with a
hideous shell of concrete in an attempt to preserve it, but one century of
exposure had proved more destructive than the sands of a thousand
years. The fabric went on falling to pieces until 1980, when St Piran
must have heaved a thankful sigh from Heaven as his little retreat was
reburied and left in peace.

From the oratory you can walk east for a few hundred yards to the old cross, its four rough holes showing where the carved head once was, and the low granite remains of the church just below it (772565). The best route back to Perranporth is the way you came – down the face of Penhale Sands and along the beach. Before you go, however, dig a hand down into the dunes – you may come up with gold from the great city of Langarrow. Like Lyonesse off Land's End, like Cantref-y-Gwaelod off the Powys coast, like Atlantis itself, Langarrow paid for a golden age with a cataclysmic disaster – not by a roaring sea, however, but by a terrible sandstorm.

The city, so the legend says, stretched for four miles, the largest and most beautiful place in the kingdom. Its people grew rich, mining the tin and lead in the hills behind their city, and they filled the streets of Langarrow with wonderful buildings. They feasted, sang, harped and danced, and became too high and mighty for the hard work of the mines. They invited the other towns of England to send them their worst criminals, who were put to work in the bowels of the earth and housed in a squalid shanty-town outside Langarrow's splendid walls. The new-comers dug the precious ores and built a new harbour for their masters; and as they toiled they began to grow envious – not surprisingly – of the charmed lives led within the city walls. The fair women of Langarrow could not help comparing the sunburnt, muscular bodies and the lusty manners of the labourers with their own men, flabby through feasting and blanched with luxury. Soon the gates of the city were opening at night-time for clandestine meetings between the Langarrow ladies and their extramural lovers. Gradually the workers insinuated themselves into the city, seducing the maidens and polluting the refined manners of the citizens with their uncouth ways. Langarrow turned from a golden city into a stinking den of iniquity, too corrupt and degraded to be cleansed. So, one night, a great wind came swirling down, driving the sand before it. For three days and nights it blew, and when it finally died away the wonderful city lay buried far under the heaping hills of Penhale Sands.

The golden city, founded upon a rock, was laid waste by shifting sands; St Piran's little house of God, founded on that shifting sand, survived the centuries. This most realistic and optimistic of saints might well have appreciated the irony.

16 Rock to St Enodoc's and Polzeath

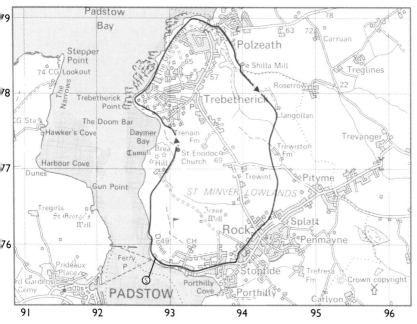

OS 1:50,000 Sheet 200
5 miles, the round trip

This ramble along the mouth of the Camel estuary takes in all that lay nearest to the heart of Sir John Betjeman. For anyone who has recognized the flavour of their own childhood holidays in Cornwall in his heart-touching *Summoned by Bells* – those nostalgic glimpses of waves breaking on cliffs, steep flowery lanes, delicious first holiday mornings on the sand before breakfast, games on the beach – his presence overlays the walk. It's hard not to view the landscape through the eyes of the poet who lies buried in the tiny churchyard of St Enodoc at the foot of Bray Hill. In later life he looked back for comfort to those 'safe Cornish holidays before the storm', a world where everything always came all right by bedtime.

The little village of Rock is still very quiet and well-bred, a place for middle-class families to come and come again in succeeding generations.

None of the bright neon of the popular Cornish resorts here; the shops sell oilskins and sailing tackle, and the emphasis is on windy cliff walks and cold plunges from Daymer Bay and Greenaway. Rock looks out across the Camel estuary to the long waterfront sheds and piled houses of Padstow, a short ferry-ride away over the river.

> The Padstow ferry, worked by oar and sail,
> Her outboard engine always going wrong

has given way to a more modern craft, but you still have to board her from a rickety pontoon.

From the car park at the end of the road (928759), climb up the track on to the top of the tall range of dunes that fill the gap between Rock and Bray Hill. From up on the sand ridge the view across the estuary is of low hills patched with cornfields, running south to the three girder spans taking the disused North Cornwall Railway line over Little Petherick Creek, and below that the winding Camel entering its green valley. To the north, a long ridge slopes gently down to Gun Point, with the cliffs of Stepper Point taking their abrupt plunge into the waves beyond. The fast currents and strong breezes of the estuary send the sailing boats scudding about, sheets of spray butted up by their bows drenching the occupants whose cries of mingled fear and excitement come up faintly from the water.

The path dips down and up along the dunes, making for the round bald crown of Bray Hill (928771) with its three pimples of tumuli on top. Soon it reaches the lower boundary of the golf course, on whose bumpy fairways and rough ground small boys caddy for their cloth-capped fathers. Just before a dark belt of pine trees the path crosses the greens, following a line of white-painted stones, to reach a little footbridge over a stream that bisects the course (930768). One of young John Betjeman's schemes on that first day of his holidays was to dam this stream, which had been struck out of the ground by the staff of St Enodoc 15 centuries before to quench the thirsts of the Cornish farmers at harvest time. Cornwall's patron saint, born a Welshman but taken to Ireland as a lad, landed here in the sixth century and built a hermitage which, some stories say, lies under the present church of St Enodoc (931772). Its stumpy, curving spire can be seen ahead as you walk along the path from the footbridge, standing out of a thick tamarisk hedge that encloses the churchyard.

Unlike the lost city of Langarrow under Penhale Sands, there is solid proof of a village which once stood under Bray Hill and was buried in a disastrous sandstorm. Many remains of the vanished settlement have come to light, including the carved stone mortars for grinding corn which now flank the path from the lych-gate to St Enodoc's. Sand half buried the little church, too, and by the nineteenth century had drifted up its walls and was slowly filling its dark interior. Custom and ecclesiastical law demanded that the vicar hold service in the church at least once a year, and a hatchway was cut in the roof so that he could clamber down and preach among the mouldering pews, bat-droppings and sodden sand drifts – not his favourite visit of the year, one imagines. Local people called St Enodoc's 'the sinkininny church', and, but for the Rev. Hart Smith, it would have sunk beyond recall. Mr Smith, however, decided that the little Norman church was worth saving, and in 1863 he set about rescuing it from its long neglect, a task that took him a good year. He was too late to save the superbly carved fifteenth-century rood-screen which had been sliced down to a set of stumps some time earlier, but together with the local masons he carefully cleaned and restored St Enodoc's.

There is an ancient Cornish cross in the porch, and a touching memorial in slate to John and Alice Mably, a father and daughter who died within six days of each other in July 1687. Their portraits stand stiffly over a verse composed by the grieving wife as if spoken by her departed husband:

> Here is the loue of my
> wife ſhown: that where
> wee ly by this
> it may be known
> my wife and I did in
> loue ſo well A gree
> yet muſt i part: For god
> would haue it ſo to be.

> From my wife Ann Mably.

The interior of St Enodoc's has no electricity; on the infrequent occasions when it is lit, candles and oil lamps do the job, as they have done

'*Monarch of miles of sand*', *a young holidaymaker enjoys the safer end of the surf on Polzeath Beach.*

ever since the church was built. On dull days it can be hard to make out any details in the gloom. There are flat granite arches supporting the roof, a chubby Norman font with what appears to be a carved stone dressing-gown cord around its waist and some beautifully worked kneelers showing local wildlife: crab, lobster, flatfish, starfish, whelk and snail, as well as various wild flowers and birds. In the south wall is an oval plaque to John Betjeman's father, but no memorial to the poet himself. No need for one, either, as his plain grey slate gravestone lies by the path outside, facing westwards towards the hump of Bray Hill and the sound of the waves breaking in Daymer Bay.

The beach where young John ran alone, 'monarch of miles of sand', is reached by following the white stones across the end of the golf course. Across this course he searched for treasure hunt clues, and on the sands in Daymer Bay he played with his holiday friends at games organized by the bossy Miss Usher, who thought him 'a common little boy'. The path runs from the beach up along the top of the cliffs where he was trapped by the incoming tide, below Trebetherick – a tiny hamlet in his day but now sprouting sideways along the ridge. Even as a young man, John dreaded the arrival of his father at their holiday home in Trebetherick, and the ensuing rows during which 'black waves of hate went racing round the room'. Ernest Betjemann (he resumed the Germanic -nn after the family had prudently dropped it during the First World War) was a tense, demanding, rather unhappy man who took out his disappointment in his dreamy, impractical son by insisting that the boy knuckle under, caddying on the golf course, weeding and digging bait to teach him a lesson. John finally snapped under the pressure, slamming the door and running away to indulge in that seductive adolescent self-pity:

> An only child, deliciously apart,
> Misunderstood, and not like other boys,
> Deep, dark and pitiful I saw myself
> In my mind's mirror...

From the clifftop path there is a peep behind of Padstow's houses between the green shoulders of Bray Hill and Gun Point, before the eye is drawn forward to the 250-foot cliff of Pentire Point rearing above the waves, and the jagged bulk of Newland Rock rising offshore. You walk above little coves of shining black rock, where in rough weather

> ... enormous waves
> House-high rolled thunderous on Greenaway,
> Flinging up spume and shingle to the cliffs.

Dramatic as this high viewpoint is, a better one is just around the corner – the half-mile depth of beach below Polzeath, where in a stiff wind at high tide the rollers generate enough force to come storming in one behind another, smashing at the cliffs of the narrow bay and filling the air with a haze of spray. The tall houses and hotels of Polzeath stand along their headland above this furious sea activity, in the middle of which canoeists wait for the right wave to bring them racing in towards the shore, paddling frantically to keep up with the white crest before disappearing in an explosion of arms, legs and paddles. There are surfboarders standing upright and splendid in fluorescent wetsuits half a mile from land, and shrieking six-year-olds with plastic lilos flailing around, five yards out from the beach. Everyone who comes to Polzeath comes for the surf, and the lightest onshore breeze brings them all out into the water in high excitement. From the cliff-path it's a wonderful sight, and seductive enough to add at least half an hour to the walk – much more if you decide to hire a board and have a go yourself.

After sampling a Cornish ice-cream on the seafront, turn down the lane beside the post office (937789). It runs to the left of a caravan park, the screaming and splashing from Polzeath beach fading behind you, to come to Shilla Mill (940783), where it crosses a stream on a bridge made from lengths of old railway line. A stony track climbs on the far side up through the cornfields, passing a house (945778) to reach a stile at the top of the ridge. Here you look across the valley to the buildings of Trewiston Farm standing on the next rise of ground. The path drops through a field to a wooden stile in the valley bottom, then climbs again over slate stiles to come to the farm (944773) and a far view over high ground to Bray Hill and the Camel estuary. Cross the lane here and bear left above a barn over more slate stiles to a road (944770), beyond which helpful waymarks lead you on through the fields to cross the road above Rock (942762). A shady lane on the other side drops gradually into the village, where you turn right (939758) to walk down to the ferry and the car park.

17 Clovelly to Mouth Mills and Brownsham Farm

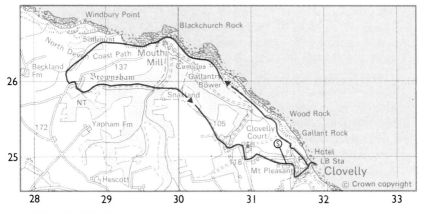

OS 1:50,000 Sheet 190
5 miles, the round trip

Clovelly is the sort of place that people fall in love with. Charles Dickens's Captain Jorgan, lounging on the quay and looking up at the houses climbing their narrow cleft, pronounced it 'a mighty sing'lar and pretty place as ever I saw in all the days of my life!' In 'A Message from the Sea', one of his Christmas stories, the Captain's creator produced a gem of detailed description for Clovelly, a word-picture that sums it up today as it did nearly a century and a half ago: 'The village was built sheer up the face of a steep and lofty cliff. There was no sound in it, there was no wheeled vehicle in it, there was not a level yard in it . . . no two houses in the village were alike, in chimney, size, shape, door, window, gable, roof-tree, anything.'

There are a few wheeled vehicles there today, Land-Rovers that ferry exhausted tourists up a steep lane on the edge of the village to the car park at the top; but the plunging, twisting descent of the cobbled main street remains closed to all traffic but donkeys and Shanks's ponies. The donkeys still carry the luggage of hotel guests 'upalong' on panniers strapped to their backs, stolidly facing the clicking camera-shutters and sticky, stroking hands of children. Clovelly in summer becomes a jam-packed corridor of tourists, but out of season you can walk down the street and along the tiny cobbled alleys that run among the maze of cottages each side, and hear nothing but the seagulls and your own footfalls.

All cars park – at a charge – above the village (315249). You walk down past the gift shops which have sensibly been sited up here away from the main street, past the Mount Pleasant public park and war memorial and on to those famous cobbles. The view is tremendous as you start the descent, over the cleft where Clovelly lies to the green knees of the cliffs one beyond another, falling hundreds of feet to a black, pebbly shore. The red earth of Devon stains the cobbles, which bend in a sharp angle to the left at the top of the village street (317247). Everyone's fingers feel for the camera button at this point, for the scene below is ready-posed for a photo: white cottages leaning on each other's shoulders, their tiny front gardens, window-boxes and hanging baskets bright with flowers as they descend the hill, the shallow steps of the street framed in their double row. Clovelly is uniquely quiet for such a popular tourist trap, thanks to the absence of cars.

As you walk down the street, many of the houses carry dates and the initials C.H., recording their restoration by Christine Hamlyn of Clovelly Court. This far-seeing lady was passionate in her purpose, to guard the village from the worst effects of tourism when motor cars and charabancs began to open up the district in the early years of this century. The Victorians had discovered it when it was a herring-fishing community, and came by excursion steamer to the harbour to rhapsodize over the 'village like a waterfall'. Clovelly added a couple of hotels and a rash of boarding-houses, but it was the advent of the petrol engine that made Clovelly Court tremble. Christine Hamlyn could not stop the tourists coming; but by carefully restoring and maintaining the cottages and roadways, and then excluding all 'trippery' from Clovelly, she kept the wolves of commercialism at bay. The Clovelly Estate Company, run by Christine Hamlyn's great-great-nephew, still follows the same line. You won't see many electricity cables in the place – almost all are laid underground. The few shops in the village are neatly kept and don't intrude large signs into the street. There's a price to pay for this preserving of Clovelly in aspic, though; there's no incentive for young locals to stay around, and the place is in real danger of becoming just another retirement haven – a bright and hollow jewel in North Devon's crown.

Halfway down, the cobbled street bends, and you look over the grey

*Beautiful Clovelly at 7 a.m. on a summer's morning: a few visitors and a
lot of cobbles in view. After breakfast it's the other way round till dusk. Note the goods sled.*

roofs below into the sheltered harbour behind its two-tiered stone wall (319249). It was built in the sixteenth century by George Cary, a member of the family that held Clovelly Court before the Hamlyns took it over in 1738. George Cary was proud of the harbour – the only safe haven on all this exposed coastline – which cost him £2000 and set Clovelly on its feet as a port and fishing community. The Red Lion Inn stands at the entrance to the quay, from the end of which you get a wonderful view back over the boats drawn up under the inn to the pile of houses rising and spreading into their cleft like the branches of a whitewashed tree.

Walk through the archway of the Red Lion and up the steep little lane outside the village, a stiff haul rewarded by glimpses through the trees of the cliffs marching away round the long curve of the bay. Just before reaching the road at the top of the hill, bear sharp right and through a gate (316250) into the grounds of Clovelly Court. The coast-path soon leaves the estate track at a wooden fingerpost to plunge into the trees (sweet chestnut, oak, lime, sycamore, ash) which clothe the cliff edge for the next two miles. The path runs briefly into the fields with a glimpse to your left of Clovelly Court and the top of the church tower next to it, before dropping down into the trees again past a little stone summer-house (310257), placed right at the lip of the cliff. From its rustic bench there is a superb view forward to the tilted strata and knife-edge descent of the cliff under Gallantry Bower, a straight fall of almost 400 feet.

The walk continues through rhododendron bushes under the twisted trunks of enormous oak trees to reach another summerhouse (306260). Here a central column of wood carved with foliage is surrounded by a hollow square of bench and supports a pagoda roof. Under the eaves are wooden angels with outstretched wings which give the summerhouse its name, wholly appropriate in this high and heavenly spot, 'Angels' Wings'. It was built in 1826 and restored, as its plaque records, in 1934 in memory of Marion Stucley 'who loved Clovelly' – one among many. Visitors have carved names and dates into the wooden structure, but there are no football or racialist slogans. Some of the graffiti are 50 years old and more; 'Rose and Len, 1937', 'J. W. and J. C. of the Yorks and the Worcs Regiments (1943)' and 'Gertrude & Billie, 1945' have antiquity's seal of absolution for their little acts of vandalism.

As you continue along the cliff-path you look ahead to the dark bulk of

Windbury Point and, nearer at hand, the buckled sandwich of the cliff above Blackchurch Rock. The map doesn't do justice to this out-thrust of contorted sandstone. The haunch of rock is sliced clean through to reveal the swirls of red sandstone and white quartz in its heart, bent almost double like a folded pack of streaky bacon – impressive seen from above, but only a prelude to the dramas of Mouth Mill beach (298267) into which the path drops by zig-zags.

You don't need to be an expert geologist to see that something extraordinary has happened here. The plates of rock that make up these great cliffs are bowed and bent into arches, one face of packed slabs stacked together like table mats and leaning inland, the next in enormous wavy lines arching out over the beach, the one beyond curved completely over to form a solid archway of sandstone wafers. These folds are known as synclines, formed when gigantic pressures in the earth's crust took the still-pliable sandstone and bent it back on itself. Blackchurch Rock, standing clear of the cliffs, is a perfect example: twisted, layered and forced into an inverted 'V' shape whose top has fallen away. The gentle wash of waves on the beach and the chuckle of a stream among the boulders only accentuate this mind-boggling scene of petrified violence.

There was a quay here once, built by the owners of Clovelly Court for the ships that brought Welsh limestone to be burned in a kiln whose ruined walls and archway stand on the far bank of the stream. The ships came in as far as they could on a high tide and dumped the limestone on to the beach, to be collected at the following ebb by horse-drawn carts. After burning, the lime was taken up the woodland tracks to be spread as a fertilizer on the acid soils of the estate farms. Today all this bustling activity has vanished, and Mouth Mill must be one of the quietest places under the sun: the tumbledown kiln, a cottage next to it and a handsome old mill house just upstream stand silently between the flanks of the cliffs under a rounded, tree-covered hill.

Continue up the coast-path, climbing steeply through the trees and over a couple of fields at the top to look down into a narrow cleft under the long, slanting, chewed-off snout of Windbury Point. Here the coast-path goes over a stile and down into the valley; but you keep straight ahead, following 'Brownsham Farm' fingerposts over stiles equipped with sliding dog-passes, to drop into the woods and climb again to the National Trust car park (285260) above the farm. Now the signposts change their message to 'Clovelly', pointing the way past the large old farmhouse with its surrounding wall of cob under a slate hat and into a bridleway through the estate woodland. It's a stony lane that runs pleasantly under the trees, with not one mechanical sound to be heard among the trickling of streams and singing of birds. After a good mile of easy walking, the path leaves the trees and heads over the fields to a farm and a pair of gatehouses at the entrance to one of Clovelly Court's drives (306252). The lodge on the left of the path carries an inscription in Latin, translating as: 'The Law of God, the Light of God. Christine Hamlyn, mistress of Clovelly ["Clausae Vallis" or Enclosed Wall], rebuilt this house in 1924.'

Between the oaks, cedars, firs and pines of Clovelly Court's parkland the drive winds up to the house (309251), lived in today by relations of the Hamlyns who still run the village on a tight rein. Mostly Georgian, the house incorporates some of the fourteenth-century mansion that was burned down in 1943. All Saints' church beside the drive is the parish church of the village, a dignified building with a Norman tower, though most of the church dates from about the fifteenth century. The interior walls are heavy with monuments to the Cary and Hamlyn families: George Cary, the builder of Clovelly harbour, is here, and so is the later benefactor of the village, Christine Hamlyn. A sad story is unfolded on the south wall of the chancel in a monument to Elizabeth Cary. This young wife died in 1677 aged 21 – presumably in childbirth, as a little plaque below hers records the death of her infant son Robert in the same year. He lived less than a month.

Bear right up the drive beside the church to reach the road by a red-brick gatehouse inscribed 'Go East – Go West – Home's the Best. FH – CH – A.D. 1900'. Turn left along the road to reach the car park, passing the entrance to the Rectory where Charles Kingsley's father lived. Charles Senior was curate here from 1826 to 1832 when he became Rector, an office he held for the next four years. Young Charles spent much of his boyhood at the Rectory, absorbing the atmosphere and getting to know the countryside and people of North Devon that would one day come together in *Westward Ho!*.

18 Lynmouth and Lynton to the Valley of Rocks

OS 1:50,000 Sheet 180
2½ miles, the round trip

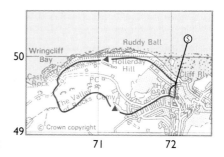

No book of coastal walks would be complete without this one, short though it is. Its tremendous popularity is well deserved, running as it does through one of the most spectacular stretches of clifftop scenery in Britain. The outward path along the North Cliff Walk from Lynton to the Valley of Rocks was laid out back in 1817 when Wordsworthian appreciation of 'lofty grandeur' and 'craggy splendour' was beginning to grip the holidaying public. The poet, his sister Dorothy and their friend, Samuel Taylor Coleridge, had visited Lynton when all three were living in North Devon, and they wrote enthusiastically of the beauties of the 'English Switzerland'. In those days, visitors to the Valley of Rocks who started their walk down on the quayside at Lynmouth were faced at the outset with an aching climb up to the start of the cliff walk nearly 500 feet above. Today, however, thanks to the enterprise of a Victorian publisher and a local designer, you can travel up from the shore car park to the clifftop by the rattling old cliff railway.

Lynmouth lies spread along the beach under the towering sides of the valleys which bring the waters of the East and West Lyn rivers down to their confluence in the harbour mouth. The village was founded on herring fishing, and became a popular resort in the early nineteenth century when continental tours were barred to British travellers by the Napoleonic Wars. Looking around for a suitably scenic substitute for the Alpine landscape, the tourists discovered Lynmouth and flocked here. High above, the twin village of Lynton began to expand in sympathy; those who stayed up here on the plateau behind the cliffs were denied easy access to the seafront, but they were compensated by Lynton's position right in the mouth of the Valley of Rocks. Some easier means of communication than the stiff climb between the low and high villages was needed; and in 1890 Sir George Newnes, the eminent publisher who lived near by, put his money behind a scheme for a cliff railway dreamt up by a local man, Bob Jones. The railway was built in a channel hollowed out of the cliff-face, its cars linked by cables and operated by gravity and water; the one at the top filled its ventral tank while the lower car emptied out until the force of gravity did the trick.

Rising up the 30-degree slope aboard the cliff railway (721497), you look out from the square car, glassed in like a flying greenhouse, over the houses grouped around Lynmouth Bay to the great promontory of Foreland Point sticking far out into the sea. It's not uncommon for mist to roll in waves over Foreland Point while the inland moortops stand out in the clear under a blue sky. On such days the foghorn by the lighthouse gives three mournful moos every 20 seconds, warning ships off the rocks at its feet.

You pass the descending carriage halfway up in the bulge of the passing place and jerk to a stop at the top of the incline. Walk up the lane to turn left into the village street and left again beside the ornate portico of the Valley of Rocks Hotel. Walking down North Walk Hill, you look out over the wall to a splendid view into the steep-sided Lyn Cleave, with the East Lyn River sparkling at the bottom.

On 15 August 1952 this quiet little river was hugely swollen by 36 hours of continuous rain on Exmoor, which culminated in nine inches falling in a single night. As darkness fell, the villagers of Lynmouth became uneasily aware of a growling roar as boulders and tree-trunks began to tumble down the rising rivers. As the electricity cut out and plunged the village into pitch darkness, a wall of water ten feet high came charging down the West Lyn River, sweeping houses, people, animals and roads away as it battered its way towards the sea. When morning came, the people of Lynmouth – those who were still alive – came out of their houses to find a muddy swath cut through the middle of their village. Nearly 100 houses had been smashed to pieces, and 34 people were dead, crushed in the ruins of their houses, drowned along the riverbanks or swept out to sea. Lynmouth had experienced this kind of tragedy back in 1607 when water coming from the opposite direction during a great sea-surge had wrecked part of the village, but the ancient disaster paled into insignificance beside the devastation of that August night. Many people who had never heard of Lynmouth until they picked up their newspapers or switched on the radio contributed to the disaster fund which helped to rebuild the broken village. Today, looking down on Lynmouth, there are no visible scars of the great flood; but local men and women, if they feel inclined to talk about it, can prove how deep that wound goes in village memory.

A bridge takes you over the cliff railway and on above the gardens of houses below the cliff walk. These soon peter out and a narrow tarmac track leads westward on a ledge halfway up the cliffs which angle down sharply beneath you towards the sea and rise on your left, covered in heather and bracken, to the crown of Hollerday Hill. There are benches and shelters along the way, each looking out over the fall of the cliffside to long sea views. Then the rock faces and pinnacles of the outer wall of the Valley of Rocks appear ahead, the very stuff of Welsh or Cornish cliff walks, but striking here among the rounded slopes of the North Devon coast. Under the grey limestone stacks the path divides (710500); the old signpost here has three arms, two pointing the same way and the other in the opposite direction, and all suggesting different ways of getting back to Lynton. Take the right fork and walk on around the headland, where vibrations of the sea hammering the base of the cliff make the path quiver beneath your feet. A fine view opens up ahead over the small cove of Wringcliff Bay to Duty Point, the promontory of Wringapeak standing next in line and concealing the curve of Woody Bay. Castle Rock (703498) rises in the foreground, its green back sloping steadily up to the fort-like limestone blocks perched on top, then falling sheer away to the wave-worn boulders 800 feet below.

The path runs through the defile under Castle Rock, where a stony track climbs up to the summit 'fortress' for an even better view, east, west and south. The limestone blocks here are piled against each other, looking as if a good push would send them crashing – though they have probably lain this way for the best part of 10,000 years. Back on the road in the valley bottom, a track marked 'Mother Meldrum's Cave' climbs steeply through the heather of the great bank opposite to reach a cold little hollow among the blocks of an outcrop (705495). This cheerless den, high above the valley, was the occasional lodging of a local 'wise woman' or witch, Aggie Norman by name, whom star-crossed lovers and sick people would consult and wandering children would avoid like the plague. R. D. Blackmore based his wise woman, Mother Meldrum, on this character, and brought Jan Ridd up here to seek a ruling on the progress of his love for Lorna Doone.

Above the cave a well-marked and extremely steep path will land you,

*There's a lung-racking climb to this breath-taking view
over the Valley of Rocks as it curves towards Lynton.*

with every leg muscle twanging and lungs aflutter, on the ridge (705493)
some 500 feet above the valley floor. The much longer and easier
alternative (an extra two miles) is to walk along the road past Lee Abbey,
taking the lane on the left here which elbows back on itself and climbs
more reasonably to the ridge. As you face the Valley of Rocks, over on
the left the concertina folds of cliffs advance to the green tooth of Duty
Point. Peeping above the trees at the summit is what seems to be the
tower of a dramatically sited church (695496), an impression reinforced
when you consult the map and see 'Lee Abbey' marked at the base of
Duty Point (698493). But the abbey is no abbey, and the tower never
had a church attached. It was put up by Squire Bailey of Lee Abbey, a
mansion built in about 1850, to give his invalid wife a viewpoint over the
sea. Lee Abbey lies among its fields, tucked securely under the downs in a
high saddle of ground above the cliffs. When the squire died, his large
house was taken over as a hotel. During the Second World War it housed

a boys' school, and when peace came it became a Christian work and holiday centre, a role it still fulfils.

The eye runs east from Lee Abbey down over the bare head of Castle Rock and its adjacent crags, before dipping down into the bottom of the Valley of Rocks. The rocks lie along the sides and floor of the U-shaped valley, dumped there when the East and West Lyn rivers, their natural mouth blocked by ice, swung round the corner and burrowed here behind the cliffs to reach the sea at Lee Bay. The rains of millennia have softened the rivers' crude handiwork into this half-cylindrical shape. The valley makes a perfect stronghold, guarded on the west by the downs, on the east by a right-angle bend, and to north and south by the steepness of its sides. Hut-circles among the bracken show its use as a refuge since at least the Bronze Age, and in later lawless times on Exmoor the Valley of Rocks made a good ambush spot for outlaws. Present-day occupants include ravens, hawks, fulmars and razorbills from the cliffs, and a herd of wild goats. They tolerate the July and August invasion by holidaymakers, who are neatly siphoned off into car parks and on to side paths in the bracken.

It's a breath-taking view from the ridge, opening up as you walk round the boomerang shape of the turn in the valley over the houses and church tower of Lynton, sitting pretty above the meeting place of the East and West Lyn rivers. Small vegetable gardens comb the lower slopes of the hillsides with dark and bright green ranks of beans, cabbages and lettuces. The path drops through woods where squirrels jump from sycamore to beech branches, becoming a stony track, then a tarred lane which enters the outskirts of Lynton (715492). Follow the 'Old Village' sign down Lydiate Lane towards the church tower. At the bottom, a wooden sign on a house wall points to the tiny, cramped and crammed Exmoor Museum opposite the primary school. It contains a graphic account in words and pictures of the Lynmouth flood disaster, the full story of the epic overland journey of the lifeboat one wild night, and exhibits ranging from photographs, through farming tools, to household equipment, which call to life the old customs and atmosphere of the Exmoor that began to sink out of sight as roads, railways and electricity came over the horizon.

Just beyond the museum a lane on the left brings you back to St Mary's church, its Norman tower and part of the south wall the only survivors of a rebuilding in 1741 and a thorough restoration when the Victorian town began to grow. On the most north-westerly pier of the nave is a simple slate plaque to 28 victims of the great flood, including two families who lost four members apiece, babies, young children and, at the bottom of the list of names, an Unknown Woman. From the church you walk back past the Valley of Rocks Hotel to take the cliff railway down to Lynmouth. A poster of Victorian vehemence on the wall at the foot of the incline advertises the Glen Lyn Gorge: 'Devastated by the Flood 1952 – Now Restored and Pathways Extended. Nature has healed many wounds but Vivid Evidence of the Flood's Fury can still be seen.'

19   Around Brean Down

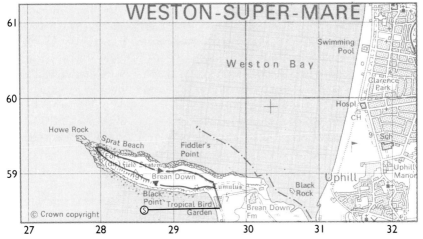

OS 1:50,000   Sheet 182
2 miles, the round trip

Primitive man was a hardy being, but the Iron Age subsistence farmers who made the fortified settlement and network of tiny fields up on the back of Brean Down must have been among the toughest. The winds that come hammering in all year round off the Bristol Channel can make this walk around the Down more of a horizontal than a vertical progression; and they don't blow any more strongly now than they did 300 years before the Romans arrived.

As you drive along the flat coast road from Brean village, Brean Down blocks the view ahead in a great wall of limestone, the last effort of the Mendip Hills to dip their western feet in the sea. Until the draining of Bleadon Level during the Dark Ages, Brean Down was virtually an island, cut off from mainland influences. The Romans had built a temple on the Down in about 340, but it was soon abandoned – perhaps in favour of more local gods as the invaders' culture began to disappear while they themselves melted away south to the last defence of their Empire. The flatness of the surrounding fields and sea emphasizes the island character of the Down, a place of refuge for present-day wildlife and walkers alike.

The road runs through a line of drab red-brick houses and bungalows past the Brean Down Inn (bar meals and a very friendly welcome) to the car park, close under the eastern end of the Down by the Brean Down Cove shop and the little tropical bird garden (296587). From down here the long bulk of the Down, stretching out to the west into the water in complete contrast to its surroundings, looks even more like something improbable out of a dream.

For those who delight in such things, there is a fine example of a Twyford's Adamant in the gents' urinal behind the shop, each stall handsomely crested. After paying your respects, make for the zig-zag steps (208 of them) that climb the side of the Down to the saddle of ground below the east knoll of the central ridge. To your right is the raised earth bank (299589) that protected the west and south sides of the Iron Age settlement – no need up here for a northern fortification, as the slope of the ground to unclimbable cliffs was protection enough. On the left is the site of the Roman temple (293588), hard to make out among the low scrub bushes; it was probably a squarish building with a pillared porch, flanked by two other square structures. Turning west into the teeth of the wind, climb up the spine of the knoll to one of the most impressive sea and land views anywhere around the coasts of Britain.

The enormous sweep all round the horizon that the Iron Age farmers saw has changed considerably in detail since they rested on their spades up here, but very little in outline. To the north across Weston Bay stand the two piers of Weston-super-Mare, running back into the long ranks of hotels and houses under Worlebury Hill. The slender bill of Sand Point sticks out beyond, the waters of the Severn Estuary connecting it with the great 70-mile line of the southern underbelly of Wales. The coast prospect runs west from Newport to Cardiff – with binoculars you can pick out the ships and cranes in the docks – and on around the curve to a far-off blotch which is Swansea. A pencil-line of Gower coastline ends in the Bristol Channel, the whole land panorama rising to the faint outlines of the Brecon Beacons. Looking due west now, your gaze moves across the linking line of sea over the white exclamation-mark of the lighthouse on Flat Holm Island, before the perspective suddenly shortens to swoop over the green nose of Brean Down's west knoll where the Iron Age field banks make square mounds in the turf. Then the distant land reappears – the tiny red huddle of Minehead under Exmoor's shadow, another long

Swathed in mist, Brean Down's limestone whaleback
rises from the mud-flats of the Bristol Channel.

curve of coastline moving nearer past the grey boxes of the nuclear power
station at Hinkley Point to the silver tongue of the River Parrett where it
meets the sea below Burnham. After all this coastline and brown estuary,
streaked into white lines by the wind, it's a shock to see green fields below
you as you look eastward at the rump of Mendip, end-on to you and
running away as it climbs inland.

This is a view to stand and savour, but the wind probably won't allow
you too long a respite. The path runs on out to sea, its grass nibbled short
by the rabbits that have colonized Brean Down, safe here from shotguns
and snares. Other forms of wildlife share their refuge, too: foxes and
weasels (could those rabbits have something to do with it?), hedgehogs,
badgers and the moles whose red earth mounds scar the turf. Plants enjoy
the solitude, too, notably the lovely white rock rose (its most northerly
site of only three in Britain) and wide drifts of cowslips. These prefer the
northern slopes of the Down where the soil is deeper; the white rock rose
thrives on the southern side where the anchoring rock is only a couple of

109

inches below the surface. Ravens and peregrines nested on Brean Down until recently – the hope is that they'll return one day.

The path descends to a neck of land between the two knolls where a couple of battle-weary elders are still just about on their feet in their fight against the wind. The turf here is full of sand blown up from the beaches below. You climb up again over the ridges of the stony pre-Roman field boundaries to the trig point at the top of Brean Down where the hitherto missing component of the view is suddenly revealed ahead: the upturned-boat shape of Steep Holm Island out in the Bristol Channel, sanctuary for breeding sea-birds. Down below you are the square-windowed blocks of the old fort at the tip of Brean Down (280593), reached by a steep descent mined with molehills which leads on to a narrow bridge over a moat. On your left as you enter the fort are the bleak barracks of the common soldiery, on your right the equally forbidding-looking officers' quarters, both buildings still offering a hollow threat to intruders with their empty rifle-slits. You can explore the cold, bare little rooms with superb views from their windows, and the vaulted tunnels of the magazines beyond which supplied the seven 7-inch muzzle-loading guns that were sited here. One of the gun positions still stands with its racer rail in front, apparently made by bending a piece of ordinary railway line. The gun mounting, made of the muzzle of a cannon from the previous century, is still in place in the centre of the position.

The fort was completed in 1870 to defend the Bristol Channel ports (both Welsh and English) from the invasion that many feared was being planned by Napoleon III. It didn't happen, and the fort's only dramatic event was when Gunner Haines, one summer dawn in 1900, decided to end it all by letting off his carbine into No. 3 magazine. Quite a lot of the fort, and two of its guns, went with him. There's also another piece of military history which I failed to find, to my regret: part of the mounting of a weapon dreamt up by the Department of Whizzbangs during the Second World War. Most of these aptly titled 'Miscellaneous Weapons' were far more dangerous to their experimenters than they would have been to the enemy – the wonderful Great Panjandrum, a kind of rocket-firing mobile catherine wheel, proving perhaps the most spec-tacular of the breed as it ran riot during beach trials, careering over the sands and vomiting rockets in all directions while the assembled boffins and brass hats ran for cover, before plunging into the sea and tipping over for a final orgy of wild explosions. Brean Down's Expendable Noisemaker seems to have been in the same anarchic tradition. Intended to make funny noises under water to puzzle incoming acoustic torpedoes, the problem was to fire it in a straight line. One local farmer had his chicken run blown up around his ears when the Expendable Noisemaker arrived unexpectedly from the Brean Down fort, having decided to deviate from its planned course by 90 degrees.

I hope you can set the seal on your walk by finding that elusive relic before turning up the old road from the fort along the northern side of Brean Down. Views of Weston-super-Mare and the coast of South Wales accompany you to the point (296589) where you climb, over the neck of the Down, to the steps back down to earth again.

20 Penarth to Sully Island

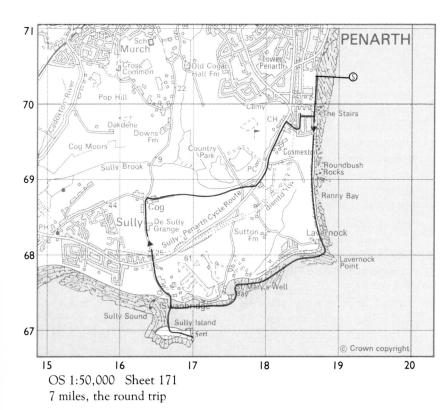

OS 1:50,000   Sheet 171
7 miles, the round trip

CONDITIONS:

The section from Lavernock Point to Sully Island is really a low-tide walk. The unfrequented estuarine beaches and long curves of cliff give the low-level walk a kind of understated charm, for these are not the golden sands of West Wales, but red-brown marl and limestone sands and muds. The tide comes in fast up the narrowing Bristol Channel, cutting off Sully Island completely and reaching the cliffs – so plan your walk with an eye on the tide-tables.

Penarth owed its Victorian Age boom to tourists, commuters and docks. Steamers left every day for excursions to Lundy Island, Ilfracombe and the other resorts on the north coasts of Devon and Somerset. Families from Cardiff, just up the Bristol Channel, flocked to Penarth each weekend in summer for the bathing, the safe beaches and the amusements: pierrots, bands, floral gardens and the pier. Well-to-do Cardiff businessmen found Penarth a pleasant place to live, ten minutes by rail from the city centre but definitely countrified. At one time the town could boast ten millionaires.

As for the docks – they were opened in 1865 to cope with the overspill from Cardiff's crowded waterfront. There was an insatiable demand for Welsh steam coal to power the factories, ships and trains of the rapidly industrializing countries. Coal came pouring in down the Taff Vale Railway extension from the valleys of South Wales and went out on each tide in the square-rigged sailing ships that arrived from all corners of the world to fill Penarth Roads. The new dock handled nearly 300,000 tons of the black diamond in the year it was built. The boom went on until the early years of this century, but a gradual decline set in, accelerated by the Depression of the 1930s. In 1936 the dock closed, and Penarth settled back into the comfortable arms of tourism.

From the car park on the cliffs at the southern end of Penarth (186704) a tarmac path runs southwards; it is a favourite stroll with visitors and with the many old folk who have retired to the seaside here. It passes that necessary facility of any respectable coastal resort, a doggy toilet, and then a courteous notice in good round municipal-speak: 'Dog owners are requested to endeavour to ensure that their dogs utilize the dogs toilet.' Soon the tarmac surface ends, and the path goes between bushes out on to the cliffs, with a view over the estuary to the islands of Flat Holm and Steep Holm, lying in the fairway between Penarth and Weston-super-Mare. Behind you the Welsh shore sweeps round the mouth of the River Taff to the crane-jibs in Cardiff Docks. Flat plates of rock run out from the pebble sheet under the cliffs, sloping into the water at the steep angle to which they were pushed by volcanic upheavals. Parts of the cliff here are made of alabaster, which was quarried together with the grey limestone. These cliffs are full of fossils: remnants of fish, ammonites and even Ichthyosaurus, the giant fish lizard. You need to watch your step along this section of the walk, as the bushes that have seeded themselves on the path have been cut off a few inches above the soil and make excellent stumbling blocks.

You pass a little castellated tower – use your nose to divine its

Fractured cliff under Lavernock Point stands over its eroded fellows
that run in plates out towards the distant line of Flat Holm Island.

function! – and come to Lavernock Point, from where the red marly nose of Sully Island can be seen poking out from the mainland. Lavernock Point is an elbow of land jutting into the British Channel at the place where ships make their turn into the mouth of the Severn. For sailing vessels in stormy weather this was a treacherous spot, and many came to grief on the Point.

The village of Lavernock has its place in history, for it was here on 11 May 1897 that the world's first radio message was received. Guglielmo Marconi, transmitting from Flat Holm Island, three miles out in the Bristol Channel, had no 'giant leap for mankind' statement rehearsed; his epoch-making words were simply: 'Are you ready?'

At high tide you will have to turn inland up the road and take the footpath across the fields (182682) to join the road above St Mary's Well Bay; but by scrambling down to the beach at low tide you can follow the shoreline around the feet of the cliffs. The rock strata make a long up-and-down sweep round the bay, with bungalows discreetly peeping

114

over the edge of the cliffs. Halfway between Lavernock Point and St Mary's Well Bay, the site of a slip is marked by a great fan of rock and mud which funnels down the cliff-face, its foot planted on the beach. Rock-pools in the limestone slabs, bladder-wrack in carpets, oystercatchers and black-backed gulls feeding on the tideline – these are the lonely pleasures of this rather bleak foreshore.

You pass a burnt-out old house among trees on the headland of St Mary's Well Bay – it housed officers during the Second World War, and was a nursing home after that – and reach the rough causeway connecting Sully Island with the mainland. The earthwork rings of the old encampment on the eastern end of the island can be clearly seen – a perfect place for defence, surrounded by water for much of the time and with unrestricted views over both land and sea approaches. These advantages were appreciated by attackers as well as defenders: Sully Island was a base for pirates between the sixteenth and eighteenth centuries; they would dash out from its shelter to snatch prizes going up and down the channel and have their booty hidden away on the mainland before retribution could descend. A warning notice where the causeway joins the island makes a dramatic introduction.

WARNING! YOU ARE RISKING YOUR LIFE BY VISITING THIS ISLAND.
Avoid being caught on the causeway by a fast rising tide. If in doubt, stay on the island. The causeway is a death trap.

The warning, however, is not a joke, as many visitors have found out the hard way. That notice is the most remarkable feature of Sully Island, a quiet retreat of reed beds and bramble bushes, with a fine platform of rocks on the south side where the topsoil has been nibbled by the waves as much as 20 feet back from the underlying rock.

Safely back ashore, the little community of Swanbridge offers hot dogs, ice-cream, a shop and the Captain's Wife pub, very popular in summer. Follow the lane to the left to the B4267 road, which you cross to go under the solid stone bridge of the disused Sully–Penarth railway line, with views opening up over Penarth and Western Cardiff to the industrial valleys beyond. At the hamlet of Cog, turn right at a tall wooden public footpath sign (163688) up a farm drive and over a stile, keeping to the left of the farm buildings. Ahead to the left are the trees and gleaming water of Cosmeston Lakes Country Park, a limestone quarry until 1971.

Underground springs flooded the pit and the whole area was transformed into a country park, which Cardiff families use today in the same way as they used Penarth 100 years ago. There are water sports of all descriptions on the eastern lake, while its western neighbour is a nature conservation area.

The footpath, not clear on the ground, bears to the left under the crest of a hill and slants down to reach a gate (177689) opposite the site of Cosmeston medieval village. The village was abandoned in the fourteenth century, perhaps because of contamination by the Black Death, and is now being excavated for eventual display. Bakehouses, farmhouses, barns, a dovecot and a manor house have all been located.

Walk through the site to the B4267 road, which you cross, and turn left along the Sully–Penarth Cycle Route, a tarmac strip beside the road. Pass the entrance to Cosmeston Lakes Country Park and the Schooner pub (or not, as the case may be) and turn right up Brockhill Rise (182698) over the old railway; then left along Caynham Avenue and right down Craven Walk to reach the clifftop path back to the car park.

21 Col-huw Beach to Tresilian and Llantwit Major

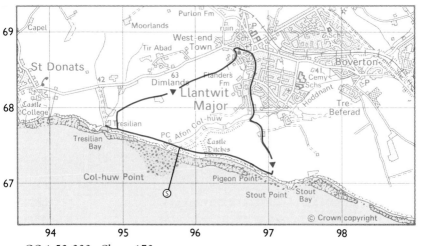

OS 1:50,000   Sheet 170
4½ miles, the round trip

CONDITIONS:

The usual care needs to be taken along the clifftop path; otherwise, field-paths and lanes. Allow a good three hours for the walk, as there are many fascinating things to see and explore.

Col-huw Beach below Llantwit Major sticks a tongue of sand and rock out into the Bristol Channel. This shelf in the sea is composed of debris brought down the Col-huw River by melting glaciers at the end of the last Ice Age. The Romans used it as a landing point for wine and other luxury goods, as did the monks for more basic necessities for St Illtud's famous 'university' monastery just inland. Norman merchants landed goods here, too, before the whole harbour was devastated by storms in the fifteenth and sixteenth centuries. Today a beach shop, café and public lavatories stand in the car park (955674) where the laden carts once began their bumpy journey inland. A display case contains a large coloured map and notes on the whole area.

A few yards back from the beach, the path climbs up to run along the cliff edge. In stormy weather, waves break right over the 100-foot cliffs, throwing pebbles into the fields beyond. Ahead, the long arm of St Donat's Head sticks out into the sea, covered with trees which hide Atlantic College. The Californian newspaper multi-millionaire Randolph Hearst bought the house in the 1920s before it was taken over by the college, where students from all over the world find time amidst their studies to run their own inshore lifeboat station. The white finger of the lighthouse stands clear of the trees, its light visible from the Exmoor hills that form the far boundary of the Bristol Channel. The hard yellow of gorse and softer gold of buttercups make patches on the grass of the cliffs, where birdsfoot trefoil, pink tufts of thrift and sea lavender grow.

The path runs down into the tiny Dimhole Valley formed, like Col-huw Beach, by Ice Age meltwater, and up again to pass a Second World War pillbox, built against the threat of Hitler's Operation Sealion in 1940 and camouflaged with blocks of limestone to blend in with the surrounding stone walls of the fields. You walk on to a fine viewpoint over Tresilian Bay, a diminutive inlet where many an illicit cargo was landed during the eighteenth and nineteenth centuries. The large white block of Tresilian House (948678) stands in the crook of the bay, looking very French with its blue slatted shutters and grey roof. It was built as an inn, and had a long and exciting connection with smuggling. An underground tunnel is reputed to connect the house with Reynard's Cave, the larger and more seaward of the two caves that face you on the far side of the bay. The pirate Colyn Dolphin met a nasty end in the cave, buried up to his neck by rivals to taste the rising tide. It was also the scene of secret marriages between local lads and their girls; every lass knew that if she could throw a pebble, first go, over the rock bridge inside, she would be wed before the year was out. You can explore the cave at low water, but remember the fate of Mr Dolphin and keep an eye on the tide.

Retrace your steps for a few yards to a stile which you cross to go along the side of a stone wall, over the remains of an old lime-kiln into a lovely shady dingle. Stone steps, running with water, lead up to another stile (949680), from which you cross a field to the left of an old roofless building with slit windows. This is Sheeplays, which once belonged to the Grange farm near Llantwit Major. This little corner of Wales has a long connection with the Church, beginning with the Breton saint, Illtud. He came over the sea to christianize the wild, heathen Welsh in the fifth century and established a teaching monastery here. This huge

Roman traders, Dark Ages monks, Viking marauders and Norman merchants all used the harbour at Col-huw Beach before it was destroyed by storms.

educational establishment (a kind of Atlantic College of the Dark Ages) had seven halls and 400 houses catering for 2000 pupils, among them perhaps St David himself. The fame of St Illtud's university spread all over Christendom as the years passed. But the tenth century brought the Vikings who, though no great scholars, knew enough to smash and burn the whole settlement to the ground.

From the eleventh century onwards, the Abbey of Tewkesbury revived Llantwit as a Grange farm, the monks cultivating the fields and putting up many buildings, including the old barn. The path runs on across the fields by stone stiles to reach the outskirts of Llantwit Major among more ruins of the monastery farm. On your left is a curved wall of masonry, usually with a jackdaw perched on top, which is all that remains of another barn. Cross a stile into the narrow Church Lane (964686), the monks' main highway between Grange and fields, with the round stone thimble of their dovecot standing over the hedge on your right. The Old Vicarage on the left was built partly with stones from the medieval buildings. At the junction of Church Lane with the village road, the Grange's gatehouse stands on the left. This is the longest-standing building in Llantwit Major, some 800 years old. The blocked-up arch of the gate entrance can be seen in the wall of the building.

The church of St Illtud (966687), just ahead, is one of the most remarkable buildings anywhere in the British Isles. Within its small frame, 1500 years of history lie side by side. Since St Illtud's day, people have been buried in its churchyard. Celtic memorial shafts and crosses, intricately decorated with interlacing patterns and carved with still-legible Latin inscriptions, stand next to Tudor effigies in the West Church. On the walls of the East Church are medieval paintings – a fifteenth-century one of St Christopher, turning to look up at the Christ child on his shoulder, and one 100 years older of Mary Magdalene about to pour ointment from her alabaster jar over the feet of Christ, an expression of delight on her face. The cross is represented throughout the church in just about all the styles of the centuries, from the square-tipped flowing Celtic tracery through crude early-medieval gougings to elaborate seventeenth- and eighteenth-century designs. There are three sections to the building: the abandoned, crumbling Lady Chapel on the western end, the now disused western church (which is a storehouse for many of the treasures), and the eastern church where services are held.

Whatever the strength of your religious feelings, spare plenty of time to savour this feast of history and craftsmanship.

Llantwit village grew rich alongside the Grange, and it contains many sixteenth-century houses – some considerably older. You reach the triangular centre of the village by walking up from the church along Church Street. Each side of the triangle contains an old pub: the Old White Hart, the Tudor Tavern and the Old Swan – part of which is 900 years old. There are also antiques and gift shops, a fish-and-chip place and a war memorial in the form of a Celtic cross.

From the village centre, walk along Church Street past the Town Hall, which was probably built to serve as a courthouse at the end of the thirteenth century. The steps outside were used for centuries by town criers to announce the news of the day before newspapers came along. Turn right down Colhugh Street (968687), which you follow for a good half-mile down the Col-huw valley to a bridge under which the Hoddnant flows to join the river. Beyond the bridge, turn left up a lane signposted 'Rosedew Camping Site' (967678), keeping straight ahead through a gate by a fine group of old stone barns. A clear path has been tractored across the field down to the cliff edge, from which you look across to the West Country hills. Turn right over a hob-nailed stile to the path along the clifftop, where yellow flowers of wild cabbage tremble in the wind. The path passes into the shelter of a thick thorn hedge and crosses the outer ramparts of Castle Ditches (962673), an Iron Age fort where mounds in the turf show the shape and position of the huts that sheltered as many as 50 families. There is a good view ahead of the narrow bands of horizontal rock that form the cliffs, and of the inlets cut into the coastline by the sea, before the path runs down in zig-zags to the car park at Col-huw beach.

The countryside around Llantwit Major bulges with interest – wildlife, geology, history, conservation – which I have only touched on during this walk. A really well laid-out and interesting series of leaflets, detailing walks in the region and each with a different emphasis (the cliffs, the beach, the countryside, history) can be obtained from the Glamorgan Heritage Project, which looks after this section of coast. Their address is: Seamouth, Southerndown, Bridgend, Mid-Glamorgan CF32 0RP (Tel. Southerndown (0656) 880157).

22 Oxwich to Port-Eynon Point

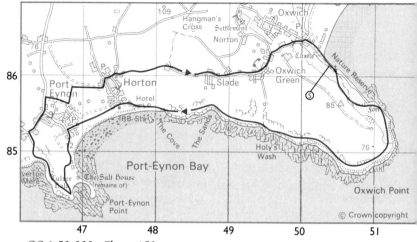

OS 1:50,000   Sheet 159
8 miles, the round trip

CONDITIONS:
Woodland path, clifftops, field-paths and lanes. No difficulties, but be careful on the cliffs above Port-Eynon Point.

Oxwich lies tucked away on the south-eastern corner of the Gower Peninsula, too small and straggling to be truly a resort village, bathed in peace and seclusion. There is a superb beach curving north-east, and behind it the Nature Reserve at Oxwich Burrows, a treat for anyone with an hour or two to spare. Sand blown by the sea-wind has piled into dunes, blocking off the mouth of the river and forming an area of salt-marsh, dotted with reedy pools of fresh water. There are many species of ducks, geese and swans; buzzards and sparrowhawks hunt the woods and marshes, replaced at night by owls and nightjars. Several rare species of plants grow here, and hundreds of more common ones. The excellent Reserve Centre is in the car park at Oxwich, and leaflets for the nature trail through the reserve can be bought there.

The clifftop walk to Port-Eynon starts at the Oxwich Bay Hotel (502863) – restaurant, snacks, teas on the terrace overlooking Oxwich

Bay, 'children welcome'. Follow the road round to the right in front of the hotel to the church of St Illtyd among the trees (504861). The tall, battlemented tower of rough stone is thirteenth-century, and the body of the chancel is built up over the remains of a Celtic cell. From the church the path runs on a wooded hillside with a steep drop to the sea on the left. This area of cliff woodland is a National Nature Reserve, the path carried up and down the hillside by wooden steps. With the bird-song, dappled sunlight and sough of wind and waves, it is rather like the Undercliff at Lyme Regis, without that slippery stickiness underfoot.

You climb up to a path running south-east along the top of the woods, seamed across with tree-roots, past the bleached skeleton of a large ash tree whose silvery-grey, barkless arms are flung up skywards, a few green leaves still obstinately sprouting from them. An ancient oak, hung with lichen and fungi, makes an arch over the path with one of its branches whose tip has taken root in the soil. Soon the path plunges down again by more steps (I counted 176 – get your children to check!) and runs out on to the open hillside, with a view back to the sweep of Oxwich Beach, across to the steeply cut mouth of Penard Pill, and forward to Pwlldu Head and Mumbles Head. As you round Oxwich Point, far across the Bristol Channel rise the faint outlines of the Devon and Somerset hills.

As trees give way to bracken and gorse, a stile leads you out of the Nature Reserve, under outcrops of rock on the top of the cliffs and above the grey rock slabs that jut out into the sea from their feet. A right-hand fork in the path (510849) leads up over Oxwich Point and back to the village – the left turning runs on towards Port-Eynon. Quite suddenly a vista opens up ahead, of the houses of Port-Eynon crowding down to the sea, and beyond them the long snout of Port-Eynon Point. Hardly a roof breaks the skyline in the sheltered village, packed down out of the wind in its valley.

The path drops down, to run along a landslip terrace a few feet above the rock perimeter. The little bays are pebbly, with a toenail of sand below Slade. You enter the outskirts (or downskirts) of Horton past immaculate white seaside villas, and come to a road opposite the 'Ship-wrecker's Shop/Gower Superstore/Beachcomber Boutique', where you turn right. The track runs behind sand dunes into the narrow streets of Port-Eynon, where the Ship Inn could tell a smuggler's tale or two. Smuggling and shipwrecks loom large in the history of this coast: the

The dunes of Oxwich Burrows undulate behind a superb
beach of digging sand, uncrowded even in summer.

church of St Cattwg has a fine memorial in its churchyard to a lifeboat-
man in sou'wester, oilskins and cork lifebelt, in memory of three of the lifeboat crew who drowned going to assist a ship on New Year's Day 1916.

You reach the cliff above the old lifeboat station (469847) (now a
Youth Hostel) by turning left at the main road and walking through the
car park. On the beach beyond the Youth Hostel, the remains of an old
building can be seen at low tide (470846); this was the Salt House, built
in the sixteenth century for one John Lucas, a man of 'furious and
ungovernable violence', who became the leader of a far-feared smuggling
gang. He fortified the house against his many enemies; but wind and
wave were eventually too much for it, damaging it beyond repair in a
great storm in the early 1700s. The John Lucas then living there saw not
only his house but also his fleet of ships smashed by the sea, and is
reported to have died on the spot through literally bursting with rage and
grief – evidently a chip off the old block! The claw of rock that curves out
into the sea beyond the Salt House was used for loading limestone
quarried near by, and for unloading oysters from the one-time fleet of 40
boats.

Take the right-hand path above the Salt House up over a stony clitter to the granite memorial to two of the founder members of the Gower Society, on the top of Port-Eynon Point. From here, turn inland along the edge of the cliffs, where a few purple orchids sway, somehow surviving the salt spray and the wind. Below you, and accessible at low tide, is Culver Hole (465845), an inlet enclosed by a 60-foot wall of masonry, pierced with 'windows'. It was probably built as a dovecot, but inevitably local legend makes it a smugglers' hideout, and connects it to the Salt House by a tunnel running under the Point.

Walk down to Overton Mere, and up to your right over stiles to Overton village green. Turn right, past the massive barns of New House Farm, to the A4118 road, where you go left up the hill. Take the drive on the right (464857) into Highfield's Holiday Park; 300 yards down the hill where the drive forks, a stile on the left (468856) takes you up through bushy dells and over stiles into a lane, past caravans and into Horton. A tiny shop, post office and off-licence is run from Bank Farm. You come to the road by a telephone box, where you turn left to pass the village hall, and right into a stony lane at a green fingerpost marked 'Eastern Slade 1.34km' (474860). This reckoning of distances by continental scales on Gower's footpath signs is rather chillingly efficient. In a few hundred yards the lane forks; take the central gate in front of you and walk forward through more gates, keeping parallel with the cliffs. Aim to pass below the green-roofed farmhouse ahead, where a stile marked 'Oxwich' shows the way into the lane to Slade.

While going down the hill into Oxwich, you will see the tall ruins of Oxwich Castle standing in a field to the right of the road. It was built in 1541 by Sir Rice Mansel; really a fortified manor house, not a true castle, its six-storey tower and pigeon house still stand.

Take the right-hand fork in the lane and walk downhill, a steep, narrow and winding descent, to pass a field completely pink with campion in season, and return to the Oxwich Bay Hotel.

23   Rhosili to Worms Head

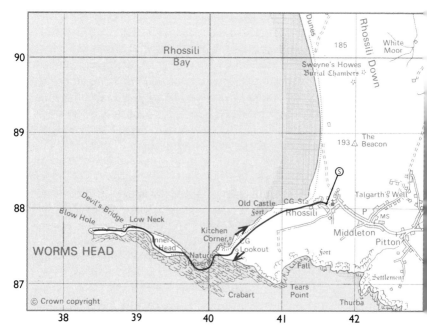

OS 1:50,000   Sheet 159
4½ miles, there and back

CONDITIONS:

The northern edge of this walk is all unguarded cliffs or steep slopes. Keep well inland and take great care, especially if you are with children or dogs. It is extremely dangerous to bathe from the promontory. Worms Head is accessible for only 2½ hours each side of high water. Check times with the coastguard (Tel. Rhosili 202). The South Wales Evening Post publishes times daily, relating to high tide at Worms Head. The causeway between the mainland and the promontory is very rough going, over large broken slabs of rock, and is slippery with seaweed – allow at least 15 minutes to cross it, much more if with young children. This rough going makes the whole expedition more tiring than it might seem from the map, particularly on the return journey. To enjoy fully what is one of the most spectacular and exhilarating coastal scrambles in Britain, allow yourself at least 3 hours between leaving and regaining the mainland, and

126

another 30 minutes each way for the steep route to and from the car park.

Not to be recommended is the following scenario: ten minutes to cut-off time, still on the Inner Head with a tired toddler in tow!

From the car park opposite the Worms Head Hotel it is easy to see why the Norsemen called it 'Wurm', or dragon. The promontory noses out into the sea with its back to the mainland and a bald patch on its head which lies canted south-west among the waves. There are two official heads to the dragon, the Outer and Inner, although the Inner is more like a sharp-spined body, grass-green and steep, which leads out over the rocks of the Low Neck to the 200-foot crest of the Outer Head. In rough weather a jet of water spouts high out of a blow-hole in the Outer Head and the spray dashes in thick sheets over the dragon.

A few weather-beaten houses, an ancient church and a hotel make up the tiny community of Rhosili. It perches 250 feet above a great three-mile scimitar of silvery sand that curves away north below the 630-foot Rhosili Down. In the eighteenth and nineteenth centuries, Excisemen were fully stretched by the inhabitants of this outermost tip of the Gower Peninsula. The Customs officers kept seizing kegs of wine and brandy landed on the beach, and the local folk kept bringing more ashore. The lying lights of wreckers also brought goods to the beach, as did the weather. From the path to Worms Head you can look down at low tide on the skeleton of the cargo ship *Helvetia* (412882), driven ashore in a south-easterly in November 1887.

The path from the car park (415880) slopes down past the Gower Information Centre and shop, running to the left of Old Castle (409880), the remnants of an Iron Age village defended by earthworks, which stands right on the edge of the cliffs in a superb, if extremely dangerous, defensive position. Warning notices reinforce the hazards of the cliff edges: do keep well inland! The land up here is wind-scoured all the year round, a treeless plateau of short grass and gorse bushes where you may spot stonechats and redstarts. The path runs over the down to the coastguard lookout hut (403875), then drops abruptly downhill by zig-zags to the causeway.

The rocks of Worms Head were tilted at an angle of 60 degrees or more by violent upheavals in the earth's crust, and the jagged rock plates of the causeway lie awkwardly for the average scrambler. Near the mainland,

Worms Head from the causeway, with the incoming tide
about to surround the Norsemen's 'dragon'.

they are stained orange with lichen; further out, grey with barnacles, they support rock-pool communities that are revived twice a day by the tide washing over them. Once over the first barriers, the causeway becomes easier underfoot, its rocks worn and smoothed by the action of the sea. Millions upon millions of mussel shells make a crackling carpet underfoot as you crunch your way towards the Inner Head's stripy bands of tilted rock under their green coat of grass.

Once on the Inner Head, you can make your way round the southern side along a path above the rock platform that juts out into the sea. It is tempting to scramble up the back of the dragon to the top of the spine; but the whole of Worms Head is a Nature Reserve whose survival depends on not being overrun by its visitors. The constant mewing of gulls tells you of its popularity with sea-birds, and the noise increases as you approach the Low Neck which connects the Inner and Outer Heads.

Here the path keeps to the rocks well above the water, an exciting route by the wave-worn arch of Devil's Bridge on to the massive hump of the Outer Head. Take great care at the very nose of the dragon, which falls vertically down into the sea. The ledges formed by the rock strata here make good nesting places for the gulls and their cousins the kittiwakes, the dark bars on their necks and V-markings on wings showing up as they glide over the water. Razorbills are seen on the Outer Head too, and shags in summer. Many other birds make a landfall at Worms Head, an easily visible aiming point from out at sea.

From the dragon's head you can look back inland to the great upsurge of Rhosili Down. Viking tombs from pre-Christian times lie on the top of the down, and modern-day adventurers in the graceful shapes of hanggliders swoop and plane on brightly coloured wings from their jumping-off point on the peak.

Returning from Worms Head to the mainland, notice as you walk up the clifftop path the long, thin fields on your right. These are known as the Viel, remnants of strip farming that have survived from the Middle Ages, and perhaps from Saxon times. The best land in the district lies here, and is shared between the local farmers by this method.

You can lengthen the walk, if you have the energy, by climbing up the path over Rhosili Down; but junior members of your party will certainly want to scamper down the steep path to the magnificent beach to explore the remains of the *Helvetia*, to swim, or to dig for the Peruvian silver dollars of King Philip IV of Spain, treasure from another of Rhosili's many wrecks that reputedly lie buried somewhere in the sand.

24   St Govan's Head and the Chapel in the cliffs

OS 1:50,000   Sheet 158
4 miles, the round trip

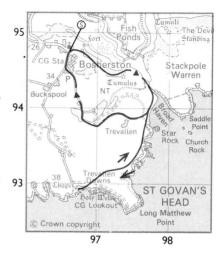

CONDITIONS:

If the red flags are flying, don't do this walk! *Most days they aren't, and Bosherston Post Office will let you know the hours of Armageddon.*

Even saints can't sleep in peace these days. St Govan probably tolerates the steady tramp of tourists' feet through his resting place during the summer season, but the crump of the military's artillery and thud of Royal Navy bombs must have him revolving in his grave below the altar slab of his tiny chapel in a cleft of the cliffs at this southernmost tip of Pembrokeshire.

This flattish limestone pensinula, running out from the underside of Wales into the Atlantic, attracts visitors in huge numbers. They come for the wide sandy beaches, the long headlands that breast the waves and the area's atmosphere of being not quite connected to the rest of the world. The grey stone hamlet of Bosherston stands at the end of a narrow lane going nowhere, and just about copes through July and August with the cars that line its little road and the invading array of holidaymakers demanding tea and ice-creams after a long, thirsty day on Broad Haven beach. In spring or early autumn, the chances are you will have the place to yourself.

The thirteenth-century church of St Michael and All Angels at Bosherston (966948) is roughly built of lichen-blotched blocks of limestone, its narrow tower standing tall in a low landscape. Inside are the stone effigy of a fourteenth-century Crusader knight, a fine Norman font and a stained-glass version of St Govan as a beatific, white-bearded old man. The saint came to the district in fear and trembling some time during the sixth century, chased into refuge among the cliff inlets by pirates who had attacked his coracle during one of his missionary voyages

130

from his native Ireland. Having built a hermitage into the cliff-face, he set about preaching and converting among the farmers and fishermen of this remote corner of Wales. When he died in 586, they buried him beneath his altar slab – and then healing miracles began to happen.

Our walk to the tiny chapel of St Govan starts at the car park below Bosherston church. A sign points downhill to a well-trodden path that skirts the lily ponds which probably attract more visitors to Bosherston than the fame of its holy man. The ponds radiate like miniature inland lochs from Broad Haven in long fingers of water, covered with the broad floating leaves of water-lilies. When these are blooming, the ponds seem to be alight with starbursts of white petals. They were created a couple of centuries ago as fish ponds by the Earl of Cawdor, who had a sea inlet dammed above Broad Haven and the resultant channels lined with white marl to retain their water. The marl enriches the ponds with lime, and many species of aquatic plants grow there as well as the famous water-lilies. Kingfishers and herons enjoy free fishing rights for perch, tench, roach and pike; and by taking out a fishing permit from the Olde Worlde Café in Bosherston, you can join them if you wish.

At the bottom of the slope from the car park, bear right around the ponds above the little inlets, almost every one holding a couple of boys fishing and exchanging the usual young fisherman's pleasantries:

'You lost my effing spinner, dincha?'

'No, I effing didn't.'

'Yes, you effing did.'

Rafts of coots and gulls float on the ponds alongside which the path runs among blackberry bushes to reach Broad Haven. This is a splendid beach, as broad as its name promises, sandy, sheltered, looking out between limestone headlands to Church Rock just offshore (983937). The rock exactly resembles a church, too, with a pitched roof and yellow stone tower – though the belfry looks to be in need of restoration. The incoming seas crash around its slimy black base, sending creamy spouts of water shooting up around its walls.

A narrow path climbs up to your right; don't take it, but walk across the beach and mount the wooden steps at the far end of the cove to the top of the cliffs, where an ice-cream van is usually parked during summer (977938). Turn left here along the clifftop path and walk out to the end of the headland, from where you can see that Church Rock is only a church when seen from Broad Haven beach. Viewed from up here, it loses its unity and is revealed as a set of wave-eroded, steeply tilted blades of rock, the furthest one like the head and shoulders of a grizzly bear gazing out to sea. Beyond Church Rock stands the thick yellow-grey limestone neck of Stackpole Head, the strata nosing down into the sea at a shallow angle; and immediately below you is Star Rock, a chunk of cliff split away from the land which forms the southern breakwater of Broad Haven.

Cross a stile by an MoD red flag (provided it isn't flying – if you see what I mean!) beyond which the path runs over Trevallen Downs towards the fort-like coastguard lookout on St Govan's Head. The downs are a plateau of wind-blown gorse and bracken, their flat green sweep broken by deep gullies where the bare rock pokes through. Offshore rise stacks of limestone as high as the cliffs from which they were separated by the interminable action of the sea, their tops accessible only to gulls and climbers.

Below the large car park at St Govan's Head, a white-painted six-pointed star marks the top of the 74 steep, worn steps down the narrow inlet to the slate roof of St Govan's chapel (967929). It's a remarkable building, measuring only 18 feet by 12 feet and made of clumsy blocks of stone pierced by tiny windows. You enter it through the low back door and look out of the south window from the cool, dark interior to a bright square of daylight, a patch of green sea, a rock stack and a jumble of great boulders fallen from the cliffs to the shore below. At the east end is the plain altar slab below which the saint's bones are supposed to have been reburied when this thirteenth-century chapel replaced his even humbler cell. In the walls are a piscina (a stone basin) and an aumbry (a niche to hold the sacraments). Behind the altar, steps rise through a rough archway to a narrow recess which may have been St Govan's original hermitage. There are broad indentations in the walls of the recess – the marks of the saint's ribs, according to legend, moulded into the rock during his long hours of prayer.

Below the chapel stands a low stone canopy shielding the holy well to which cripples from all over Wales made pilgrimages. Another well lies under the floor of the chapel near the north door. After receiving their cures, the pilgrims left their crutches on the altar as a thanks-offering and skipped nimbly up the steps, whole again. Nowadays, the well is empty of

*Frogs' paradise – Bosherston lily ponds,
covered with a thick mat of lily pads.*

water and blocked with stones, but still damp and fresh enough to
support a thin green backcloth of algae.

Looking back up at St Govan's chapel from the well-head, it's easy to
see how it inspired believers. The extreme solitude; the soothing, regular
rush of the waves; the extraordinary position of the building, wedged
tightly in its gully with the pale stone cliff walls rising high behind and on
each side; the tiny, dark interior which the light never fully penetrates;

133

the isolation of the whole area from the outside world – these gave the little chapel in the cliffs a magnetism which it still exercises.

From the car park above, a road leads through the military ranges to Bosherston; but in the holiday season it can be unpleasantly crowded with cars. A pleasanter return route goes back to the car park above Star Rock, where you turn left on to the narrow lane which curves round the head of a gully to reach the village (965945) a few hundred yards below the church.

25 St David's Head

OS 1:50,000 Sheet 157
4 miles, the round trip

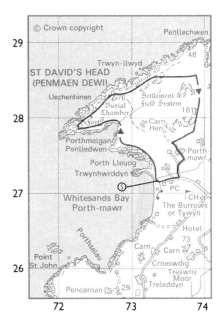

Sailors who got safely in between the nutcracker jaws of St David's Head and Point St John to make a landing in Whitesands Bay used to make straight for the little chapel of St Patrick on the cliff, there to fall on their knees and give thanks. If they were prudent, they would come back to the chapel before their next voyage to ask for St Patrick's protection against the dangers of the sea. The saint was likely to lend a sympathetic ear to any seafarer, especially in this rocky bay where he must have prayed fervently before setting off to convert the wild Irish at the turn of the fifth century. The upper jaw of the bay was named in honour of his contemporary, St David, whom he is said to have met at the monastery on Ramsey Island, just offshore.

On the long spit of St David's Head are the tightly clustered circles of stone huts, long crumbled into ruins by the time the two holy men came to this western tip of Wales. Iron Age tribes were shrewd judges of a good defensive position; securely housed with a full-circle view from their clifftop settlement, they laid out a rough system of fields in the valley below. But long before they farmed the peninsula, Stone Age men were burying their chiefs here in stone chambers within sound of the sea. Saints, sailors, Iron Age farmers and Stone Age mourners all shared the same experience of life as a hard task-master, draining body and spirit of energy. Sites like St David's Head – high, lonely, guarded by sea and land – satisfied the practical and the religious needs of people for whom rock, wave, wind and storm meant both inspiration and danger. Walking here among the remains of their settlements and monuments, one marvels at the strength of feeling that drove them to build chapel and tomb with minds and muscles already stretched to the limit by the business of just staying alive.

The outline of St Patrick's chapel stands on the right of the path (733272) just above the car park at Whitesands Bay. As you climb up along this section of the Pembrokeshire Coast Path, the glistening curve of the bay falls away below and the hedgehog back of St David's Head, bristling with lumpy rocks, stands out in the sea ahead. Inland on your right, the flat coastal countryside sweeps up to the rocky top of Carn Llidi (738280), the steeply rising ridge which forms the centre of this circular walk. The path runs along the edge of the cliffs high above the surfers and paddlers in Whitesands Bay and the scramblers along the craggy neck of Trwynhwrddyn (try saying *that* through a mouthful of ice-cream!), the Cape of the Ram (731272). A glance down at its distinctive shape should give you an idea of how it got that name. . . .

In the sea off the mainland are a scattering of islands, ranging from tiny rocks hardly breaking the surface of the sea to the two-mile-long Ramsey Island with its twin peaks of stone and low coastal strip. Behind Ramsey is a curving archipelago known as the Bishop and Clerks. One writer judged them better prelates than the notoriously absentee bishops of St David's; at least 'they keepe residence better than the rest of the canons of that see are wonte to do'. In the season of storms they were not so commendable, however, for they 'preached deadly doctrine to their winter audience, such poor seamen as are forcyd thether by tempest'. The tip of Trwynhwrddyn will one day be an island, too, by the same process that formed its neighbours: incessant erosion by the sea. The little bay of Porth Lleuog (732273) on the north side of the Ram is floored with one of these stacks of rock, ground down by the waves almost level with the sand and showing as a set of black ridges running in towards the cliff.

The path runs across a heathery shoulder and round the narrow inlet of Porthmelgan (728279) before swinging west to mount the slope of St David's Head. Grass and heather give way to stone slabs which lead to the remains of the Warrior's Dyke (723279), a double wall that once stood up to 15 feet high. Even as those clifftop settlers were walling off their stronghold, a carpenter's son in Galilee was lighting the torch that his servant Patrick would carry over the sea 500 years later. From the rocks above the hut circles and the 100-foot cliffs you can gaze round at

Poking out into Whitesands Bay lies Trwynhwrddyn, Cape of the Ram and despair of would-be speakers of Welsh who thought they were doing rather well . . .

much the same view of bays, islands, promontories and fields that the Iron Age farmers knew.

The path runs from St David's Head under the whole length of the ridge of Carn Llidi; keep well over to the left above the reddish rock faces on the north side of the peninsula. A short detour to the right brings you beside Arthur's Quoit (724280), a great stone slab hurled here in sport from a nearby hill by Arthur, that ubiquitous giant of Welsh folklore. In fact it's a Stone Age burial chamber, already 4000 years old when St Patrick left Whitesands Bay for Ireland. The capstone, as large as a ping-pong table and about 16 inches thick, is held half-open like an oyster by a slender upright, its perfectly flat and smooth underside ready to slam to earth – but five and a half millennia haven't yet managed to close it.

With a long view of the northern Pembroke coastline stretching away in front and curving round towards Strumble Head, walk on along the cliffs until you reach a stone wall (736287), where you leave the coast-path and climb up through the bracken on a clearly marked track that goes over the shoulder of Carn Llidi. A side detour leads up to the stirring viewpoint from the topmost peak, almost 600 feet above the sea: Skomer Island, 12 miles to the south off the southern tip of St Bride's Bay; the Smalls Lighthouse, alone in the wide sea some 20 miles away to the south-west; the low-lying country inland from the city of St David's right round towards Fishguard. If St Patrick set sail for the Emerald Isle on a clear day, he might even have taken a bearing from up here before starting his voyage, the best part of 100 miles over the water to the tiny pale-blue peaks of the Wicklow mountains.

Rejoining the path on the shoulder of Carn Llidi, you descend at the back of the hill and bear right to reach a footpath sign (739278). Keep straight on here around the hill until the path swings down to the left to reach Whitesands Bay car park by way of Dan y Craig farm (736275). The stony, uneven surface of the lane, the well-grown hedges full of harebells and ragged robin, are reminders of the way all country lanes used to be before the advent of tarmac and the County Council hedge-splinterer.

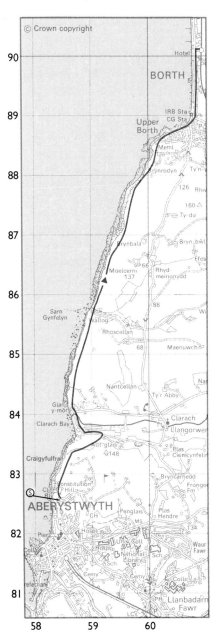

OS 1:50,000   Sheet 135
6½ miles, railway station to railway
station

CONDITIONS:
*A clear path runs all the way from
Aberystwyth to Borth, but it's a narrow way with some stiff climbs and
descents, in places very near an
unguarded drop over the cliff edge.
The route should be suitable for children, provided you keep an eye on
them, but dogs pulling on leads could
be dangerous.*

The ornate little station of the
Aberystwyth Cliff Railway
(583825) marks the start of this
superb high-level cliff walk over
the headlands to Borth. In the
little wooden carriage you sit with
your back to the cliff looking out
over the roofs of Aberystwyth, the
slanting cliffs beyond and the sea:
a view that widens out as you rise.
The short journey up the cliff is so
slow that you could easily pick
blackberries off the walls and hand
them to someone in the descending carriage as it passes you halfway
up the track. All Aberystwyth's
history is laid out below you: the
thirteenth-century castle on the
headland, taken and re-taken during English/Welsh skirmishes; the
old harbour from which lead and

iron-ore from up the Afon Rheidol went away in ships by the hundred thousand ton, until cheaper ores from abroad killed the mines; the ranks of hotels and boarding-houses spawned by the rise of Aberystwyth as a great resort (sunny, sheltered and with an iron-rich, health-giving chalybeate spring); to the south-east beyond the hill, the University and great, grand National Library of Wales.

From the 380-foot top of Constitution Hill the view is huge, and it's even better seen through the panoramic sweep of the 'World's Biggest Camera Obscura' that stands above all. From here you set off on foot, passing the tearooms, and in a short while cross over a stile on to the narrow path along the cliff edge. Wide and impressive as the view is back over Aberystwyth, it pales compared with the great arc of coastline that lies in front of you. Many miles away across Cardigan Bay the pig's nose of the Lleyn Peninsula runs as a chain of blue humps out into the sea, ending in the final blob of Bardsey Island. Tywyn is a sprinkle of white along the flat mouth of the Afon Dysynni, Aberdyfi a huddle of just-distinguishable houses under the hills on the north side of the Dyfi estuary. Borth is hidden by the jut of the headlands, the nearest of which runs in a sweep of hedged fields down to the caravan city in Clarach Bay, where the waves cream in against the grey and silver beach from which in the summer season faint shrieks, laughter and barking drift up. Tiny specks of children and dogs scamper along the shore, while the slightly larger dots of their parents move more slowly, singly or in couples.

Where the path forks, bear left downhill (588834) through the shady avenue of a Forestry Commission plantation, turning left at the bottom to reach the beach road through the caravan settlement of Clarach Bay Holiday Village. 'Village' is putting it mildly; this is a well-ordered little township with neat streets of grass, shops, cafés and most of a town's amenities. These holiday dwellings are not really caravans – that is, ready to roll at a moment's notice – they seem as fixed as houses in their allotted green spaces. Across the stream lies Glan-y-môr, the sister village, along the lower slopes of the headland. Both places have the authentic atmosphere of seaside towns with their bunting, ice-cream signs, children with buckets and spades, and grandparents cuddling babies behind the striped canvas windbreaks on the beach. The only difference is that these caravan townships are cleaner, less dingy and more open than most coastal resorts. Good luck to the shrewd farmers who harvest this seasonal cash-crop against the empty winter months.

Beyond Clarach Bay a rough but well-trodden path climbs up to run along the edge of the black cliffs with their caps of light grey clay. The cliffs, sliced into thin layers of stone, are interspersed with grassy terraces that overhang the sea where chunks of ground have slipped and stuck fast. Couples, old and young, lie spreadeagled in these sun-traps above the tilted rock stacks washed by the waves at the feet of the cliffs. Birdwatchers with binoculars stand on the path, looking up at the buzzards that circle over the high fields inland.

Over the next headland, the long pebbly bill of Sarn Cynfelyn (587858) disappears under the water, its straight course out to sea marked by a dark line on the surface. In local legend the underwater ridge is the remains of a causeway that linked the mainland with a Welsh Lyonesse or Atlantis, a great city in the sea surrounded by a wall and named Cantref-y-Gwaelod, the Lowland Hundred. The city governor was a toss-pot who neglected his duty of keeping the sea-wall in good repair, and the city paid for his carelessness in AD 520 when a storm broke down the dilapidated defences and the sea surged in to engulf the place. Low tide exposes the remains of a submarine forest offshore at Clarach Bay which, if it does not prove the tale, at any rate shows that the land once extended far out into the sea. If you are walking here during rough weather, listen for the sunken bells of the city tolling its requiem beneath the waves. It makes a better story than the geologist's humdrum explanation of Sarn Cynfelyn as a ridge of pebbles deposited here by Ice Age glaciers.

At Wallog on the shore above Sarn Cynfelyn are the remains of a lime-kiln (590857), its semi-circular mouth looking like a railway tunnel. The next section of the path is a breath-taking scramble up the steep side of the headland, the ground plunging away on your left over a grassy slope to the sheer fall of the cliffs down to the sea, about 450 feet below when you reach the second and higher summit (595870). Black-backed gulls plane around the cliffs far beneath you, and cormorants fly, necks out and stumpy wings working overtime, down to their fishing grounds. From the top you can see the green tongue of land south of the Afon Dyfi poking out seawards, the wide mouth of the river gleaming beyond it. In front, the long white and grey strip of the houses of Borth stretches along the seafront, backed by the immense, drab-coloured sweep of Cors

141

From the upper station of the Cliff Railway you can enjoy this memorable panorama over Aberystwyth.

Fochno, the 'dreary sea marsh' usually passed over by writers of guidebooks with a couple of dismissive lines. Students of botany know and love it as Borth Bog, and come here to study the rare plants that thrive in these waterlogged miles of marshland.

Between Borth and the clifftop path are a series of headlands, over which you go to reach the war memorial cross (601885) standing darkly out on the last summit above the village. A plaque on the memorial records its rebuilding by public subscription after being felled in 1983 by a thunderbolt. From here the path descends past a garden crammed with all kinds of miniature trees to reach the railway station at Borth, a village saved from over-development by its bog and steep cliffs. None of Borth's buildings is a feast for the eye, but its long sandy beach (stinking with seaweed at high tide) pleases the sand-yachters and bass fishermen, while the bay is full of canoes and small sailing boats. People come to Borth to *do* things, not to laze around. Borth is bracing.

27   Fairbourne to Barmouth

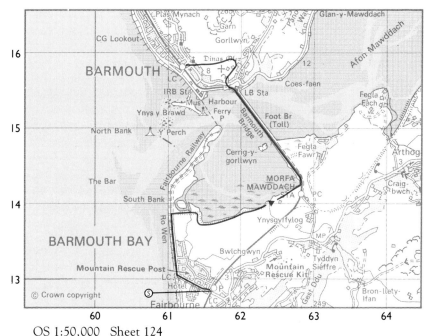

OS 1:50,000   Sheet 124
4 miles, one-way journey, returning by rail

Fairbourne and Barmouth are separated by a wide pan of sand across the mouth of the Afon Mawddach, although a narrow, scraggy neck of land leans out over the estuary from Fairbourne and fails by only a couple of hundred yards to make a complete connection. The two places could not be more different in character, though. Fairbourne lies low behind its sea-wall, throwing a scattering of bungalows and hotels over the marsh that forms the southern boundary of the river mouth. Across the sands Barmouth stretches in narrow alleys up its cliff and along the shore, standing tall with many-storeyed hotels and a grey sweep of slate cottages climbing into the hills behind. Fairbourne is unforthcoming, a quiet haven for beach strolls and sandwiches under the sea-wall; Barmouth deals in high season in fish and chips, fairs and loud laughter in its seafront streets. Between the two the wide river mouth curves under the piers of the railway bridge and runs between high, narrowing ridges that are united further inland by the long slopes and swelling peaks of the northern reach of Cader Idris.

Dignity and impudence lie side by side at Fairbourne: the standard-gauge track of British Rail that runs out over the estuary bridge into Barmouth, and the tiny Fairbourne Railway which takes summer visitors for a bumpy trip by the sea-wall to the very end of the spit of land stretching out over the sands. The miniature engines and red-painted carriages of the Fairbourne Railway rattle beside the road that runs from the BR station down to the sea-wall (611130), along the top of which you can walk above the neat little bungalows and handful of hotels that make up Fairbourne. The beach below the wall is all firm sand, dug with relish by English, Welsh, West Indian, Pakistani and Chinese children enjoying a respite from the industrial Midlands cities.

After half a mile the houses are left behind, and you come to a tall green wooden chalet building beside the miniature railway. Cross the line here (610139) and turn right over a stile on to a flood wall which skirts the marshy ground between the sea-wall and the mainline railway. The harbour at Barmouth, dotted with sailing boats, and the houses of the town are on the left as you walk along the flood wall; to the right lies the sweep of flat ground on which Fairbourne has sprouted, and ahead the mine-scarred hills each side of the Afon Mawddach. The marsh is thronged with snipe, curlews and oystercatchers feeding by the stagnant ponds and slowly flowing creeks. Knolls of rock rise out of the marsh floor like the outlying humps in the Somerset Levels – but where those are smooth and grassy, these are jagged, lumpy and patched with gorse. This is a landscape full of contrasts, containing the flavour of seaside, wetland, moor and mountain.

The path leaves the flood wall at the railway line to cross the tracks (628143) just above Morfa Mawddach station. On the far side it turns left and runs beside the railway on to the long spur of Barmouth Bridge, striding on its stumpy, barnacle-encrusted legs above the expanse of wrinkled sand that stretches away to the east and west. The railway shares the bridge with pedestrians, the tracks separated from the wooden slats of the footway by a fence. The bridge was a major feat of Victorian engineering, half a mile long and designed so that its centre section of steel girders could be swung aside to let boats through.

Strong winds blow up the river from the sea here, sweeping clouds of sand across the lines; the constant ebbing and flowing of the tide digs away at the footings of the piers, and the whole structure vibrates to the pounding of heavy trains. Yet it took a minute sea-creature to threaten the existence of the bridge. A few years ago British Rail discovered that the legs of their bridge were being munched into holes by marine worms living in the river bed, and considered closing this link between Barmouth and Fairbourne. That decision, if acted upon, would have deprived the whole western coast of Wales of its railway service. It didn't happen, and for the present the worms are being held at bay while train passengers and walkers continue to enjoy the wonderful view up and down the estuary from the middle of the bridge.

The slate-green waters of the Afon Mawddach bristle and seethe as the tides pull them to and fro, pressing them inland towards the gradually converging apex of the valley and sucking them out into the broad sheet of Barmouth harbour. On clear days Cader Idris can be seen above the eastern ridges: 'Arthur's seat' in Welsh and, according to legend, a rather risky place to sleep, since the slumberer will awaken either a poet or a madman.

Once through the central girders – shivering thoughts of the Tay Bridge disaster if there's a gale blowing! – you pay a small charge at the toll-house and walk on above the old lifeboat station – nowadays the boat is moored in the harbour, ready for action. The path climbs to the A496 road, where it turns left below a cliff blasted away to allow a tall terrace of houses to be built inside the hollow. A few yards down, you climb to the right up steep steps at a public footpath sign (618156). The steps mount achingly up the face of Dinas Oleu ('The Fortress of Light') to a metal National Trust sign, where you bear left under sheer 100-foot faces of rock and continue to climb until a slate wall runs across the path (619159). Bend left here back towards the sea, looking out from the high prospect over the whole bay, the sands, the green marsh flats and the sea beyond. William Wordsworth thought the view 'sublime', as good as anything Scotland could offer.

Soon a stone wall runs in on the left, and the path threads a rocky valley bounded by slopes of stone blocks to which heather, bracken and gorse add colour. Emerging from the valley you come to a gate high above the grey slate roofs and walls of Barmouth – like Lucy in *The Tale of Mrs*

Barmouth Bridge strides over the Afon Mawddach into the huddle of Barmouth's houses and hotels under Dinas Oleu, the Fortress of Light.

Tiggy-Winkle, you could almost drop a pebble down one of the chimneys. The path falls steeply from the gate down the hillside on to a lane which runs into the town.

If you bear to the right, you will reach Barmouth Station by way of St George's, a cluster of old cottages given to John Ruskin in 1874 so that he could practise his ideas of social reform on their inhabitants. 'My principle is to work with the minutest possible touches, but with steady end in view, and by developing as I can the energy of the people I want to help,' he wrote to Mrs Talbot in his letter of thanks and acceptance of the land and houses which she offered him. Ruskin founded his Guild of St George with the aim of 'the production of souls of good quality'. He was revolted by the materialism and worship of wealth that he saw in late Victorian society, turned his back on the art world of which he had been a leading light, and tried by the outpouring of vast quantities of money and time to set up ordinary people in trades and living conditions in

147

which they could value work for its own sake, and be valued themselves for the efforts and energies they put into their work. The Barmouth guinea-pigs fished, spun, wove and carved under the eye of their benefactor for a few years, but John Ruskin soon suffered a mental breakdown that prevented his taking any further active part in the Guild of St George. Devoted followers carried poor, tortured Ruskin's ideals into this century, after which the Guild and all its works gently faded away.

Present-day Barmouth, like every other seaside town, has exchanged its fishing and spinning for the holiday trade; but the atmosphere of that Victorian Barmouth is well captured in a eulogistic piece that appeared in the journal of the Guild of St George for 1901:

> From the time when the sun lights the morning mists on the Eastern Mountains and turns the Estuary into a sheet of silver, until he has burned all day above the open sea and sunk a copper-disk behind the hills of Carnarvonshire, the grey walls radiate his light and heat, the children climb and re-climb the stony stairways, lean cats come out and bask on the tops of the walls or creep stealthily between the great tufts of valerian and saponaria, strings of coloured garments flutter in the breeze, fishing nets dry after the night's work, and all day long the old guttural Welsh is heard about the hill.

28 Above the Gate of Paradise: Braich y Pwll, overlooking Bardsey Island

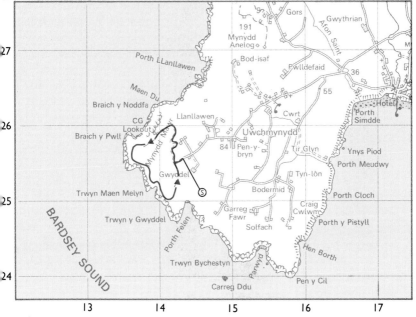

OS 1:50,000 Sheet 123
2 miles, the round trip

CONDITIONS:

The western tip of the Lleyn Peninsula is known as the 'Land's End of Wales', and is one of those places that cry out for a decent continuous coastal footpath. History and legend cling to almost every cove and headland, and the bleak beauty of the windy hills inland is better appreciated if you have the crash of waves at your feet as you view them. The National Trust owns four pieces of headland, from Mynydd Anelog on the north side of the peninsula's tip round to Pen y Cil on the south, and some loose access agreements exist with land-owners along the stretches in between; but no one has so far succeeded in knit-ting the whole line of coast together for the benefit of walkers. The walk described in this chapter is therefore restricted to a two-mile scramble around the very extremity of this neck of land; but you should allow at least a couple of hours to explore it, and will have to tear yourself away when your time is up. Shoes with some grip in their soles are necessary for the steep slopes above the cliffs.

149

In clear weather there is a wonderful view from the top of Mynydd Mawr, the 'great mountain': the island of Anglesey to the north, the great sweep of the Pembrokeshire coastline to the south, and away to the west over the sea the dim blue outlines of the Wicklow mountains in Ireland, over 60 miles away.

Braich y Pwll (135259), the 'ridge of the pool', is a narrow green spur of grassy rock that noses down from the steep seaward slope of the Great Mountain into the strong currents of the sea, forming the most westerly spit of land in Wales. It's fully as rocky and final as the wave-torn teeth of Land's End, though less visited and completely uncommercialized. In fact, in any conditions other than full sunshine you can walk up the cracked old concrete roadway from the car park (143255) and have the place completely to yourself. At the top of the roadway stands the small, lonely coastguard lookout (139259) with an uninterrupted view out over the cliffs to the sea horizon. Steps lead down as a continuation of the roadway to the bare concrete foundations of the Admiralty signalling station that once sent messages to ships passing through Bardsey Sound; beyond these, a wide sheep-track drops through the heather to a view-point over the last few yards of Wales (137257). To your left is the narrow cleft, bowl-shaped delving and spoil-heap of an abandoned quarry, and to the right the tall grey cliffs of Braich y Noddfa, the 'cape of the haven', rising out of the water. The track leads round to the left below the stony outcrops of the hill, and there in front is the main attraction of this walk, humped in the sea a couple of miles offshore like a sleeping otter, rudder fully extended and back turned on the land.

The Gate of Paradise . . . the Rome of Britain . . . the Iona of Wales . . . the Island of the Saints – Bardsey Island was a refuge for pre-Christian men, and a holy touchstone and place of pilgrimage from AD 516 when the Abbey of St Mary was founded at the northern tip of the island. Accessible from the mainland only after a perilous journey by boat across the treacherous Bardsey Sound – the last risk of a long and exhausting pilgrimage across a Wales filled with threats to the traveller from man, beast and nature – Bardsey Island meant respite from danger, freedom for the body and soul from the pressures and problems of the ordinary world, and rest for aching bones. St David, the patron saint of Wales, died on the island (aged 146, according to legend), and lay at peace there until his remains made their final journey to Llandaff.

Merlin, too, is supposed to have brought the treasures of Britain to Bardsey for safe-keeping. In the medieval chart of the soul's salvation, three pilgrimages to Bardsey rated the same as one to Rome: and the pilgrims came flocking. Their graves lie unmarked and uncounted all over the island – 20,000 of them are said to be buried there.

By the nineteenth century Bardsey had lost its monastic community and its pilgrims, but it still remained a place apart, turned from God to Mammon as a stronghold of pirates and lawless men. There were about 60 inhabitants when the new lighthouse first blazed out in the south of the island on Christmas Eve 1821, and the same number were farming, fishing and luring boats on to the rocks with lanterns half a century later. Looking across Bardsey Sound from up here on the cliffs it's easy to see how the island people could do as they pleased and fear no one. Boatmen from Aberdaron around the southern point still had the habit then of laying down their oars as they entered the 60-fathom depth of Bardsey Sound, doffing their hats and praying for a safe passage through; they called Bardsey 'Ynys Enlli', the Island of the Current, and had good reason to fear the narrow channel of swirling water. The islanders themselves lost six of their small number when their boat *Supply* capsized only a few feet from the mainland in 1882, and these were only a drop in the ocean among the hundreds who drowned here down the years.

In 1870 Lord Newborough, the owner of Bardsey, decided to take the self-determining islanders in hand, and appointed a 'King of Bardsey' from among them to enforce the rule of law. The noble kingmaker obviously had his tongue halfway in his cheek when he decided that a king was not a king without a crown, a treasury and an army: he established the dignity of his nominee with a brass crown, a silver box and a wooden soldier. The Bardsey monarchy lasted until 1926, by which time most islanders were deciding to leave the mists, gales and thin soils of Bardsey for an easier life on the mainland. Today, just a handful of islanders remain, heirs to the sanctuary and guardians of the bones of those 20,000 saints.

The path winds on along the steeply sloping hillside above the sea and drops down over the shoulder of Trwyn Maen Melyn, the 'cape of the yellow stone', on to a grassy plateau above a narrow inlet where battalions of foxgloves wash the bracken with purple. When the bracken has died back, the outlines of the foundations of the little church of St

151

For nearly a thousand years pilgrims gave thanks on this spot, looking across Bardsey Sound towards the sleeping otter shape of their Gate of Paradise, Bardsey Island.

Mary can be seen here (140252). Some enthusiastic pilgrims found enough energy at the end of their journey to build it within sight of their goal a couple of miles away across the Sound. There was sweet water to refresh them, too, down on the shore at Ffynnon Fair (St Mary's Well), covered by each tide but always staying clean and good. Memories of the pilgrims' prayers lingered on in the district long after the last of them had found a grave on Bardsey; local people knew that you would be given your heart's desire if you could take a mouthful of water from the well, climb up the cliff and run three times around the old church without swallowing it. (Given the steepness of the climb up from the inlet, one suspects that not many wishes were granted!) The sides of the cleft are pitted with indentations; science, dispassionate conqueror of myth, says they are simply the result of erosion, but the pilgrims came up with a more satisfying explanation. The Blessed Virgin, visiting the church, rode down to the well on her little pony to satisfy her thirst. Everywhere that her horse's hoofs touched the rocks, its imprints were fixed for all to see and wonder at.

From the plateau, climb up by a zig-zag path on the left on to the next headland, Trwyn y Gwyddel, or the 'Cape of the Irishman' – Paddy's Nose, in short. There is a farm just inland also named Gwyddel, a folk-memory of the settlers from Ireland who were among the first to colonize this outward-poking spur of the mainland. The seaward side of the headland is smothered in the purple and yellow of heather and gorse, tangled light-green beards of usnea (lichen that will tolerate only the purest of air) and brighter green splotches of flat lichens on the outcrops of rock. Beyond the cape, the low outline of Carreg Ddu, the 'black rock', rises out of the wrinkled sea.

A few steps up and you look over a panorama inland of cottages and farms on ridges and down in the sheltered hollows. Few trees grow at this end of the Lleyn Peninsula; the rocky ground won't let them take root, and the salt-laden wind won't allow them to stand. The narrow strip-fields are bounded by long lines of stone walls that run down to the edge of the cliffs, and the tall black spikes of telegraph poles mark the course of the twisting lanes in whose hedgebanks grow lady's bedstraw, campion, ragwort and blue drifts of harebells. A wide, sheep-cropped path runs back down to the car park above the pilgrims' church and in view of their island haven.

29   Llanfairfechan to Bangor

OS 1:50,000   Sheet 115
8 miles, railway station to
railway station

The Menai Strait, pinched into a
waist less than a mile across for
most of its passage between the
mainland and the island of Anglesey, broadens out as it reaches
the open waters to the north-east
into a wide skirt of water with a
fringe of mud and sand that
reaches far out from Llanfairfechan. Inland, the hills rise from
a fertile coastal strip up to the central peak of Moel Wnion, nearly
1900 feet high and less than three
miles from the sea. This is slate
country, carrying great wedges of
the purple stone that created the
quarry town of Bethesda high in the hills above Penrhyn and Bangor.
These steep, folded ranges overlook the route of this walk from the
south, with a contrasting view northwards over the flat stretch of sand,
mud and water to the long, low swell of Anglesey. Slate is the theme:
built into the field boundaries and farm buildings, lying in blocks and
slices on the foreshore and producing the enormous riches that built
Penrhyn Castle (602719) for the slate king, George Dawkins-Pennant.

  The little river that enters the sea at Llanfairfechan falls 2000 feet in
its short course of less than three miles. The small resort town grew up
around its mouth, thanks to the half-mile strip of firm sand which runs
out from the shore to blend with the shining muddy miles of the Lavan
Sands. Across the strait stands Beaumaris Castle, the castle of the
beautiful marsh, built in 1295 by that scourge of Welsh nationalists,
King Edward I, to command the passage between the mainland and
Anglesey. Before taking the ferry for Beaumaris at a time when the
Menai Strait was not yet bridged, travellers faced a long and dangerous

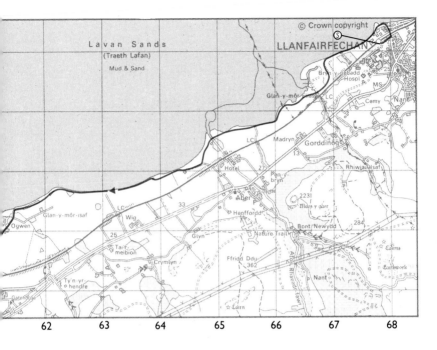

ride over the Lavan Sands with their sudden tides and treacherous soft places. Centuries of complaint finally led to the calling in of Thomas Telford, in his day unequalled as a conqueror of natural barriers all over the kingdom. By 1826 his great 1000-foot-long bridge was spanning the Strait, and travellers to Anglesey could dispense with the services of the Beaumaris ferryman – and the verger of Llanfairfechan church, whose duties included ringing the church bell to guide fog-bound wayfarers safely to shore.

From Llanfairfechan station entrance (678752) turn left, and left again under the railway to reach the seafront opposite the Pavilion Café. Walking westwards along the sea-wall, at low tide you look out over the huge, dead-level expanse of the Lavan Sands which seem to connect Anglesey to the Welsh shore. To your left the ridges rise over the boating lake, and behind you the houses of Llanfairfechan crouch under the long screes and rocky backbone of the much-quarried Penmaen Mawr hill ('Great Stone-head'). Anglesey slopes gently down to a northern spit

155

from which a lighthouse sticks up, and beyond it Puffin Island swells out of the waves. The low sea-wall curves with the coastline above the ribbed sands where bars of glinting water lie in long parallel lines across both the dun-brown sands and the chocolate mud with which they merge a few hundred yards from the shore.

Soon the sea-wall bends inland (669748) towards the railway line among its sheltering trees, enclosing saltings which are grazed by sheep that never seem to lose their footing among the slippery mud-banks and dark creeks. Ahead, the castellated tower of Penrhyn Castle looks over the trees, appearing from this angle to be not on the mainland but across the water on Anglesey. The isolated farm of Glan-y-môr-Elias ('the hillock of Elias by the sea') (667742) sits above the shoreline, the boundaries of its fields lined with upright three-foot slabs of slate, hereabouts rather more available than timber for fencing. Keep to the right of the fields along the very edge of the land, where the marsh gives way to a pebbly foreshore carpeted with cockle and mussel shells. A wall and a wire fence deny you access to the fields; instead, you crunch along over the shells, pebbles and slate chippings to reach a clump of trees (649735) in which a footbridge crosses the mouth of the narrow river below Aber – properly named Abergwyngregin, or 'mouth of the stream of the white shells'. From here the trees conceal the mound where once stood a castle built by Llewelyn the Great. Edward I sent a summons here in 1282 to Llewelyn ap Gruffud, grandson of Llewelyn the Great and the last in the line of Welsh-born Princes of Wales, ordering him to come and prove his fealty at Westminster. Llewelyn wouldn't listen, and his pride brought the English sweeping in to take his lands and birthright – and his head.

Beyond the stream you leave the salty, muddy smell of the foreshore and strike inland to a green public footpath sign (647731) which points down a lane past a well-weathered old farmhouse (644730) and back to the shore again. From here it is a couple of miles of beach-slogging on the low, crumbling cliffs or under them, before an overhanging spinney (618724) leads to a grassy path and the foot of the lane to Ogwen Farm. One feature dominates this shore walk – the great tower of Penrhyn Castle, growing gradually larger and more dominant as you approach it.

Before walking up the lane, take a look back over the narrowing channel of the Menai Straits. The acres of mud that stretch away to the

*Across the boating lake Llanfairfechan lies under
the flat-topped bulk of Penmaen Mawr.*

Anglesey hills look flat and barren today, but legend says that under
them lies a beautiful valley of fair grassy slopes and streams, where a
fabulous city stood. George Dawkins-Pennant found no fine halls or
golden bells when he came to Penrhyn to build a residence that would
reflect his power and glory – just a dilapidated old castle that had seen
better days. Built in about 1300, it inspired the poet Rhys Goch Eryri
('Rhys Red Eagle') a century later to outpourings of praise. Penrhyn
Castle caused joy every hour and honoured all minstrels; it was 'a marble
palace standing between Menai and Snowdonia'; its walls shone out 'as
bright as daylight, as white as drifting snow'.

The Gruffudds, staunch supporters of the English, took it over in the
early fifteenth century when its original owners, the Tudor family,
backed the wrong horse in Owain Glyndwr. The Gruffudds lost it, too,
two centuries later when Pirs Gruffudd had to sell up to meet his debts.

157

Pirs was a fiery, larger-than-life Elizabethan rogue, a pirate and scally-wag, brave enough to take his own ship and crew out in 1588 to beat off the Dons, forceful enough to capture a Spanish prize in 1600 and bring it in to Abercegin creek below Penrhyn; also enough of a spendthrift to pass all his gains across the gaming-table.

George Dawkins-Pennant used his money to more permanent effect. Rich from slate, he ploughed the profits into a wholesale reconstruction of the old castle, rebuilding in Anglesey stone in the Norman revival style. Begun in 1827 and finished 13 years later, the phoenix attracted as much blame as praise; heavy, wild, vulgar, tasteless were some of the milder comments. The new Lord Penrhyn, however, didn't forget the foundations of his fortune – slate found its way into the grand design, in the construction, among many other items, of two large, solid beds!

To reach the entrance to the castle (now owned by the National Trust and open to the public), follow the lane up past the reedy ponds of The Spinnies Nature Reserve opposite Ogwen Farm (613720) and on over the railway line, to turn right (610710) for another mile to the castle's mock-Norman dog-tooth gateway, flanked by appropriate towers (598710). From here you cross the A5122 road and walk up the narrow lane opposite, which runs westwards between gently swelling fields and hedges, a contrast to the mountainous aspect of the hills further east. The lane crosses a stream and goes under a bridge (586706) which carried a railway bringing slates down from the Bethesda mines to Port Penrhyn on the coast, from where they went by ship to roof the expanding towns of Industrial Revolution Britain.

Climb steeply to turn right on to a road (582709) which you follow as it bends left under a wood with wide views behind over Penrhyn Castle and the upthrust of Moel Wnion, then right by an electricity station. On the next bend (578710) a path leaves the road to the right and runs over the shoulder of the hill, looking forward over the grey roofs of Bangor. Bounded by a wall and a hedge, it drops down to steps which descend to a road (579717), where you turn left to reach Bangor railway station (575716) and a ride back under the hills and through the fields and woods of the coastline to Llanfairfechan.

30   Hoylake to New Brighton by Mockbeggar Wharf

OS 1:50,000   Sheet 108
7 miles, railway station to railway station

> The wilderness of Wirral: few lived there
> Who loved with a good heart either God or man.

Thus the anonymous author of *Sir Gawaine and the Green Knight*, writing in the fourteenth century when the Wirral was a wilderness indeed. Thickly forested in the interior, the square peninsula just across the Mersey from Liverpool looked north on to a vast expanse of lakes, mud and sand. Silt had not yet narrowed the River Dee, which separated the no man's land of the Wirral from the northern coast of Wales with a busy highway of water many miles wide. Hoylake (the 'high lake') on the north-western tip of the Wirral was guarded from the ferocious winds of Liverpool Bay by its enormous frontage of sand, and provided a safe haven for fishing and trading ships. In the late seventeenth century the Hoyle lake still stretched for miles out into the bay west of the peninsula; but in about 1725 that great protective sandbank was sliced through to allow ships better access to the Dee. In poured the sea, depositing layer upon layer of silt into the lake and reducing it over the next 150 years to a puddle little more than 100 yards across.

Until the seaside resort boom of the late eighteenth century, there were only a couple of cottages at Hoylake. Then the visitors began to arrive to walk the grassy sea-bank and stare out across the sand flats into the storms that so often gathered out in Liverpool Bay. A few more houses went up in response to the new tourists, but it wasn't until Birkenhead businessmen began to look for a congenial place in the country that the hamlet really started to expand. Once the railways and ferries across the Mersey were established, Liverpool merchants could also live on the Wirral and be only a few minutes away from their city empires.

Nowadays the village of Hoylake occupies two miles of the Wirral's coastline, a neat and quiet place a world away from the clamour of Liverpool, six miles to the east. The Royal Liverpool Golf Club near Wallasey provides Hoylake's pubs and shops with some custom, and more comes courtesy of the retired Liverpool people who settle down here with their backs to the noisy city. Those looking for fun and frolics go elsewhere.

From Manor Road railway station (222893) you turn up Manor Road, a secluded street of red-brick terraces and semis, to the T-junction. Turn left here, and immediately right into Hoyle Road which leads down to the seafront (219898). On the left is a Victoria Jubilee drinking fountain under an elaborate cast-iron canopy which carries medallion portraits of Queen Victoria in her grim senior citizen mode. The open-air bathing pool just below strikes a rather odd note in its position right on the shore, until you raise your eyes to the prospect beyond of those flat, dull-yellow acres of sand, stretching away at low tide to a horizon which shimmers with a far-off strip of water in Liverpool Bay. If you want a bathe at Hoylake that covers more than your ankles, the pool is more useful than the sea for most hours of the

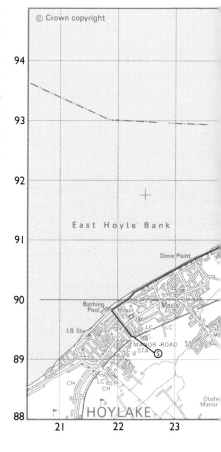

day. It was all different in King William III's day, when the Hoyle Lake was deep enough for a fleet of 90 ships to be assembled for his invasion of Ireland. Nearly 10,000 men set sail on that day in 1690 and, less than a month later, had snuffed out the hopes of the exiled James II for ever at the Battle of the Boyne.

Turn to your right above the bathing pool and walk along the promenade whose blue-painted railings run ahead in gradually converging lines like an object-lesson in perspective. Inland is a long rank of pebble-dash bungalows and semis, while on your left a few boats lie on

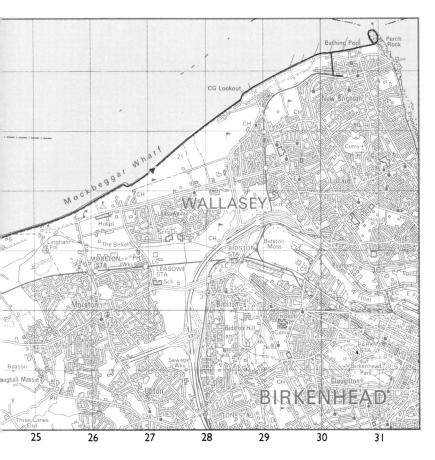

the sands waiting for the next tide, seagulls perching on their gunwales looking for lugworms. Marine worms get no peace here – the sands are also a happy hunting ground for fishermen in search of bait, their spades cutting through the thin top layer to reveal the cheesy mud below. A submarine forest lies offshore, turning the underlying sand a peat-black colour. A faint shrimpy smell comes inland from the outer sands where Hoylake men and women would walk barefoot in Victorian days, feeling with their toes for cockles which were then hawked around the back streets of Birkenhead.

*How to stop the Wirral's fragile coastline sliding
into the sea – the latest chapter in a long saga.*

In spite of those miles of separating sand at low tide, when it does get
to the land the sea has tremendous erosive power. Many schemes have
been tried in the past to prevent the northern shore of the Wirral from
being washed away by waves that have built up energy on their way across
from Ireland. Today's solution seems likely to be successful: an enormous
sloping sea-wall of concrete that runs the whole length of the shore from
Hoylake to New Brighton. Soon it appears ahead, the path running just
below the top and above the narrow ribs in the concrete designed to
break the hammer force of falling waves. The seagulls use the wall as a
shell cracker, flying over to drop cockles and mussels and then swooping
to chase and catch the shattered remnants as they roll down the slope.
Walking along the wall, you leave the houses of Hoylake for a flat,
marshy landscape beyond which stands the slight rise of the Wirral's
backbone. Ahead are the silhouettes of cranes and warehouses along the

Liverpool shore, and to the north-west the low outlines of the Lancashire coastline running away towards Formby. As the tide creeps in, the sand-spits on your left disappear one by one, and the gulls go swearing off to find drier roosts.

The path curves with the sea-wall to pass the tapering, headless tower of Moreton lighthouse (252913), in use until 1908 when the silting up of the bay denied inshore passage to ships. Beyond the tower, a great green-grey block of buildings stands a few hundred yards inland (262918); built as a tuberculosis hospital, it's now under new management as the Wirral Christian Centre. Nearer the shore is the handsome hotel (half black-and-white mock timbering and half red brick) that shelters the yellow walls and battlements of Leasowe Castle (264919). Stuck out here in the windy marshes, it makes a sombre, Dickensian scene – you half expect Magwitch to leap out from behind the sea-wall.

The octagonal castle was built in 1593 by Ferdinand, 5th Earl of Derby. The reason is obscure; some say it was put up to guard his point of embarkation for the family estates over in the Isle of Man – others, more prosaically, that he built it as a grandstand from which to watch the horse races at Leasowe, supposedly the forerunners of the Derby. It was furnished with panels taken from the Star Chamber court at Westminster, and later with oak rescued from the submarine forest. Within a century of being built, the castle was a ruin. Its imposing appearance drew beggars to the door, only to discover that the grand building was a hollow mockery. This is the origin, according to local legend, of the curious name of 'Mockbeggar Wharf' given to the sea frontage below the castle. In late Victorian times the castle got its castellations and became a hotel, then a convalescent home for railwaymen and their wives. During the First World War the German prisoners-of-war incarcerated in the castle organized an unsuccessful revolt. The old building has certainly lived life to the full – it even has a ghost, and a tame mermaid who can be seen at high tide combing her hair on Mockbeggar Wharf by the light of the full moon.

The face of the sea-wall hereabouts is full of tide-breaking devices, curiously shaped concrete curves and curls, while offshore lie long islands made of boulders and blocks for the same purpose. The path passes a shallow bowl of sand dunes, the site of a Second World War anti-aircraft gun-emplacement (277927) which helped to guard Liverpool docks against the bombers. The grass knitting the sand together has been so eroded by sliding feet and bottoms that the dunes are in danger of drying up and blowing away. Marram grass has been planted here to consolidate them with its long roots, and runs of fencing are embedded in the dunes to trap the wind-blown sand and keep it in place. Behind the dunes lies the course of the Royal Liverpool Golf Club, where in 1921 England and the United States played their first match.

The white block of the beach patrol centre stands on the end of the wide promenade which is paved in red sandstone and curves around the north-eastern shoulder of the Wirral peninsula to run south along the Mersey shore as New Brighton's Prom. The hinder and respectable side of New Brighton stands up on the sandstone bluff above the path, its fine large Victorian and Edwardian houses the legacy of those Liverpool commuters who thought Hoylake too far away from the Mersey. Where good taste came, however, bad soon followed in the shape of cheapjack stalls, funfairs and drinking dens, shovelled together for the benefit of dockers and their families who could cross the river just as easily as their masters. The shore road of the new town gained the nickname 'Ham and Egg Parade' from the number of ramshackle eating-houses that spread along its front. New Brighton was really after the title 'Blackpool on the Mersey', and the Ham and Egg Parade was pulled down at the turn of this century in favour of a copy of Blackpool's best-known landmark, a great tower of steel lattice-work 621 feet high, which stood even taller than that other one up north. They tried to replace vulgarity with culture, too, in 1899 inviting Sibelius to conduct a performance of his music for the first time in this country. The boom didn't last, though: the Tower came down in 1921 (though the ballroom beneath lived on, to play host 40 years later to four lads with guitars and funny haircuts from across the river), and New Brighton subsided from its hectic heyday to become another of Britain's fading resorts.

At the turn of the promenade, the Perch Rock runs out into the Mersey. The lighthouse at its tip (309947) was built in 1821, the same year as the sandstone fort just below it which was constructed to defend the port of Liverpool. The old fort came into its own in 1940, when an anti-aircraft battery was sited there to take advantage of its position just across from the docks. This is the place to get a panoramic view of Liverpool's dockland. The waterfront has sadly changed from the days when Cunarders would put out for America in a storm of cheering while incoming merchantmen queued up in the mouth of the Mersey. Second World War convoy crews, entering port after the dangers of the Atlantic crossing, saw the familiar skyline changing trip by trip as bombs tore the landmarks out of Bootle and Toxteth. In this generation the fires have been generated by Liverpool's own disaffected citizens, and most of the docks stand idle.

From Perch Rock you turn back and up the hill to reach New Brighton station in Victoria Road (change at Birkenhead North).

31   Blackpool's Golden Mile
   between the piers

OS 1:50,000   Sheet 102
3 miles, there and back

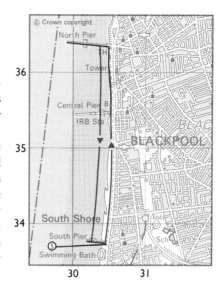

This short walk runs from Black-pool's South Pier along the famous Promenade, past the Central Pier to the Tower and the North Pier. You could stride it out in 15 minutes, or do it in five on board one of the town's grimy old trams that rattle along the Prom, one behind the other. The elderly holidaymakers in Blackpool have the right idea, however; hands behind backs or arm-in-arm, they take the best part of an hour saun-tering along the Golden Mile and soaking up the atmosphere of what is still Britain's brightest, brashest seaside resort. Blackpool still delivers what its customers demand, fresh air and fun.

Standing at the candy-striped entrance to the South Pier (303337), opened in 1893 as the Victoria Pier, the atmosphere of this walk hits you straight away – a buzz of disintegrating Space Invaders and an accelerat-ing roar of junior Grand Prix drivers in the pier's amusement arcade at your back, the polite voice of the bingo caller enquiring if all you lovely ladies are sitting comfortably before we begin, the grinding wheels of the yellow and green trams along the Promenade. Looking south, the view is filled by the gigantic fun park on South Shore, a maze of bright paintwork and flashing electric bulbs. South Shore has always been the raffish end of the seafront – back in the nineteenth century it was the site of a permanent rough and ready fairground which grew up along the sand dunes. Respectable visitors kept well away from the area with its gypsy fortune-tellers and sideshows where they were likely to have their pockets picked at best, or at worst be propositioned and even robbed. In the early years of this century, South Shore cleaned up its act to a certain extent. It styled itself a Pleasure Beach, installed a scenic railway and Big

Dipper and arranged plane flips from the sands over the town.

Turning north from the pier entrance, you look along the wide Promenade towards the distant Tower rising above the hotels and amusement arcades. From September to November the Promenade comes alive at dusk in a blaze of colour as the Illuminations are switched on. People travel to Blackpool from all over the country to wander along the Prom and enjoy 'The Greatest Free Show on Earth'.

The Promenade itself was a strip of green turf 200 years ago when Blackpool was just a handful of cottages on the shore. Visitors had begun to arrive in the 1730s when the seaside boom had just got under way, taking lodgings in the cottages and strolling along the green walk above the crumbling cliffs. 'Rich, honest, rough manufacturers ... whose coarseness of manners is proverbial even among their countrymen', these early holidaymakers had to put up with dirty lodgings, uncouth hosts like Tom the Cobbler who dispensed bread with filthy fingers from the pockets of his apron, and such a shortage of basic supplies that meals could be suspended halfway through while the boy was despatched on horseback to the next village for whichever commodity had run out.

The grass promenade went on deteriorating into the nineteenth century as the numbers of visitors increased. To celebrate the eighteenth birthday of young Victoria, a more substantial walkway was opened in 1837, but it was regularly ravaged by the storms for which this coast is famous. After extensions in the 1870s, the present Promenade was opened in 1905 on land reclaimed from the sea. A million tons of sand had been dug from the South Shore to buttress it, and the whole venture had cost £300,000. It was worth the time, trouble and expense – the visitors crowded into the town to get that special feeling of walking above the water. Second World War servicemen had a different impression of the Prom as they drilled up and down its length under bawling sergeants.

On your right as you stroll the Promenade, the hotels – Queen's, the Seafield, the New Waterloo – are interspersed with little Blackpool Rock shops and fish-'n'-chip cafés. On the pavement are stalls divided between the new American-influenced fast foods such as burgers, thick milk shakes and fried chicken, and the more traditional seafoods: jellied eels, cockles, mussels, whelks and winkles. Down on the beach there are still sandcastle competitions, deckchairs and shrieking toddlers dashing in and out of the sea, but it's a pale shadow of the noisy, crowded scene of Victorian days when 'none here need complain of lassitude or ennui – there is amusement and employment for all'. The bathing-machine proprietors mostly kept to the South Shore, but here on Central Beach were pierrots, Punch and Judy shows, minstrels, hawkers, purveyors of quack medicines, oystermongers and photographers who would take your picture and present it to you in a gilt frame for sixpence. Eventually Blackpool Corporation, mindful of the town's good name, banned all such operations from the beach and thereby brought the Golden Mile into being in all its glory – for the travelling shows simply moved a few yards inland and set up permanent shop. Their heirs are the present-day amusement arcades where young holidaymakers spend all day in semi-darkness wrestling with Martians and one-armed bandits – more profitable for the lucky few, but perhaps less fun than the open-air providers of food and jollity who would come down to serve you on the beach in those good old days.

As well as the ubiquitous Belmonts and Oakdenes, some family names still exist among the closely packed hotels of the Central Beach: Harper's, Colin's, and Crewe's Original, for example. There is great variety in the architecture of these establishments, from the cream-coloured tiles of the art deco Seafield Hotel to the modest terraced Stretford Hotel, presumably named to catch the eye of Mancunian visitors in thrall to United. As you approach the Tower, however, the number of hotels decreases and the glittering mouths of the arcades gather closer and closer together: Tony's Prize Bingo ... Texas Star Amusements ... Slots of Fun. Youngsters throng these dark halls which boom with metallic voices and gibber with video games, while their grandparents hold hands in the ornate shelters on the other side of the Prom.

Maggie May's Show Bar fills the pavilion at the tip of Central Pier (304355) – 'The Non Stop Pier Head Party'. There's a helter-skelter in the middle, together with Circus USA, The Twelve Minute Thrill Show. Central Pier was opened in 1868, and extended later to its full 1500 feet. Victorian holidaymakers came roller-skating here or took a sixpenny ride aboard the *Queen of the North* over to the Isle of Man. Next to the pier stands Blackpool's lifeboat shed, looking like the entrance to a London tube station in its coat of shiny cream tiles.

Strolling along the Prom-Prom-Prom:
what Blackpool is all about.

Now the hotels fade almost entirely from the scene, and the advertisements from the arcades shout more stridently. The Best!!! The Most Exiting (*sic*) Sound and Light Experienc. . . e!!! Eyes down, ladies! You pass Funland and the Golden Mile Centre, then the Palace Night Club and, rather surprisingly in this world of holiday fun, the huge art deco store of Price Busters. Next to that stands the magnificent red-brick chocolate-cake of a building from which rise the crimson legs of the Tower (306360), gradually converging as they climb to the platform and galleries on top, 518 feet above the crowds at the entrance. Back in the good old days 'The Wonderland Of The World' was emblazoned proudly across the building; nowadays there's only a disappointingly discreet little sign.

Blackpool Tower was opened in 1894, its spreading site obliterating or incorporating several old attractions: The Royal Arcade market with its penny stalls, Blackpool Aquarium and Menagerie, and the Beach Hotel where Charles Dickens enjoyed a sound night's sleep in 1869 after working up a good appetite with a 'delicious walk by the sea'. Just 100 years later, Blackpool Tower's most famous entertainer, Reginald Dixon, retired after half a lifetime at the keyboard of the Mighty Wurlitzer. The entertainment goes on, however – comedians, bands, dancing, a water spectacular (Animals Galore!), Jungle Jim's Adventure Playground and Good Time Emporium; and community singing to the organ, too. It's a pity that the Big Wheel no longer turns on the front, jerking 1000 riders 220 feet into the air, stopping each car to embark more than 30 passengers and taking a frustrating half-hour to make one revolution. Depicted in so many Edwardian photos (you could get Wheel and Tower in one snap) the Big Wheel opened two years after the Tower, but only lasted 32 years. You could enjoy twice the view from the top of the Tower, and the half-hour circuit was too boring for most pleasure-seekers. Next to the Tower on its north side, where Lewis's store now stands, was 'The People's Popular Palace of Pleasure'. It started life as the Prince of Wales Baths and Theatre, and then became the Alhambra, where 6000 people at a time could dance the night away, go to the theatre or enjoy the circus.

Beyond the Tower, North Pier (305364) sticks out, cut off short at its seaward end and carrying only one pavilion in the centre and four little shelters. That central pavilion is a makeshift job, put up after the original one was neatly separated from the rest of the pier by a wayward ship in 1984. Blackpool has too much pride invested in its piers – and too much money – to let it go at that. By the time you walk this way, the North Pier should have been restored to its former glory.

You can either catch one of the Corporation's old trams back along the Prom to South Pier, or walk there; but the beach offers a new perspective of the Golden Mile. The racket from the arcades diminishes, though it doesn't vanish, once you are on the beach; and it's fascinating to pause under the Central Pier on your way back and look up into the dripping shadows above. The influence of the Railway Age on the pier's designer shows in every cast-iron pillar, girder and bracing strut – all now green with weed and encrusted inches thick in barnacles. At the end of the day the donkey owners sometimes give in to the children's demands for a race, and run behind their sedately cantering assets, whooping like wild men, while the jolting young riders are nearly sick from shrieking and giggling. The only drawbacks of the beach walk are its sprinkling of small, smooth, olive-green donkey turds, and a tideline almost entirely composed of cigarette-ends.

If neither beach nor Prom appeals as a return route, you can get a glimpse of the domain of the fabled Blackpool landlady by crossing under the Tower and making your way back via the inland streets. Literally hundreds of small boarding-houses line these streets, ranging from the spick-and-span to the downright shabby; 99 out of 100 display 'Sorry – no vacancies' notices in their windows from June throughout the summer and on until November when the Illuminations are finally switched off. Landladies no longer lie in wait at the railway station to kidnap tourists fresh off the trains, nor do they charge extra for cruets and the morning milk – but there are still notices on stairs and in hallways requesting guests to refrain from eating fish and chips in the bedrooms, to prevent their children playing on the stairs and to pay up on arrival ('In God We Trust – Others Pay Cash'). Cheap, cheerful and accommodating, the boarding-houses do more than Tower, piers, Promenade and Golden Mile to keep the old Blackpool holiday spirit alive.

32 Crossing the Sands of Morecambe Bay

OS 1:50,000 Sheet 97

Between 5 and 10 miles, depending on the state of the tide and the course of the River Kent

CONDITIONS:

Private enterprise is strictly out on this walk – don't try it without the Guide. The tide comes in here with the speed and noise of a train, and rises between 20 and 30 feet; so if you are caught in the middle of the bay you have had it. The route is not along a straight line, shore to shore – it bends and curves through most points of the compass to avoid quicksands and sudden hollows which only someone with expert local knowledge can place accurately. Before you make the crossing, write to Cedric Robinson, the Sands Guide, at Guides Farm, Cart Lane, Grange-over-Sands, Cumbria LA11 7AF, or ring him up (Grange-over-Sands (044 84) 2165) and settle on a date and time. You can also buy one of the excellent books he has written about the Bay, and get his autograph on the title-page when you join him for your trek. Then prepare to get wet – up to the knees if you are lucky – up to the waist if not. The crossing involves many splashes through wet patches and the fording of the River Kent, whose powerful current in bad weather can put the wind up the boldest spirit. The crossing may be a four-hour epic from Morecambe to Grange, or a two-hour stroll from Silverdale to Kents Bank, depending on the whim of the river – either way, the return journey is by train.

If the Dutch could only get their hands on Morecambe Bay, just think how many polders they could squeeze out of the 117 square miles of flat, muddy sands. Luckily for walkers who like a spice of adventure with their outings, and for naturalists and lovers of wild open spaces, all the various schemes to enclose the Sands have so far come to nothing. Cut across by three rivers (the Kent, Keer and Leven), the vast expanses of sand remain the province of the oystercatchers, knot, dunlin and black-backed gulls, the fishermen and the parties of walkers who venture the crossing under the watchful eye of the Guide.

Only 100 years ago it was a different scene. Then a mass of scurrying, stooping figures covered the sands at low tide: cockle and mussel pickers, shrimp catchers, fluke and dab fishermen. Shallow-draught ships made for the quay at Hest Bank; horses and carts trundled the cockles and

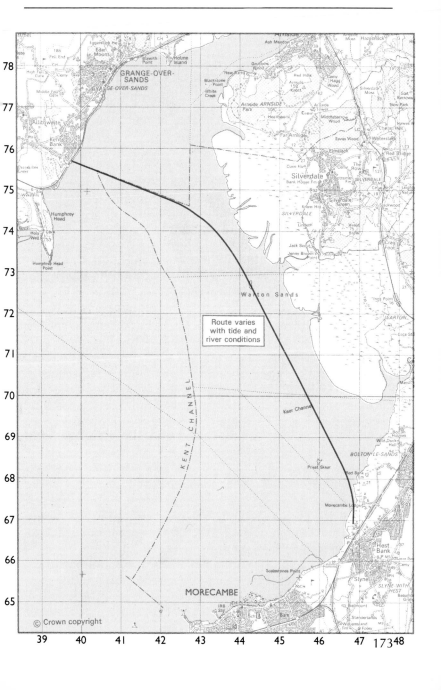

Route varies with tide and river conditions

© Crown copyright

Crossing the Sands. Cedric Robinson leads the faithful through the River Kent towards the Promised Land of Kents Bank.

mussels from their beds on the 'skeers' (rock outcrops) or under the sand to the villages under the low cliffs; carriages full of sightseers rattled across from Morecambe to Grange-over-Sands. The gradual silting-up of the bay and the ever-shifting courses of the rivers were responsible for emptying the landscape, the River Kent being the chief villain of the piece. This fast-running waterway through the sands has been known to swerve from one side of the bay to the other in the space of a couple of days, piling up sandbanks and bars as it goes. The silting has been accompanied by sewage pollution in recent years, the one burying the cockle beds and the other poisoning the mussels. Other watercourses run under the sands, too, converting them into treacherous quicksands in which a cart or tractor can be completely swallowed between two tides.

The unpredictability of the route across the bay led to the early establishing of a guide across the Sands. The monks at Cartmel Priory, on the tongue of land poking out into the top of the bay, provided a guide service, as did the State from King John's time onwards. The guides took the generic surname 'Carter', and in the mid-sixteenth century were paid

£5 a year, with a house and three fields thrown in, for a duty 365 days of the year which lasted 12 hours out of every 24. The essential nature of their work is shown by the sombre statistics for drownings: 140 travellers met their deaths on the sands between 1559 and 1880, and these were only the ones whose bodies happened to float ashore. A visitor asking a guide whether any of his calling had been lost on the crossing was told: 'There's yan or two been drownded, but they're usually foound agean when t'tide gaas oot!' John Wesley, William Wordsworth and Mrs Gaskell all made the crossing: the impetuous Wesley raced the tide against local advice, while Mrs Gaskell made a more sedate journey behind a guide blowing a ram's horn and mounted on a white horse so that he could be seen in the gathering dusk. In spite of frequent boggings-down and some fatal delays at high tide, a coach service operated across the Sands until 1857, when the newly opened railway offered a safe and convenient alternative route.

The old-time guides always marked their paths across the bay with sprigs of laurel known as 'brobs'; and the present Guide, Cedric Robinson, keeps up the old tradition. He has a tractor to help him get out on to the sands and survey his routes, which change as the course of the Kent changes, from day to day. Otherwise the job is as it always was: demanding, wet, cold, tiring, grossly underpaid (he gets £15 a year, and the house and fields from the Duchy of Lancaster) and enormously satisfying.

Once over the green and dun shelf of salt-marsh that sticks out in a ledge from the shore, you step down on to sticky, sloppy sand. Here you have to decide whether to cross barefoot (bruises) or in shoes (blisters). Probably the best compromise is to wear trainers or gym shoes without socks. Mr Robinson goes barefoot – but he's been doing it since 1963, so his soles are well pickled by now. Soon the sticky surface becomes firmer, and you walk on ribs of sand raised by the wind and tide, under which lie the beds of cockles. At certain times the cockle shells rub together and produce the famous sound of the 'singing sands'.

In a small party there is time to chat to the Guide and hear some of the legion of stories about the bay, its people, industries and legends connected with the crossing of the Sands. When a crowd of people turns up, Mr Robinson becomes a human sheepdog, racing around blowing a whistle to herd his unwieldy flock along his chosen route. If he is too busy to talk, you can admire the wide view as you walk. If you have set off from

175

the hospitable Silverdale Hotel, for example, to the south lie Morecambe, the cooling-towers of Heysham power station and on clear days the spindly stick of Blackpool Tower; to the north, the sleeping-dog shape of Holme Island and the promontory of Arnside; behind you the Silverdale shore; and in front the houses of Grange-over-Sands running south to the spit of Humphrey Head Point, backed by the outlines of the southern fells of Lakeland. Between you and these blocks of land around the bay stretch the miles of dead-flat silver-grey sand, wrinkled and ridged, barred across by shallow sheets of water where the gulls and waders congregate. Every so often the party halts while Mr Robinson checks his 'brobs' and bearings, then sets off in a new direction. The River Kent, whenever and wherever you reach it in the tableland of sands, has its safe crossing place marked with 'brobs' between which you wade across, smiling cheerfully through gritted teeth as the water reaches those parts that other rivers don't even approach. There is no turning back, either – if the Guide isn't fully confident at the start of the walk about the state of the river, you won't even set out. The Kent has Mr Robinson's full respect: 'It can be really frightening, the river. It's one of the fastest flowing rivers in England – and it doesn't always play your way.'

Safely across, you pass the long, curved nets of the fluke-catchers waiting to trap the fish as they go down the Sands with the tide. A surprising number of salmon-shaped flukes apparently end up in these nets.

My crossing was in company with hundreds of people sponsored to raise money for leukaemia research and a body-scanner. You may not, as I did, have the red-sweatered Brass Band of the *Lancashire Evening Post* to welcome you ashore at Kents Bank to the strains of 'It's a long way to Tipperary' and 'Oh, I do like to be beside the seaside' – but you will linger long over memories of your wet, filthy, delightful walk across the sands of Morecambe Bay.

33   Whitehaven to St Bees

OS 1:50,000   Sheet 89
7½ miles, railway station to railway station

The first thing that strikes you about Whitehaven as you come out of the railway station (974188) is that it has a working waterfront. The docks lie just down the road and their noises claim attention. They hiss and clank as the phosphate rock rumbles up conveyors from the holds of ships on its way to the vast chemical works that is one of the town's most important employers. The Marchon works stands to the south of Whitehaven, beyond an area of clifftop burrowed and honeycombed by coal mines – the last of these, Haig Pit, closed in 1984. These industrial concerns have benefited Whitehaven not only in terms of employment for the townspeople; without the sponsorship of the National Coal Board (now British Coal) and Albright and Wilson, the firm that runs the chemical works, the Cumbrian Coastal Way, of which this walk is a part, would not have come into being.

As you walk around the perimeter of Whitehaven Harbour, you'll notice tall Dutch-looking buildings lining the streets of the town among the Victorian shops and terraces. Many of these are survivors of the original town, laid out in the seventeenth century by the Lowther family, Earls of Lonsdale, around the harbour which was built in the 1630s by Sir Christopher Lowther. The family owned the local coal mines, and Whitehaven provided a sheltered haven for the ships that took the coal over the sea to Ireland. The new harbour gave other trade a boost as well, and Whitehaven was soon importing tobacco, sugar and rum from the Americas. It developed a bustling waterfront with pubs, boarding-houses and large warehouses. The lighthouse on the Old Quay at the southern end of the harbour was put up in 1730, by which time the town had risen to become Britain's chief coal port. Today, with the coal, ironstone and sandstone businesses all dead or dying, Whitehaven people look to the chemical works for their bread and butter, or further south to the nuclear reprocessing plant at Sellafield. Like Barrow, Workington and other Cumbrian coastal ports, the town is feeling the pinch of declining industry and rising unemployment: it's too remote from Carlisle or Lancaster to attract well-heeled commuters as residents, and it retains a strictly local atmosphere along with its fine old buildings.

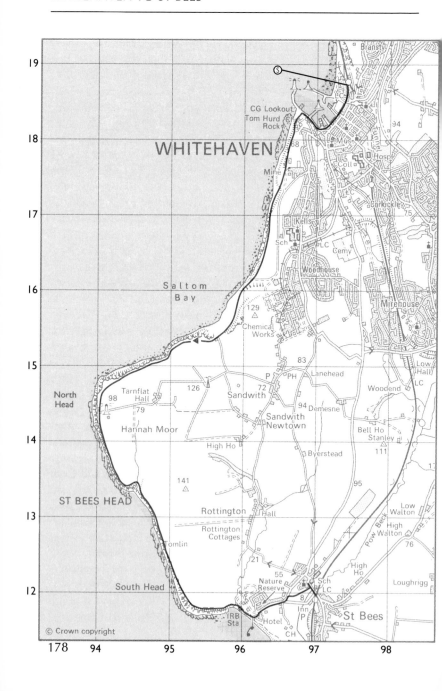

You pass the splendid old sandstone Public Baths with their relief figures of Neptune and a chubby mermaid, and walk round South Harbour to the feet of the cliffs by the Wellington pub (967184). A large mural on the cliff wall shows John Paul Jones, the Scots lad turned ardent American patriot who sailed into Whitehaven Bay in 1778 in his ship *Ranger* to attack the town. Jones had inside knowledge of the layout of Whitehaven's defences, having trained here as a seaman; and he led his 31 volunteers ashore in a daring raid, spiking the cannon that guarded the harbour and trying without success to burn the shipping in the shelter of the jetties. Jones withdrew without achieving a victory, but the dashing attempt gave him a lasting reputation in the town. Beyond the Wellington stands one of the cannon he spiked, pointing out over a low wall towards the stone-carrying ships out at sea.

The path curves round to go through a doorway in the cliff wall and up steps, emerging under a tall industrial chimney known locally as Candlestick Chimney. It gained this name when it burst into flames after being struck by lightning. The chimney had been put up as a vent for the Wellington Pit in the cliffs below, sunk in the 1840s, and in 1910 the scene of the worst disaster in the history of Cumbrian coal-mining when 136 men and boys lost their lives. The coast-path now runs past the sites of several of the Lonsdale family's pits; but before entering this industrial wasteland, take a good look at the little cottage (967182) that stands beyond Candlestick Chimney on the edge of the cliff. The stucco is flaking off the walls, exposing patches of rough brickwork filling gaps in the original purple sandstone blocks. Dilapidated, shabby and crumbling, this little house deserves a better fate – for here as a boy lived the author of *Gulliver's Travels*, Jonathan Swift.

Wellington Colliery closed in 1933, as did the Ladysmith and Croft pits further south where the Marchon chemical works now stands; and they were clearing away the remains of the Haig Pit (967176) when I walked here in 1986. A 75-year-old ex-miner, bent and wheezing with chest trouble, pointed out the conveyor belt, coal washery and pit-head gear. He carried a shooting stick on which he had to sit down every so often to recover his breath. 'Ah'm ninety per cent dusted,' he told me. 'Can't walk more than fifty yards. Ah worked forty years in these pits. This one used to run oot five mile under the sea. These modern cutting machines have a kind of spray to dampen doon the dust. When Ah was

Looking back over the black sands and red sandstone cliffs
of Fleswick Bay to the lighthouse on North Head.

working doon the pit ye couldn't see the coal face at all most times, and
we used to breathe it all in.' He was upset to see the young men cutting up
the rusty old girders of the coal washery with oxy-acetylene torches.
'Look at them lads wi' them blow-pipes. Nae masks. Fumes off those
won't do their chests any good.'

The intention is to convert the tall pit-head buildings and winding
wheels into a mining museum, and to landscape the great plain of dusty
black heaps and scars into a recreational park on the cliffs. By the time
you walk here, all this desolation will be under the turf – and so, I
suspect, will my guide, one of the last victims of the old style of mining.

Before you reach the beautiful country on the open cliffs to the south,
there is one more industrial site to be got round: the giant chemical works
and the polluted beach below it. On top of the cliff above Barrowmouth
stand the fuming chimneys and square buildings of the Marchon works,
sending out a strong soapy smell over the surrounding fields and houses.
Here they make the chemicals that go into shampoo and bubble-baths,

and the fall of water that pours down the cliff-face is as foamy a cataract as any romantic could wish for. It's stiff with soapsuds, crashing down on to the rocks on the shore which are black and slippery with chemicals. A sluggish reef of suds lies offshore in a great white arc, rocking with the waves and covering the surface of the bay with a greasy film. There is icing on the chemical cake, too – black icing in the shape of coal spoil which is tipped over the cliff edge by trucks to join the appalling stew below. Barrowmouth must be the beach least likely in all England to tempt you to bathe. It's a sobering and horrifying sight; but each fall of foam and shower of black dirt means another meal on a Whitehaven table. Old men get their coal here, too, picking over the heaps of spoil and filling their sacks with nuggets for the fire.

Somehow nature battles on, clothing the cliffs beyond with harebells, thistles, gorse, ragwort and clover. A stiff climb up steps, and you have put the wasteland behind you and can look ahead to the red sandstone strata of the cliffs running up to the protruding nose of North Head. The beach below exchanges its slimy black coat for a green one of algae; and the razorbills and kittiwakes, which avoid the noxious waters of Barrowmouth, are seen again gliding over the sea. You pass a row of three sandstone cottages (956154) which were built for the foremen at the quarry in the cliffs just beyond. These old quarries, now all disused, form a series of rough ledges where golden saxifrage, heather and mulleins are sheltered from the sea-wind, and where local lovers can lie out of sight. One sandstone face is covered with initials hacked by couples who have used its shelter, their names intertwined with hearts or just carved side by side. William Pink took a lot of trouble gouging his name in neat capitals in 1933, and J. and R. Williams immortalized themselves in copperplate and curlicues back in 1910. J.L. in 1946 proudly added his RAF wings above his signature.

The view from North Head is wonderful: Scotland to the north and the Isle of Man to the west on a clear day. The squat white lighthouse on the tip of the Head (941144) was built in 1822 when the previous coal-fired one burned to the ground. Here the cornfields and pasture run in yellow and green patches to meet the dark-red face of the cliffs, the purple earth of the ploughed fields dotted with white pinpoints of seagulls. You walk on from the lighthouse along the cliff edge to look over Fleswick Bay (945132) to the promontory of South Head. The curve of sand in Fleswick Bay comes as a shock – it's not the regulation gold, but a silvery black, running down to dusky red plates of sandstone that have been pitted into holes by the waves. Maybe it's the colour of the sand that puts people off – there are few strollers and diggers in this small, sheltered crescent. Those who do venture down the steep cliff-path on to the beach may be rewarded by picking up blood-red garnets under the cliffs.

If you don't relish the scramble into and out of Fleswick Bay, bear left along the field edge to an easier crossing at the top of the gully and walk on towards South Head. The fields here are canted so steeply seaward that the skyline in front tilts alarmingly, and you have the feeling of being just about to slip over the cliffs. The path is worn into a deep, narrow groove in the turf, evidence of the softness of the underlying sandstone. Suddenly the view ahead opens out to a widespread prospect over the straggling village of St Bees above its beach – this one *is* gold – with the high fells of Lakeland as a backdrop. The eye runs down the mountain ridges towards the sea, and pauses to take in the steaming cooling-towers, chimneys and pylons of Sellafield nuclear reprocessing plant on the low cliffs to the south. In this gorgeous setting of sea, fields and fells, the nuclear plant over its quiet shore makes a bizarre focal point. Perhaps after all there is one beach less conducive to bathing than Barrowmouth.

The cliff-path drops down to the seafront at St Bees, where you walk along the little promenade, to turn up by the Seacote Hotel (963117) and bear right into the road which passes St Bees Rugby League pitch. Soon the road divides (966119); just beyond the fork, a footpath leads over a field to the B5345 road and St Bees railway station (970119) by the level crossing on the right. Before catching your train back to Whitehaven, however, spare half an hour for the beautiful old church and school which stand opposite each other just up the road on your left. The school (970121) was founded in 1583 by Edward Grindal, Archbishop of Canterbury and a local boy. His original building now forms the left-hand wing of the quadrangle, the other sides made up of handsome sandstone Victorian additions.

Across the road is the church of St Bees Priory (969121), founded in 1120 by the Benedictine order and named in honour of St Bega, the Irish girl who ran away from an arranged marriage with a Viking chieftain to bring the Gospel to Britain's north-western wilderness, some time in the seventh century. There are few remains of the priory itself, but the church stands as a superb example of Norman and Early English architecture. Built of red sandstone, naturally, it dominates the village with its Italianate tower. You approach it from the school quadrangle along the north side; up in the bank above the path is the shaft of a Viking cross which is more than 1000 years old, the interlacing tracery still standing out clearly. The west door of the church, built some 30 years after the founding of the priory, has four diminishing Norman arches of great dignity; and inside, the sandstone of the pointed nave arches and piers has paled to a delicate rose colour through eight centuries of standing in the dim interior of the church. A Victorian wrought-iron screen leads into the transept crossing and the chancel, where the effigy of little Maria Lumb lies pale and calm, her ankles crossed and one hand resting lightly on her chest.

Outside the church are two more items to detain you before your train. In the wall opposite the west doorway, an old sandstone cross stands in a niche whose arch is decorated with a carving of St Michael battling the dragon of evil, probably Norman in date though Viking in spirit. On the south side of the church is the ruined wall of a chapel where in 1981 a fourteenth-century burial site was excavated. Inside a lead casing was the almost intact body of a middle-aged, greying man wrapped in a shroud, his beard still attached to his chin. Round his neck was twined a rope of long hair – perhaps a parting gift from his wife. You can see both shroud and hair in the museum in the new Civic Hall when you get back to Whitehaven.

34   Craster to Dunstanburgh Castle

OS 1:50,000   Sheets 81 and 75
4 miles, the round trip

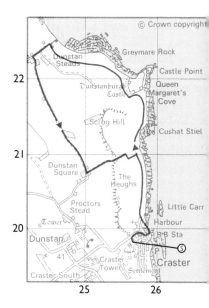

A strong thread of history has recently been broken: Crasters no longer live at Craster Tower. The family has been in Northumberland for at least 800 years, and may well pre-date the Norman Conquest. They can be reliably fixed at the tiny fishing village that carries their name from the end of the twelfth century onwards, sending their sons to follow military careers all over the world. They survived, where other great and ancient families fell, by never quite coming centre stage; the Crasters kept their feet firmly on the ground and themselves in the wings of bloody and dramatic Northumbrian history. Now most of their medieval stronghold just inland of the village has been converted into flats, and members of the family visit it only occasionally.

The village of Craster owes its fine small harbour to the family, who built it in 1906 as a memorial to a son killed in Tibet. It also owes most of its houses and all its modern amenities to the same source, though its past prosperity came in silver from the sea. When the great herring shoals began to desert the western coasts of Scotland and move round to the east-coast waters in the nineteenth century, Craster cashed in. In 1880 there were 27 fishing cobles and 20 herring drifters operating out of the village, bringing back fish to be turned into kippers in Craster's famous smokeries. Today just a couple of cobles go out to set crab- and lobster-pots and try to intercept the home-coming salmon. The herrings are brought in – sign of the times – not by the village's own fleet but by trawlers from North Shields, away down the coast. They are soaked in brine 'just strong enough to float a potato', in the vivid words of the excellent open-air exhibition in Craster car park; then smoked slowly over oak-chip fires. 'Nothing could be better', goes on the anonymous writer, 'than a pair of kippers served hot with an accompaniment of freshly baked bread slapped with butter, and washed down with an ample pot of tea.' Mmmmm! That homely panegyric must have sold hundreds of Craster kippers to hungry walkers completing this popular round walk to Dunstanburgh Castle and back.

The great craggy ruins of the castle are seen to spectacular effect from the harbour wall (259199), framed in the jaws of the concrete break-waters. This is a favourite place for the senior citizens of Craster to lean and chat on sunny days. Crab-pots are piled on the wall, their mesh these days woven out of orange plastic but their framework still made of the traditional twigs. Beyond the breakwaters lie the long, flat limestone ledges of Muckle Carr and Little Carr, lined with gulls and cormorants which depart as the waves advance, to fly in screeching crowds over the water. Inside the harbour, the slipway, with log rollers for the cobles, rises to the houses of Craster, some painted white and others in their natural colours of black and orange stone. The car park above the village stands in the hollows of the quarry from which whinstone, a hard volcanic rock, was carted to ships in the new harbour and taken away for road building. In this way the harbour benefited both the Craster family and the local fishermen. Just up the hill is Robson's herring smokery, fragrant white smoke curling out of its tarry vents.

The grass path to Dunstanburgh Castle leaves Craster through a gate on the northern edge of the village, above which a spick-and-span house named 'Kia-Ora' faces the sea. The cliffs here wouldn't be recognized as such by Welsh or West Countrymen; they rise only a few feet above a pavement of fractured rock, blotched yellow with lichen, which runs out into the water. Where it lies flat, the waves have smoothed away the angles and rounded the blocks, but the upstanding segments are sharp and hard-edged. The pools between cliffs and pavement hold tall tufts of marram grass, more commonly seen knitting together sand dunes. Two kinds of small, tubby, greyish shore scavengers, turnstones and purple sandpipers, run along the tideline looking for titbits; and in the deep, narrow cleft of Nova Scotia Bay (258212) you may be lucky enough to see black-and-white eider drakes and their drabber brown mates. The bay was once a harbour deep enough to hold a Tudor fighting ship, but over the years its depth has gradually been reduced as erosion of the nearby cliffs has diminished the force of the waves.

From Craster harbour, Dunstanburgh Castle on its promontory (257218) looks almost near enough to hit with a well-aimed stone. As you walk towards it, however, the intervening ground drops to reveal a wide valley on its southward side. Immediately the castle seems twice the size, an enormous fortification which fills the view ahead. The jagged spikes of its ruined gatehouse, pierced with dark window-holes and arched gateway, are so dramatically outlined against the sky that they might be part of some Hollywood film set. A long line of wall runs seawards to the Margaret Tower, named after Queen Margaret of Anjou; the formidable wife of King Henry VI, she was imprisoned here in 1462 during the Wars of the Roses. She captured and lost the castle twice in her campaign for the red rose of Lancaster, and the castle was not strong enough to hold her even in defeat. She climbed down or was let out of the tower, and made her escape by boat from Queen Margaret's Cove in the cliffs below the castle.

Entering the gatehouse from the path, you can climb up 67 spiral stairs to a superb view from the top: northwards over the golden curve of Embleton Bay and the spits of rock beyond to a distant glimpse of the Farne Islands out at sea; southwards to Coquet Island off Amble and the tall chimneys of Lynemouth power station; westwards over the fields towards the long blue line of the Cheviot Hills. The north–south prospect is all of 60 miles, the inland one at least 50. Around you rise the broken pinnacles of the gatehouse, which became the keep of the castle when it was strengthened against the marauding Scots by John of Gaunt in 1380, some 70 years after the castle was built. Only the southern approach was vulnerable, the north and east being guarded by cliffs rising to 100 feet and the west by the 45-degree slope of the outcrop; so the gatehouse was raised to five storeys high, 80 feet of grim defiance. A century later, battered by artillery during the wars, the old fort subsided into steady decay and was a ruin by 1550.

Before you descend the stairway, look down on the Great Ditch or moat, dug in 1314 from Cushat Stiel across the promontory to Greymare Rock on the north, and pity poor Sir Guy the Seeker, victim of one of those false-choice episodes beloved of legend. Sir Guy, so the story goes,

The view inland towards the Cheviot Hills from the top of Dunstanburgh Castle's gatehouse.

ended his days wandering around the walls of Dunstanburgh Castle, grieving for his lost love and lamenting his bad luck. He was a crusader knight on his way home after fighting in the Moorish wars in Spain. A terrible storm blew up as he was passing Dunstanburgh, forcing him to knock at the castle gates and beg shelter. He was admitted, fed, dried out and shown to bed, where he fell gratefully asleep. As midnight struck, Sir Guy awoke to find a giant standing by his bed. The monster led the knight along the cold corridors of the castle until they came to a chamber where a jewelled sword and a great horn hung on the wall. On a crystal bier in the room a beautiful princess lay in an enchanted sleep. The giant informed Sir Guy that she could only be awoken by one who would wield the sword or blow the horn – he must make the choice. The knight, astounded by the beauty of the sleeping girl, took down the horn and blew a mighty blast. The room reeled about him and he fell to the floor in a swoon. Next morning, cold and heartsick, Sir Guy awoke to find himself alone outside the castle gates, condemned to tramp a lonely round of the walls for the rest of his life. If anyone decides to film the tale, the castle ruins are made for the job.

The path continues from Dunstanburgh around the castle mound and under the tall shell of the Lilburn lookout tower, to reach the shore on the north of the promontory (257221). Here the cliffs of black basalt are splashed with the droppings of kittiwakes, fulmars and shags, whose cries reverberate around the rocky bay between Castle Point and Greymare Rock. The shags fly a lower circuit than the other birds, flicking over the sea with fast wing-beats like miniature torpedo planes. You walk west-wards along the landward edge of a golf course, and turn left (245224) up the lane to the farm at Dunstan Steads. The farm is open to the public in the evenings for tours around its land and visits to its animals. From here a green public footpath sign marked 'Dunstan Square 1' points down a concrete footpath which runs over the cornfields to pass the ruins of a lime-kiln (247214) and rise to a view forward over Craster. At Dunstan Square farm (250208) turn left down a field to reach The Heughs, an embankment of rock outcrop that separates the farmland from the shore. The walk back to Craster on the landward side of The Heughs is rather dull; a better return-route is over a little pass through the outcrop (254209), turning right through the first gate you come to and left through the next one. Here you drop down the grassy bank to the coast-path back to the village.

On the south side of the harbour, the road climbs up to the Jolly Fisherman pub, which serves sandwiches of locally caught crab and salmon and has an upper bar with a view through large windows over the harbour and rock pavement of the foreshore. Walking up the road to the car park, don't miss The Choughs Café on the right whose porch is made of an old fishing coble. Upstairs there is a small and carefully laid-out exhibition of tropical shells. Another café, the Bark Pots by the car park, offers home baking and a friendly welcome.

35 Marsden Bay and Whitburn

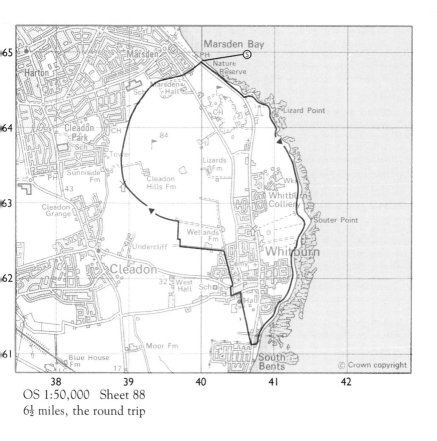

OS 1:50,000   Sheet 88
6½ miles, the round trip

Marsden Quarry must have been an efficient training place back in the 1780s. Jack the Blaster learned enough there to take his explosives down to the beach and practise on the limestone cliffs that rear up out of Marsden Bay. By the time Jack had finished, he had excavated a whole series of caverns in the face of the cliffs, enough to be opened as a public house in 1828. South Shields folk poured into Marsden to drink in the 15 underground rooms and dance the night away in the ballroom, with the sea right below their boots. They called it 'The Grotto', and it still attracts the crowds today. It must be the only pub in the world entered by going down in a lift, housed in a tall brick tower that stands clear of the cliff-face, the publican's licence-plate over the lift doors. There are 131 steep steps as an alternative – but going down thirsty is rather easier than coming up at closing time.

The Grotto is the starting place for this walk southwards along the cliffs. From the car park beside the lift entrance (400649) you look north to the long pincers of the North and South Piers that enclose the mouth of the River Tyne where it meets the sea after its loud and dirty journey through the Newcastle dockland. Marsden makes a welcome contrast to the city, small and quiet after the long, noisy industrial outskirts south of the Tyne. A row of modest red-brick houses faces the sea and the large offshore stack of Marsden Rock, severed by wave action from the mainland and only reachable at low tide over the sand. Its domed top is a mass of black and grey blobs: cormorants, fulmars and kittiwakes that share their windy roosting place. There are many lesser stacks along this coast, and each has its crook-necked black guardians resting between fishing expeditions. As you walk south over the smooth grass lawns between houses and cliff edge, the great wave-cut arch in Marsden Rock is slowly revealed, running halfway up the height of the stack and breaking the waves that surge through it into foam. Each wave takes its mite of soft sandstone, increasing by a fraction the process that will eventually make two separate stacks of Marsden Rock.

The cliff-path passes a long structure on the right like a derelict warehouse (406644). Two large, cylindrical, brick ovens on the end show its original function as a lime-kiln, burning the limestone quarried just behind where Jack the Blaster worked, two centuries ago. The limestone was burned in a sandwich with coal from the adjacent Whitburn Colliery, and the lime collected for fertilizer. Beyond the old kiln stands the stout red-and-white-striped tower of the lighthouse on Lizard Point, 75 feet high and topped with a diamond-latticed light that looks like a giant storm-lantern. Below the tower stand the twin black amplifiers for the foghorn, and behind it is the usual large, trim, white-painted lightkeeper's house. Before automation several families lived here, but lime dust and noise from the quarry drove them out.

Strong tides push into the bay beyond the lighthouse, the rollers rushing up the shingle to smack against the cliffs. Here the path enters the newly made coastal park, through which it runs as far as the military firing-ranges below Whitburn village. As you stroll along this pleasant green plateau you can look inland and marvel at the speed with which man can ruin a landscape and then restore it. If you had come this way ten years ago, you would first have passed through the huge derelict craters of a quarry and then the black heaps of spoil from Whitburn Colliery which stood just up the bank. The whole area was a scene of devastation; and, worse still, seams of coal underground had caught fire decades before and were still burning, staining the sides of the quarry pits a fiery red. In the ground were blow-holes a few inches across, wisps of steam curling out of their mouths and crusts of sulphur ringing them – but just below the surface the blow-holes opened out into craters several yards across and many feet deep. If you stamped hard you could feel the earth quaking under you. Seawater was pumped into the burning seams to try to put the fires out, but it brought powerful jets of oxygen in with it and only made matters worse.

In the view of the danger to walkers and the need to deal properly with the fires, the coast-path was closed in 1985 and the diggers moved in. They cut enormous valleys into the ground (200 yards deep in places) and removed the burning material. The remaining coal was harvested from the acres of spoil, and then the cooled earth and rock were shovelled back again and the Dantesque craters disappeared. I walked here when the cuttings were at their deepest, and was staggered by the vast extent of the wasteland and the sight of an army of yellow machines grinding their way down 45-degree ledges into the shadows far below or lumbering in circles on the very edges of the red-sided valleys. Now, looking over the grassy plain, it is hard to believe it's the same place.

The height of the cliffs steadily diminishes as they run down to Souter Point (415628) above a pebbly beach with a strip of salt-marsh backing it. Above the Point, the path passes the long mounds of a firing-range, each carrying a string of numbers identifying the targets. From here there is a wide view forward over Sunderland sprawling back inland – ranks of identical red roofs, chimneys, cranes, warehouses and the lighthouse on the end of the harbour breakwater. The path runs on below Whitburn's smart clifftop bungalows to meet the A183 road at Whitburn Bents (408612), a neat little crescent of 1930s houses with curly gables at each end and in the centre. Cross the road here and follow a green public footpath sign up over the fields towards the tower of Whitburn church and the leafy face of Southend House (405616). The square Victorian

Marsden Rock, digesting station for thousands of cormorants, fulmars and kittiwakes.

building was the dower house for Whitburn Hall, home of Sir Hedworth Williamson, the builder of Whitburn Bents. The Hall stood just over the lane to the right before it burned down in the early 1980s. The land runs up the side of Southfield House to pass the eccentric Red Cottage, a fine piece of self-indulgence by its architect, Benjamin Green, dated 1842 and incredibly over-elaborate in red and black brick.

Whitburn church, above Red Cottage, was built in the thirteenth century but suffered at the hands of zealous Victorian restorers; it stands in a beautiful position, though, looking seaward below the village green with its many tall trees and polished granite drinking fountain (put up to commemorate Queen Victoria's Diamond Jubilee). This older part of Whitburn village is lovely – pleasant Georgian and Victorian houses on a neat little street – a haven for rich Sunderlanders to live, ride, shop and stroll in. The workaday world creeps in, however, as you cross the village street and turn first left up Sandy Chare (404618) and Wellands Lane above it. Here the houses are just plain brick semis, where the rest of Whitburn lives. Ordinariness is relative, though – in Wellands Lane I met a three-legged dog, and immediately afterwards a one-armed man.

Near the top of the lane you turn left (403624) on a path waymarked with yellow arrows, which runs past the stone-built old house and barns of Wellands Farm (401624). To the south beyond Sunderland's outskirts you can see a windmill still standing, sails and all, above Fulwell, while to the north the cornfields roll up to a skyline from which pokes up a tall red-brick Italianate tower – not a church or a rich man's folly, but a water pumping tower built in 1863 to supply South Shields with a million gallons a day. The path climbs the side of the hill in a series of right-angle turns through the fields, and comes out at the top to a view which stops you in your tracks. All the industrial north-east coastlands are spread out below you – Newcastle to the north filling its low-lying bowl by the Tyne, the red splashes of Gateshead and Washington New Town leading the eye west and south over Sunderland to the flaring chimneys and pipework complexes of chemical Teesside. Running from industry through housing to rural patches and back again, this enormous panorama has the Penshaw and Boldon Hills to give it height and space and, far beyond them, the pale-blue hills of Teesdale and Northumberland.

Cleadon Windmill (389632), capless and ruinous, stands facing all this by the path. The only thing that could take my eyes off the view was the sight of a man, middle-aged, balding and bespectacled, climbing slowly round the sides of the windmill five feet off the ground, spread out like a spider as he felt for hand- and toe-holds between the stone blocks. Having completed his circuit – about 15 minutes of silent concentration – he gave a little grunt of satisfaction, dropped lightly to earth and marched smartly away downhill.

From the windmill you pass the water tower (387636) and make for the right-hand corner of a green wire-mesh fence which marks the boundary of a golf course. A faint path runs diagonally down over the fairways, making for a thin black pole sticking up just where the houses of Marsden are hidden by the rise of the ground. The pole stands beside a stile in a stone wall, from which a well-marked path goes down above a school to pass the grassy hummocks of a limestone quarry (395646). Wild mint grows here, its hairy leaves giving off a strong smell to refresh you on the last leg of the walk. Cross a road (398647) and walk down by a caravan park to the A183 road, below which is the clifftop car park opposite Marsden Rock and a swift descent to your reward in the dark bars of The Grotto.

36 Robin Hood's Bay to Ravenscar

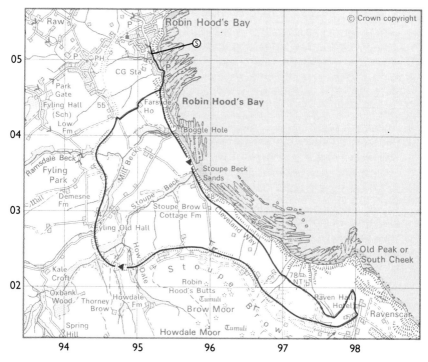

OS 1:50,000 Sheet 94
7½ miles, the round trip

This yah neet, this yah neet,
Ivvery neet an' all:
Fire an' fleet an' cannul leet,
An' Christ tak' up thi saule.

If ivver thoo gavest hosen or shoon,
Ivvery neet an' all,
Clap tha' doon an' put 'em on,
An' Christ tak' up thi saule.

But if hosen an' shoon thoo nivver ga' neean,
Ivvery neet an' all,
T' whinnies'll prick thi sair to t'beean,
An' Christ tak' up thi saule.

So sing those hardy 'saules' who complete that purgatory among long-distance walks, the Lyke Wake Walk from Osmotherly over the North York Moors to Robin Hood's Bay. Some 40 miles in 24 hours is the requirement, and many are the casualties. Their dirge is centuries old, and used to be sung over corpses in this part of the world before the souls of the departed began their journey to judgement by way of Whinney Moor.

No one knows if the outlaw of Sherwood ever came to the little cliff-encircled inlet between Scarborough and Whitby, but old tales say that he and his merrie men would retreat here when hard-pressed, to lie out at sea in boats until their pursuers had given up and gone away. He also spent many a summertime fishing holiday in the bay, going under the name of Simon Wise. Some stories even cite him as the founder of the village, which was built to commemorate the spot where the arrow fell which Robin fired from Stoupe Brow, more than a mile away – he must have had his shooting boots on that day.

The village is in constant conflict with the sea. Between the eighteenth and the twentieth century, 200 houses were taken by the waves; the red-roofed survivors stand on each other's shoulders up the ravine which leads to the bay. Ships were often driven ashore in Robin Hood's Bay in the days of sail: the drinkers in one waterside pub are reputed to have had a sobering shock when their window was smashed by the bowsprit of a ship being swept up the street by a monster wave. A 600-foot-long sea-wall was built in the 1970s, which has helped to reduce the threat from the sea.

As you might imagine, tourism is now the mainstay of this picturesque little village. In 1860 there were no fewer than 173 sailing vessels based at Robin Hood's Bay, and at the turn of the century the village could count 16 master mariners among its inhabitants. The large families of those days provided hands for the fishing boats and coasters, and there were eight grocers, five bakers and six butchers to cater for them. Then the size of families began to dwindle, coinciding with the expansion of the steelworks and factories on Teesside. Young people drifted away up the newly metalled roads, and the family fishing businesses declined. Tourism revived the village, but its isolation was ended, along with the close community atmosphere in which everyone knew everyone else (they were probably related): often claustrophobically so during the long winter months when the village was sealed off by its slippery, steep tracks from the outside world.

We start our walk at the lower car park (952051) – if you do drive down the 1-in-3 road into the lower village, you'll have nowhere to park and the greatest difficulty getting out again. Walk down the steps beside the road which runs between the narrow little cobbled alleys, flights of stone steps and maze-like passages behind the piled houses. Boutiques, bistros and gift shops now occupy many of the old fishermen's cottages, but somehow the place manages to cling to its dignity. At the bottom of the hill on the right is a telephone box, behind which stands the old lifeboat shed (954048). Large, ten-oared rowing boats with a 14-man crew were used in the 1900s, being hauled by horses up and down the steep little slipway on high wooden carriages on to which they had to be lifted by muscle power alone. The lifeboat was withdrawn in 1932, to the regret of the community, though perhaps not of the crew's wives and children. Beside the slipway is the former coastguard station, now occupied by 'Marine Activities'.

Here you make a choice: either to walk along the beach as far as Stoupe Beck (check the tide times displayed at the car park), or to climb up to the clifftop path. You won't find any fossils this way, but you will get some stunning views. For the cliff walk, turn right between the two old buildings and walk up cobbled Covet Hill, from the top of which wooden steps lead down, then up the cliff to the path along the top. This path forms part of the Cleveland Way, 150 miles of moorland and clifftop tramping from Helmsley to Filey Brigg, which was opened in May 1969; hence the large number of helpful signposts and waymarks. You look forward along the sweep of the bay round to the rising crests of South Cheek, on the top of which Raven Hall Hotel stands proudly above all; and behind you to a memorable view of the houses of Robin Hood's Bay seemingly in the act of toppling in a pile on to the beach. The path runs on wooden walkways clinging to the sides of recent falls, and as a grassy track on the cliff edge where it is firm enough.

Steep wooden steps descend to Boggle Hole (a 'boggle' is a sprite or goblin in local parlance), a narrow ravine so thickly wooded that you don't see the cluster of buildings at the bottom until you are right on top of them. This is Mill Beck Youth Hostel (954051), famous among travellers of all ages for its peaceful, secluded position. It was once a mill

The village street begins its 1-in-3 plunge down among the tightly-packed houses of Robin Hood's Bay.

to which grain was brought from the nearby Farsyde House farm and other farms in the district along paved tracks over the cliffs.

The path crosses the beck and climbs up again, over the cliff brow and down into the valley of the Stoupe Beck (958035). On the far side, a pavement of concrete slabs mounts up the cliff beside a very steep rough track. This was once tarmacked and, believe it or not, open to motor cars. At a gradient of steeper than 1-in-3, the ghosts of boiling radiators, burnt-out clutches and swearing drivers are all around you.

Pass the farm at the top and walk up the road to go through a stone stile opposite Stoupe Brow Cottage Farm (959031). Now the path runs below the vast scoops of the disused alum quarries which ate away the seaward face of Stoupe Brow, the long hill directly in front of you from which Robin Hood made his prodigious bow-shot. Alum mining was an important industry in the district 100 years ago, and has left its scars in many hillsides. Shale was dug from the quarries and burned with brushwood in great multi-storey sandwiches 50 feet high. The burnt shale was mixed with an alkaline liquid and evaporated to form the precious alum crystals: 50 tons of shale produced one ton of alum. The crystals were then loaded on to boats and shipped away, to be used as a fixative in the tanning and dyeing processes.

Pale mauve orchids grow in damp runnels in the cliff-face, along the top of which the path goes for another half-mile before climbing gently by stiles and field tracks to reach a lane (970022). This mounts steeply among gorse bushes, sycamores and mountain ash below the quarries to reach a level path (974016), where you turn left and walk along to a bridge which spans a disused railway line. Go down the path, which curves round to the right to reach the Raven Hall Hotel on the highest point of the cliffs, 600 feet above the sea (981018).

The Romans, with their canny appreciation of a good site, built a signal station up here; and the peerless view over the coast to south and north led to the building of Ravenshill Hall in the 1770s. Shortly after it was built, King George III came to try another in the long line of psychiatric cures that might help to ease his tormented mind, being nibbled away by the family curse of porphyria. The house became a hotel, nowadays patronized by those lucky enough to be able to pay for that wonderful view. Bram Stoker is supposed to have dreamt up Count

Dracula on this cliff, and late-Victorian property developers also saw a vision here. The Peak Estate Company Limited planned the clifftop resort of Ravenscar, and got as far as laying down roads and drains and auctioning off plots of land. 750 acres were up for grabs, and the shops, houses and hotels began to go up. There was even a railway station (on the Whitby and Scarborough line) at which new purchasers alighted, fares paid by the company, to inspect their investment.

Then reality began to creep in. Could they really settle on a bare, wind-whipped peak, 600 feet above the beach and often swathed in the mists called 'sea-frets' that any local fisherman could have told them were more frequent than sunny days along this coast? They thought not, climbed back into the train, and left the Peak Estate Co. Ltd to pick up the pieces. A few houses, lengths of roadway and pipes in the cliffs are all that remain of the grandiose dream.

Fancy a trip back to Robin Hood's Bay by railway? Then step – literally – aboard at the bridge below the Raven Hall Hotel. The Whitby and Scarborough line was a favourite with holidaymakers who would crane out of the carriage windows as their train negotiated the sharp curves of the line, looking down over the fields towards the toy-town houses of Robin Hood's Bay. The line was opened on 16 July 1885, and immediately established itself as a 'must' for summer travellers. Summer – there was the problem. Revenue came pouring in between June and September, but for the rest of the year the single-track railway had to rely on the handful of local market-bound women and farmers who needed its services all the year round. Ravenscar Station was approached from the Scarborough direction through a curving tunnel up which the trains had to struggle on a gradient of 1 in 39. Any slope of more than 1 in 50 was always a tough battle for a steam locomotive; and when the rails were greasy with sea mist the climb could become a nightmare, slipping and stalling in the sulphurous fumes of the tunnel. The line limped on into the twentieth century, surging briefly into the black during the summer, before plunging back into the red for the remaining eight months of each year. On 8 March 1965, Dr Beeching called 'time', and the track reverted to a weed-choked channel along the cliffs. It was too good to be wasted, however, and when the undergrowth had been cut back and the track bed surfaced, it emerged as a footpath running for 16 miles between

Scarborough and Hawsker Bottoms, a couple of miles short of Whitby, with some marvellous views out over the cliffs and sea for the new users of the railway: walkers and riders.

You walk back to Robin Hood's Bay along the old line, from which there is a close-up view of the powder-grey faces and spoil-heaps of the alum quarries above the railway. Wild thyme and heather scent the air, and the four-mile tramp back to the starting-point of the walk is enlivened by those long views eastwards over cliffs and sea which the passengers in the excursion trains enjoyed. Below Fyling Old Hall a three-arch viaduct is followed by wooden steps which carry the path over a road (944028). On the far side you walk on for another mile, with orchids growing in the shaded sides of the cuttings, to a lane which crosses the line of the railway (947042).

Here you turn right, then left down Mark Lane which leads to Farsyde House, a farm and stud (950044). Bear left around the house, then right down the fields, walking on ancient paving slabs over whose hollowed centres generations of feet passed between Farsyde and Robin Hood's Bay. On the clifftop again (953045), turn left for the last few hundred yards into the village.

37   Flamborough Head

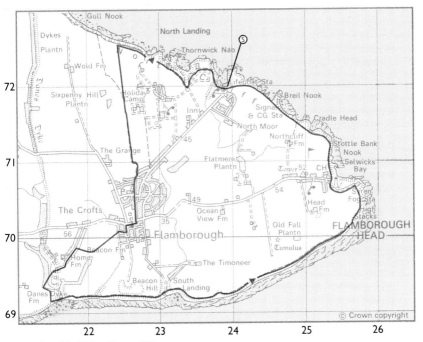

OS 1:50,000   Sheet 101
8 miles, the round trip

Flamborough Head, a great chalk thumb poking out from the top corner of North Humberside into the North Sea, receives the full force of the wind from all points of the compass but the west. The sea-birds don't seem to mind; they swoop and wheel around the narrow ledges, bringing food back to their precarious roosts in sheltered crevices. Guillemots, gulls, razorbills, puffins, fulmars, and kittiwakes screeching out 'Kitti-WAKE! Kitti-WAKE!' fill the air with their various cries, and the cliff-faces are smeared with their droppings – which also contribute a certain fishy tang to this walk.

Local men have had to learn to cope with the vagaries of wind and tide, too – the fishermen of Flamborough village have developed specially shaped cobles with narrow sterns and bulging midriffs which can be

201

launched backwards into the waves and winched out forwards. Tide and wind can switch direction suddenly, driving the boats unexpectedly into danger. This coast has a long history of wrecks, some of which are illustrated in photographs and newspaper cuttings on the walls of the lifeboat shed at North Landing, where this walk starts. A mile and a half north-east of Flamborough village, North Landing is a natural sandy harbour, squeezed between headlands of chalk that shield it from all but direct north-easterlies. The lifeboat shed stands hard back against a steep slope above a concrete slipway down which the boat is launched on its frequent missions of rescue. The public are welcome to inspect the shed and boat on the occasions when it is open; here you can read the roll of 'services rendered' back to 1889. They include a large number of 'boys cut off by tide' and 'man over cliffs', testimony to the rashness of holidaymakers on these dangerous headlands and to the efficiency of the lifeboatmen at their hazardous calling. The tough, individualistic faces of the Flamborough fishermen who have manned the boat since it was inaugurated in 1871 smile or stare out of the faded old photos on the walls, beside pictures of the dismasted barques and beached steamers whose crews they rescued with enormous bravery and no fuss.

Beside the slipway is a sloping hard on which the fishermen work at maintaining their cobles – and beyond that rise the chalk cliffs, burrowed into arches, caves and stacks by the waves.

From the car park above North Landing (238720), you turn westwards along the top of the cliffs, looking north over the screaming ledges of Gull Nook to the distant arm of Filey Brigg. The path dips into gullies and climbs out by flights of steps, or steep scrambles down which you can 'boldly go'; or you can walk the longer but easier way inland round the lip of the cliffs. Far below, the aquamarine water is clear enough to show the rocks, weeds and sandy bottom of the sea. A tan-coloured rock pavement runs back to a tumbled mass of white chalk blocks below the grey, salt-encrusted cliffs which rise to a brown fringe of soil and a green cap of turf. Concrete pillboxes in the inlets are reminders of the invasion threat for which this coastline braced itself during the early days of the Second World War. Inland above the fields rise the bright white spear of the lighthouse on Flamborough Head and the tall grey-chalk tower of its older, retired neighbour.

The path runs on the very edge of the cliffs – do be careful! – before turning left over a waymarked stile (224726) to cross three fields to a cart-track. Turn left, then right down a hedge to reach Woodcock Road (227708), down which you walk past the splendid chapel of 1889 and some old barns made of chalk blocks, to reach the monument at a crossroads in the centre of Flamborough village. It was erected to commemorate the 'conspicuous act of bravery' of the three-man crew of the coble *Two Brothers*, who during the great gale of 5 February 1909 lost their lives trying vainly to save the crew of the *Gleaner*, a father and his two sons. Flamborough lost six of its men that day; and three more on 7 May 1984, who were searching for the missing crew of a coble from Bridlington. Altogether seven men died in this tragedy, their names recorded on a memorial slab beside the monument. Like pit villages, fishing communities are prepared for the occasional deaths that their always dangerous profession brings about; but multiple tragedies like these devastate not just the families involved but the whole village.

Carry on down Tower Street past the ruins of the Constable family's castle. The Constables were lords of the manor here for nearly five hundred years until Sir Robert Constable forfeited his head to King Henry VIII after taking part in the Pilgrimage of Grace in 1537. From the castle bear right down Church Street to reach Flamborough churchyard, where fresh flowers decorate another memorial to the men who died in 1984. The Church of St Oswald contains a fine Norman arch into the chancel, a beautifully carved sixteenth-century rood-screen, and two curious pieces of local history. One of the memorials to the Strickland family incorporates in the family's coat of arms a turkey with long red wattles; and at the back of the church is a reproduction of a pardon issued by King Charles II to Walter Strickland, evidently a keen supporter of Parliament until he saw the light. It covers just about every crime known to man – Walter must have been quite a fellow.

Walk on through the churchyard to the gate and turn right to reach Water Lane, up which you walk for 100 yards to a wooden fingerpost (224701) which points left across the fields. Follow the waymarks to a road running under large sycamores, and turn left (218698). After about a third of a mile, the road cuts through an old earth-bank (215696) and bends left. This bank is 'Dane's Dyke', an earthwork which runs for $2\frac{1}{2}$ miles right across Flamborough Head, cutting it off from the mainland. Although the name testifies to the healthy respect in which the Norse

The Flamborough lifeboat stands poised for action above the narrow inlet and wave-worn chalk cliffs of North Landing.

ravagers were held in the district, the earthwork pre-dates them by 2000 years, and was probably thrown up by an Iron Age tribe to protect their stronghold on the tip of the peninsula.

Walk forward at the bend with a brick wall on your left to drop down into the depths of a dry gully, on the far side of which a path climbs up to a signpost marked 'Sewerby'. Go left here along the top of the bank to a footpath sign pointing to the right. Don't follow it, but carry on ahead down a flight of steps to a little beach of chalk boulders (215692), where you cross a road and climb up more steps to the clifftop. The view back is along the great arc of the East Yorkshire/Humberside coastline towards Spurn Head.

The path along the cliffs runs far above the fishing cobles in the comparatively sheltered waters under the south-facing side of Flamborough Head, and the long lines of floats marking the position of crab-pots on the sea bed. At South Landing (231692) there is a little strip of sand above the chalk pebbles, some salt-rusted tractors used to drag the cobles to and from the water, and a brick shed which once housed a lifeboat. It was stationed here so that a rescue attempt could be launched from either side of the headland, depending on the state of tide, waves and wind; but reorganization of the service has done away with it.

Bear left beyond the shed and climb up the steps to the clifftop, from which there is a glorious high-level walk of $2\frac{1}{2}$ miles to the lighthouse on Flamborough Head, seen over the ridge to the left drawing gradually closer. The view swings slowly round from the southward coastline through a segment of flat sea horizon to a prospect northwards over the coast as far as Filey Brigg. The 85-foot white light-tower stands on the left of the path above a square block of housing, its lantern meshed in against the weather (254707). It is open to visitors on most weekday afternoons. On the right of the path is the square white-painted building which houses the fog-siren – vital for seamen in thick weather, it can be one hell of a shock for walkers.

Turn left up the lighthouse road, then right through a kissing gate, to skirt below the lighthouse and continue along the clifftops. There is a sudden increase in the noise of wind, waves and sea-birds, whose raucous colonies crowd these north-facing cliffs. Away to the left the old abandoned light-tower, built in 1763, overlooks the smoothly shaven greens of a golf course. The clifftop path runs on for another mile and a half above the green shallows and the wheeling kittiwakes with their black-tipped wings outstretched, to return to the car park above the lifeboat station at North Landing.

38   Skipsea Sands to Barmston Sands

OS 1:50,000   Sheet 107
4 miles, there and back

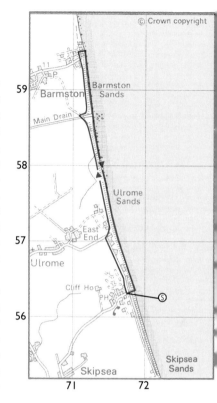

If your perception of this walk differs from mine, don't blame my poor descriptive powers! The sea is gobbling up this eastern coastline at the rate of at least six feet a year, and any clifftop path is liable to have vanished over the edge between one year's end and the next. Fences have constantly to be realigned, caravans moved further inland and cliff-edge houses abandoned as the winter storms lick away the ground they stand on. During this walk from Skipsea to Barmston along the coast of North Humberside, one is constantly reminded of the sea's capacity to overwhelm any defences man can pit against it; and of a sea-borne danger, invasion, which has threatened this coast down the ages.

Skipsea village is sited a good mile inland, safe from the sea for the next few hundred years. But the Skipsea Sands Caravan Park, where the walk begins, sits right on the edge of the cliffs and is losing its parking sites at the rate of several a year. The well-ordered ranks of the caravans stand beyond the car park at the end of the road from Skipsea (178563), from which you turn left to pass Mattsson Cottage, built just before the First World War. Its seaward extension is already on the beach; and the rest of it, teetering right on the brink, will soon follow. Those who named Cliff Top Farm, a few yards further on, probably didn't guess just how accurate that name would prove.

Where the road turns sharp left for Ulrome (175571), bear right past the Seaside Caravan Park notice-board and the Southfield Café ('Fish 'n' Chips * Chips 'n' Dips') to turn left along the clifftop between the caravans and the edge. In spite of the warning signs of concrete hardstandings cut in half and hanging over the brow of the cliffs, holidaymakers still come here to perch above the beach and the sea. The cliffs, of unstable clay, stand not much more than ten feet above the beach; they form a ragged chain of indentations bitten out by the waves, their course paralleled by the fence and the winding path. Railway sleepers and loads of bricks are jammed at the foot of the cliffs, shoring them up until the next major storm.

Beyond the caravan park the path widens out, thanks to the prudence of the farmer who has left a good margin of safety between seed-drill and cliff edge. Inland, the wheat fields curve gently to the skyline, their smooth green line broken by the tops of Second World War pillboxes which are quietly crumbling away among the corn stalks. Hereabouts the evidence of how seriously Britain was threatened by invasion in 1939/40 lies on both sides: the pillboxes in the fields and, below you on the beach, the concrete blocks of beach defences, their sharp angles softened by half a century of sea erosion but still a potent reminder of the vulnerability of this coastline. A long line of them sticks above the water, slowly exposed by each receding tide, guarding Ulrome Sands from the landing craft that never came. More lie scattered haphazardly along the beach, half buried in the sand.

The path drops to cross Barmston Main Drain (172587), a deep channel which drains the fields inland. The cliffs are too unstable to support a mouth for the drain, so the water runs out along the beach and into the sea, enclosed in a concrete casing that looks like a jetty. Some of the wartime defensive blocks are piled along the drain to give it some protection against the tides, and others have been extracted from their sandy beds and dumped against the cliffs for the same purpose.

The path rises up the cliffs beyond the drain, then dips down to arrive at another bungalow and caravan site below Barmston (172594). From the top of the wooden steps down to the beach there is a fine view northwards all the way to Flamborough Head. Beside the steps more concrete blocks have been heaped up from beach to clifftop – an unsightly but effective way of bracing up these shaky cliffs, at least

Going . . . going . . . almost gone. An abandoned house waits for the next storm to send it sliding down on to Skipsea Sands.

temporarily. You scramble over these to walk back along the beach to Skipsea Sands – there is a long, narrow strip of firm walking sand between the cliffs and the slimy foreshore.

The cliff-line may change from year to year, but this beach changes every day, from sand to pebbles and back again as each new tide decides. Fossils of ammonites, nautilus shells and bivalves lie among the bladder-wrack and pebbles – they are washed out of the cliffs when the sea sucks them at very high tides. This part of the coast lay under the sea until Ice Age glaciers laid down a coat of sand, clay and gravel. Scandinavian visitors came across dry-shod up to about 9000 years ago – then melting glaciers raised the sea level and severed the land connection. Coal, from the measures that lie under the water offshore, is deposited here by the waves, too. The crumbling of the cliffs is accelerated by springs of water which flow out of them, leaving pale grey trails down the reddish clay.

Approaching Skipsea Sands and the steps up from beach to car park, you can look up to see the corners of cottages and bungalows sticking out from the clifftops into thin air – dramatic evidence of the sea's hunger for England's eastern coastline.

39 Spurn Head

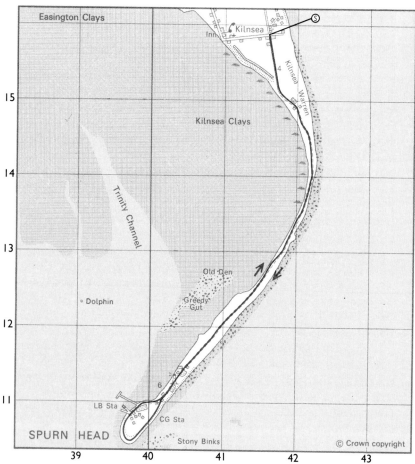

OS 1:50,000   Sheet 113
8 miles, there and back

I'll give my vote to any wind-blown spit of sand that is home to plants bearing these names: Canadian Fleabane, Buxbaum's Speedwell, Rayless Sea Aster, Dark-green Mouse-ear Chickweed, Suffocated Clover, Fool's Watercress, Toad's Rush, Crested Dog's Tail, Sand Cat's Tail and the Duke of Argyll's Tea Plant.

Spurn, three miles long and only 100 yards wide for most of its length, is a strange place however you look at it. For a start, it disappears once every 250 years and re-creates itself half a mile to the west. Wave action chafing against the flow of the River Humber works this sea change, gradually building up the long, curved spit until in another mood the tides rise up in fury and break the bar. Then the depositing of sand and shingle starts all over again. The former Spurns lie out to the east in the North Sea in parallel lines beneath the waves – the most recent one of these was the place where Henry Bolingbroke landed in 1399 to depose King Richard II. William Shakespeare knew of it, and has Northumberland hurrying there in Act II scene ii of *Richard II*:

> The banish'd Bolingbroke repeals himself,
> And with uplifted arms is safe arriv'd
> At Ravenspurg.

Ravenspurg, or Ravenspurn, was a prosperous town (with a representative at Parliament) which had been washed away along with the contemporary Spurn spit in about 1360; so Bolingbroke's landing-place was a newly arisen bar of barren sand – 'the naked shore at Ravenspurg', Harry Hotspur calls it in *Henry IV, Part I*.

In the next century, Edward IV also made a landing on Spurn on his way to ending the Wars of the Roses and the hopes of the House of Lancaster at the Battle of Barnet. Further out to sea lies the Spurn where one Hrafn, a Norse invader, landed to give it his name ('Hrafnseyr' = Ravenspurg). The present-day Spurn is liable to be more permanent than its predecessors, thanks to man's efforts at shoring it up with timber and concrete. It's a favourite place for bird-watchers, who come in busloads at all times of the year to spot the rare species, often exhausted after long flights across a stormy North Sea, that make a landfall here. Sooty Shearwaters visit in summer, Little Auks in autumn and Snow Buntings in winter, and representatives of each species are ringed at the bird observatory established in 1945 at the northern end of the peninsula. Ornithologists have proved that Snow Buntings return to the same wintering area every year – one bird came back four years out of five.

At Spurn Head, the southern or seaward end of the spit, is a small community of lifeboatmen, coastguards and pilots, connected to the mainland by their slim three-mile lifeline of roadway along the top of the sandbank. They live amidst a jumble of old army jetsam – concrete blockhouses, walls, gun emplacements and barracks – with only the sea, the birds and the passing ships for company. It is a lonely world apart, where some of nature's shyest species thrive side by side with some of military man's ugliest detritus.

Our walk begins at the Bluebell Café and shop, once a pub (417158), in the hamlet of Kilnsea, which has itself a predecessor that now lies under the sea to the east. The long, straight road runs south to a gate (418151), beyond which you enter Spurn. The Yorkshire Wildlife Trust's Information Centre stands on the left; spare a few minutes to enjoy its display on Spurn's wildlife and battles past and present with the encroaching sea. From here the way is unmistakable, a narrow road of tarmac and concrete which runs among bushes of sea buckthorn and elder above purple-grey mud-flats on the west and a strip of shingle on the east. Heaps of concrete blocks lie along the spit, evidence of past defences, and the stark piles of old jetties stand out into the water. A line of wooden telegraph-posts leads the eye round the long curve of the spit to the black-and-white-striped lighthouse at the southern end.

There are lengths of rusty railway line embedded in the roadway, the last remnants of the light railway which was built along Spurn during the First World War to carry men and materials for the building of Bull Sand Fort, an anti-submarine emplacement guarding the mouth of the Humber whose rounded bulk stands up out of the water beyond Spurn Head. Five steam locomotives were used on the railway, and the lifeboatmen travelled up and down on a special truck powered by a sail. An Itala racing car, fitted with flanged wheels, also trundled along the track. Local children's homes' outings to Spurn Head would include the thrill of a ride along the bumpy track to the end of the spit. The railway's only *raison d'être* was the military, however, and when they departed after the Second World War it ceased to operate, finally closing in 1952.

The road runs on through soft sand drifts from the dunes to reach the conglomeration of buildings, redundant or still in use, at Spurn Head. The lighthouse on the top of the spit (403113) closed down in 1985 after 90 years' operation; its twin stands below on the beach, headless and lifeless, with the waves lapping round its weed-encrusted base. Further on are the smart yellow houses of the lifeboatmen, whose boat is the only

The Spurn Head children's playground wall
– a little dash of the everyday world.

one in Britain manned all the year round by a professional crew. Their job is a vital one; this stretch of coast, constantly eroded by the sea and forever forming new sand-spits and bars, is extremely dangerous for the tens of thousands of ships that use it every year. The garages of the houses carry a series of boards inscribed with long lines of 'services rendered': 'Landed a sick man . . . gave help . . . took out doctor and landed an injured man . . . gave help . . . saved vessel . . . stood by boat . . . saved boat and 7 . . . landed a body . . . gave help. . . .'

Above the houses stands the tall grey coastguard and pilot centre with an ever-revolving radar scanner on the roof. Further on you pass the catching nets of the bird observatory, like fruit-cages over the sea buckthorn, and then the concrete labyrinths of bunkers and blockhouses built by the army to defend this outpost of mainland Britain. Beyond them lies a thick belt of scrub which leads to the sand and rocks at the extreme end of the spit. Standing here, you look across the wide mouth

213

of the Humber to the houses and low shoreline of Grimsby and Cleethorpes, with the chimneys and tanks of the oil refinery at Immingham away to the right.

On the western side of Spurn Head beside a disused concrete military jetty is the old corrugated-iron lifeboat shed, standing on timber piles above its slipway, and a spindly iron jetty that ends in a T-shaped head (396111) where the pilot boats tie up. Nowadays, if it is not at work, you may see the bright fluorescent-orange blob of the lifeboat moored beyond the end of the jetty.

Before returning along the road to Kilnsea, there is one poignant sight, just below the lifeboat houses, which seems to sum up the loneliness and also the continuing service of those who live and work on this remote extension of the mainland. The children of those who live on Spurn Head had their own school here until after the Second World War. Nowadays they are bused to schools inland; but their grassy, weed-strewn playground remains, enclosed by a low wall. On it has been painted a mural, its bright colours fading under the attacks of salt and wind, of the crowd at a Hull City football game, waving black-and-yellow-striped scarves. The lettering of the advertisement hoardings – Coca-Cola, the evening newspaper – has been reproduced with painstaking accuracy. Next to them is a scene from a speedway meeting, the bikes rearing up, cornering and crashing spectacularly. A little dash of the everyday world for youngsters living half in, half out of it.

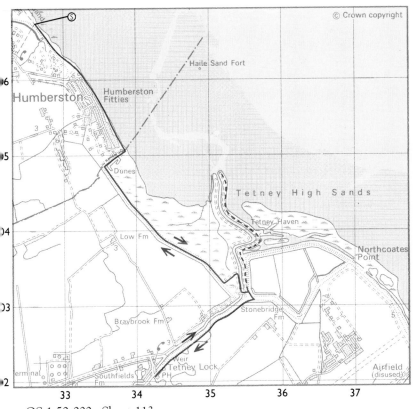

© Crown copyright

OS 1:50,000 Sheet 113
8 miles (11 miles with extension to canal mouth), there and back

Grimsby and Cleethorpes – work and play. The two South Humberside towns stand shoulder to shoulder looking out across the sandbanks and cold waters of the Humber Estuary to the curving ant-eater's snout of Spurn Head on the other side of the river. Grimsby's past prosperity was bound up in its life as a port, cut short by the sand and silt that the sea deposits slowly and inexorably along this North Sea coastline. Its present and future are founded on its fish dock and the other industries steadily creeping along the banks of the Humber.

*The Crown and Anchor stands over the disused Louth Canal
at Tetney Lock, once busy with bargemen and anglers.*

Cleethorpes is the sugar to Grimsby's salt, a gently fading playground for the factory workers of Nottinghamshire, Derbyshire and Leicestershire. Before the railway began to bring in the working-class holidaymakers with their hard-hoarded cash, it catered for genteel invalids in search of a sea-cure. Nowadays it is looking for a revival, spearheaded by 'Buster', its cheeky-chappie young Andy Capp of a mascot.

In the green, fertile fields behind the sea-wall just south of Cleethorpes, the tiny farming village of Humberston stayed small, hard-working and undisturbed until its two neighbours began to expand in the nineteenth century. It mushroomed into brick, and became a small town in its own right. The area of marshland by the sea-bank known as Humberston Fitties stayed unexploited until the twentieth-century camping and caravanning boom began. Now Humberston Fitties is a town, too – a linear town, more than a mile long, of mobile homes, caravans and bungalow chalets. This walk to Tetney Lock begins on the sea-wall just beyond the Cleethorpes Garden Stadium (greyhounds and stock cars), where you can park your car (326067).

Once on the sea-wall, the first impression is of the immense flatness of the land and sea, where every smoking chimney, crane and tanker's superstructure is a feature that claims attention. The ships – mainly oil-tankers, and fishing boats from Grimsby, with the occasional ferry from Scandinavia, Holland or Belgium – form a scarcely moving fleet a couple of miles offshore. The lighthouse on Spurn Head sticks a white finger up beyond them, leading the eye northwards to the long, low north bank of the Humber. Continuing inland, the shallow swell of the Lincolnshire Wolds rises above the coastal plain: the land of 'fens, fogs and flocks' known in ancient times as 'Lindsey' when it was famous for its fertile soil, terrible sea inundations and atrocious roads. Sandbanks break the surface of the sea in long whale-backs, some inaccessible except by boat because of the deep creeks that cross the sands on their way to the sea. Between sand and sea-wall is a narrow strip of salt-marsh, glinting with pools and small creeks. Over all are the huge skies which meet land and sea in a flat line all round the horizon. It is a strange, many-sided landscape to anyone accustomed to the cliff-shingle-sand-sea progression of the south and west coasts.

Turn right along the sea-wall past the mobile homes, accompanied by the bouncy jollity of Radio 2. The path drops to cross the outfall of Buck Beck, and becomes a tarmac track. You pass the cheap 'n' cheerful Spurn View Snack Bar and its swingboats, and walk beside the township of chalets, some with brick chimneys, all with an air of permanence with their trim, fenced gardens and brightly painted doors and window-frames. On the left the smooth, tan-coloured bank of Tetney High Sands rolls clear of the sea. Opposite the chalets stands Haile Sand Fort (349062), built during the First World War as a coastal defence along with its twin, Bull Sand Fort (370092), which stands further out in the mouth of the Humber. An anti-submarine net stretched between them, and they were garrisoned by 200 men and their officers. They survived bombing and strafing during the Second World War, but not the outbreak of peace, which saw them finally abandoned to slow death by salt and wind. Haile Sand Fort looks like a chubby submarine conning-tower, magnified at low tide when its supporting girders stand clear of the water.

At Humber Mouth Yacht Club (338050) the sea-wall turns inland and runs for nearly two miles behind a huge area of saltmarsh, an RSPB reserve where shelduck, oystercatchers, curlew, terns, waders and the inevitable larks feed and breed, apparently undisturbed by the RAF Lightnings that burn through the decibel barrier overhead every few minutes.

The path comes to an oil pipe-line (352033) that rises like a worm from the marsh, crosses above the sea-wall and buries itself in the fields inland. It brings oil from the tankers out in the estuary to the grey cylinders of the storage depot that can be seen from the sea-wall and eventually to the refinery, further up-river at Immingham. Here you turn seaward again, left and then right, to reach the concrete lock-gates (354032) on the disused Louth Canal. It was opened in 1770 and made Tetney Haven, a mile seaward, a busy place for 150 years. Declining trade, advancing silt and competition from more modern forms of transport put an end to the canal in the 1920s.

After crossing the canal and then a stile, you can turn left to walk for a mile and a half along the sea-bank to the mouth of the canal (351058), two long lips of wall pursed out into the flats of Tetney High Sands. The cargoes wound their way from the sea up the creek through the sandbanks and into the canal here. Great tidal surges were always a danger, and the concrete gates were built during the Second World War when the gates further up the canal at Tetney Lock had proved themselves unable to hold back big surges. To reach Tetney Lock from the stile by the 'new' gates, walk up to the concrete pillbox and turn right along the canal-bank to pass Tetney Weir (343023) and come to the bridge at Tetney Lock (342021).

The old lock-gates were removed from their position under the bridge, as were the wharves and the barges themselves, when the canal closed. This used to be a favourite destination for angling clubs from as far away as Rotherham, Sheffield and Barnsley, who would arrive in motor coaches for a hard day's fishing, followed by a stern evening's drinking in the Crown and Anchor by the bridge. Although Tetney Lock lost its trade, its gates and most of its visitors, the pub is still operating. It serves snacks and has a children's garden with a swing at the back.

Dear reader, the OS map is a lying jade! That footpath that runs temptingly above Braybrook Farm (344028) and Low Farm (337039) . . . there are no bridges over the creeks that bisect it. That other footpath from Low Farm to the sea-wall (340042) . . . unless you want a bootful of brackish slop, don't try it. However, as the sea-wall cuts off your best view from any inland track, you can congratulate yourself, on your way back over the outward route, on still having a grandstand view over that flat, strange, absorbing marsh, and the forts, sea-birds, sandbanks, water, ships and skies.

41   Birds, bombs and big views – the sea-walls of Gedney Drove End

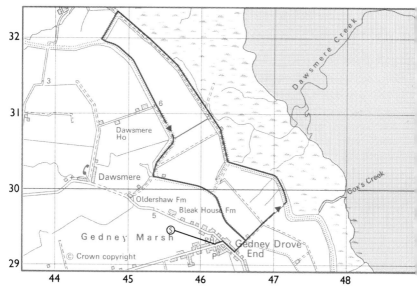

OS 1:50,000   Sheet 131
5½ miles, the round trip

There's nothing even remotely picturesque about Gedney Drove End. It's just a collection of functional brick houses, two pubs, a school and a shop stuck out on the shore of the Wash at the end of a five-mile road across the flat fields of south-east Lincolnshire. People here look after themselves, growing cabbages, onions, sprouts, sugar-beet and corn in some of the most fertile soil in the world. Tourists don't come down the drove road, though walkers and wildfowlers do. 'A bit of a funny place,' they say in Sutton Bridge (four miles away as the pigeon flies) – 'and funny people, the Drove Enders.'

The Drove Enders seem quite content to take the outside world as they find it – or not to take it at all; but Gedney Drove End is certainly a funny place. Only the great curve of sea-wall at its back saves it from the sea; for it lies on the outermost edge of South Holland, which was mostly water before the Norman monks began their wall-building. The sea lapped four or five miles inland, as far as Gedney Dyke, until the great seventeenth-century reclamations under the efficient control of Dutch experts. Then settlements began to appear over the newly dry land as the sea was gradually pushed back to reach a new coastline.

Not that the local people appreciated the efforts of the Dutchmen; they hated the idea of anyone, and especially foreigners, moving into their territory and fooling around with it. Fenmen are not noted for instant fondness for strangers, and in the case of the incoming Dutch workers they took out their injured pride of place in lack of co-operation, surreptitious wrecking of half-completed works, beatings-up and the occasional murder. History, and man's lust to have and hold, was against them, however, notwithstanding the problems that began to emerge as the new windmills sucked up the water: shrinkage of the underlying peat as it dried, and consequent lowering of the land surface below the channels into which the water was supposed to fall. It took the invention of steam pumping engines, and a revised attitude on the part of the natives to the opening-up of their secret waterland, to solve that one.

Once Drove End was established at the margin of this new world, it prospered in its own quiet way – by the mid-nineteenth century there were four inns here, as well as a school, two chapels and a full complement of village craftsmen including a blacksmith, butcher, tailor, shoemakers and shopkeepers. The Drove Enders grew vegetables, fished, shot and trapped wildfowl and worked spasmodically for the farmers further inland. They were an independent crowd, not given to pulling their forelocks to authority, which gained them their abiding reputation as 'funny people'. They led a hard life, most of them suffering at one time or another from 'marsh ague' (malaria), against which they had the habit of taking large doses of opium – which was reckoned to be better for you than boozing, the other sovereign remedy. The marsh meadows were often flooded; cattle regularly had to swim to dry grazing-patches, and during one disastrous year the Drove Enders harvested their corn from boats. No wonder some of them turned to poaching to put a little extra on the family table.

Things are rather easier today at Gedney Drove End. Modern fertilizers and agricultural machinery have forced profits out of that rich brown sea-soil which the old-timers would have gasped at. The cabbages and sprouts crowd up to the garden hedges. Drove End children still have their own school, and the post office and shop keep going. There are thriving clubs for cricket, football, darts and wildfowling. But the memories of harder times remain in old photographs on the walls of the New Inn and in the conversation of its Drove End-born and -bred landlady, whose grandfather used to wear his wife's shoes, four sizes too big for him, back-to-front to fool any gamekeepers on his track during poaching expeditions.

From the New Inn (462293) you turn right along the lane running at right angles to the drove road, then left opposite the chapel (465292) up a track which leads directly to the sea-wall (472298). The view from the top is a practical lesson in the area's history. On the landward side are enormous chocolate-brown fields that stretch away inland in a ruler-flat landscape. Eco-*Angst* is well down on the local farmers' list of priorities: most hedges have been laid low and old drainage channels filled in, the floodwater being carried away nowadays by buried plastic piping. As you turn left and walk along the sea-wall path the plough furrows flick by in a wheeling fan shape with you as the hub. Chemical fertilizers may have helped this area to play greengrocer to the rest of the country, but it's natural silt that underpins the Fenland agriculture: silt spread through the centuries from within and without, by flooding rivers and encroaching sea. All these reclaimed fields lie well below high-tide level in the Wash, and one breach in the wall beneath your boots would ruin a dozen farmers' livelihoods. The enclosures can be dated by the farmhouses and barns that give some solidity to this great disc of land: Victorian building near the wall, Georgian further inland. The seaward creep of settlement is shown clearly by a glance at the map – it's 15 miles from Gedney Hill through Gedney Fen, Gedney Broadgate, Gedney, Gedney Dyke and Gedney Marsh to Gedney Drove End.

Out beyond the sea-wall it's a different world. When a new slice of land is reclaimed and a new wall built, saltings form on the seaward side: a tufted, blotched and seamed mat of tough, bleached grass and fat-leaved sea purslane whose long roots entangle to hold the whole salt-impregnated carpet of vegetation together. The outfalls of rivers and drainage ditches wind through the saltings and the sand and mud-flats beyond them to empty into the sea. It's a treacherous place, particularly here in the bowl of the Wash, where wildfowlers and fishermen learn to keep an eye on the tide which can so easily outflank, isolate and drown the unwary. But where people fear to tread, wildlife doesn't. Some of

Observation tower overlooking the mock battleground of the marshes beyond Gedney Drove End. Nature battles on, too, miraculously undefeated.

Britain's largest flocks of geese use the mud-flats as an aviadrome, there's always a pair of ducks flapping away over the saltings, and further out the common seals arrive in early summer to produce their pups. Short-eared owls and kestrels hang over the miniature jungle of the saltings looking for mice, voles and beetles.

Man may hold the death card all the same, if his recent efforts are anything to go by. Out in the mud to the east of Drove End you'll see what looks like the sliced-off base of an Egyptian pyramid: on the map it appears as a doughnut filled with water (512295). Built in the 1970s, it was a trial run for an idea which never came to fruition: a string of offshore reservoirs from which water could be piped ashore. The logical sequel soon followed: a plan for a gigantic barrage clear across the entire mouth of the Wash which would turn the enclosed square miles of natural wildlife reserve into one enormous reservoir. Applications to enclose saltings for agriculture have been meeting a chilly response in recent years in recognition of the ecological importance of the area (the last successful one was in 1977), so perhaps these schemes, too, will come to nothing. The geese, ducks, waders and hawks certainly appear quite unperturbed by a far more dramatic intrusion already taking place: the screaming jets that bomb and strafe the MoD ranges on the saltings to the west.

In a few hundred yards the path reaches the warning notices (470302), and from here on it's a thrill a minute when the red flags are flying. The RAF, USAF and NATO flyers keep strict office hours, from 9 to 5, Monday to Friday, and provided you don't wander on to the saltings from the sea-wall or pick up any stray projectiles, they don't mind you walking through their playground. (A courtesy call to the station commander at nearby RAF Holbeach – tel: 040 68 364 – to announce your presence, though not obligatory, would be appreciated.) It's an impressive sight and ear-splitting sound as the sleek, purposeful shapes of the F111s, Harriers or A10 tank-busters roar in on a downward path, drop their little blue practice bombs with a flash or rattle away with their cannon, then strain sharply upwards and around in a blood-draining curve of exhaust-trail. The saltings are laid out like a giant athletics stadium with white blobs in lines, fluorescent orange and green cones and large number-boards. The orange-painted hulks of redundant ships are moored at intervals out in the Wash for additional target practice. Tall black observation posts on the sea-wall survey the fun, which is directed by imperturbable men with electronic equipment and laser beams from a control tower. In the middle of all this sound and fury, the shelduck and pinkfoot geese carry on with their daily lives, never seeming even to flinch as the bombs and guns go off. When the show is over and the last Harrier has snarled away in the haze, nature's own harriers come quietly back, to hover over their victims in their own deadly fashion.

One word of warning – eight out of ten cannon shells fired from the planes ricochet from their target. So far the public has walked unscathed, but the element of risk remains during these weekday practices. On Saturdays and Sundays you can inspect the marshland battleground undisturbed, and hear only the larks and geese.

The ranges extend beyond the turning point of our walk, which continues around the curve of the sea-wall between saltings and reclaimed fields to cross an outfall (448323), three-quarters of a mile short of RAF Holbeach station. Here you turn down to meet the old sea-wall (447320) that marks the outer limit of eighteenth-century Holland. The path runs parallel with the new wall but half a mile inland, bending south above the Victorian creation of Dawsmere village before heading back to Drove End and tales of long ago in the bar of the New Inn.

42 Cromer to Sidestrand through Poppyland

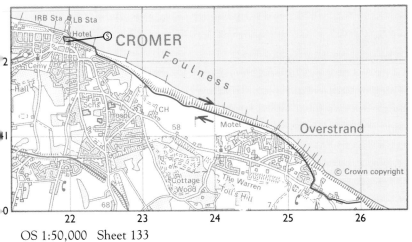

OS 1:50,000 Sheet 133
6 miles, there and back

On the grass of the cliff, at the edge of the steep,
God planted a garden – a garden of sleep!
'Neath the blue of the sky, in the green of the corn,
It is there that the regal red poppies are born!
Brief days of desire, and long dreams of delight,
They are mine when my Poppy-land cometh in sight.
In music of distance, with eyes that are wet,
It is there I remember, and there I forget!
O! heart of my heart! where the poppies are born,
I am waiting for thee, in the hush of the corn.
Sleep! Sleep!
From the Cliff to the Deep!
Sleep, my Poppy-land,
Sleep!

Not the most immortal of lines, maybe; but when Clement Scott penned them he had already opened the door through which the outside world would rush to destroy the solitude of his beloved Poppyland for ever. He had come to Cromer on the north Norfolk coast in August 1883 to write some articles for the *Daily Telegraph* on the summer season there, but neither he nor his editor could have foreseen the pulling power of those rather over-written, eulogistic pieces he knocked out during his first brief visit. By the time they had been collected into a book, *Poppyland Papers*, published in 1886 complete with Scott's little poem, everyone knew of the short stretch of cliffs east of Cromer which he had romantically christened 'Poppyland'.

This walk follows in the footsteps of Scott as he turned his back on the overcrowded seaside town that first afternoon and trudged up along the cliffs, looking for a more congenial place to stay. The Cromer that he found had emerged only six years before into the railway age from a long period of jealously guarded seclusion. A tightly knit group of well-to-do Quaker families (Barclays, Buxtons, Gurneys and Hoares) had discovered the impoverished fishing village at the end of the eighteenth century, and for the next 100 years they virtually ran Cromer as a private preserve. A trickle of respectable families arrived to rent or buy houses near the sea, disport themselves on the sand and spend their evenings blamelessly in strolling or card parties; but there was nothing in the least tripperish about Cromer until the East Norfolk Railway Company poked its nose in. With its cliffs, sandy beach, old flint-built houses and picturesque situation huddled above the sea, the place was just waiting for exploitation. The railway was the touch-paper, and Clement Scott and his articles supplied the match.

Cromer is dominated by the 159-foot tower of its church of St Peter and St Paul (220422), in the shadow of which stands the town's small and beautifully laid-out museum. It's worth spending an hour here to absorb some of the atmosphere of Cromer past and present before setting out on this walk. From the museum you turn right and right again to reach the seafront by the Red Lion Hotel. A narrow pathway and steps lead down to the cobbled slipway where the town's fishing boats are drawn up between expeditions – Cromer crabs are justly famous, and sold in all shapes and conditions around the town, from the freshly caught article in the fishermen's back yards to elaborate dishes in the hotels. From the beach there's a marvellous view of the piled houses of Cromer above the pier, the church tower climbing above their roofs, the cliff end commanded by the verdigris-ed copper cupolas of the red-brick and terracotta Hotel de Paris.

At the end of the line of beach chalets a zig-zag ramp climbs the face of the cliffs, to run eastward through thickets of yellow-headed alexanders and spiky sea buckthorn. The path passes the coastguard station, keeping close to the edge of the cliffs, and crosses a sandy hollow to climb up to the stumpy, octagonal tower of the lighthouse (230415). This is a viewpoint to delay you, looking back across the intervening swell of ground to the ever-dominant church-tower above the red roofs of Cromer running inland towards the distant rise of the Cromer Ridge. Clement Scott, fleeing the crowded pier and rude hoteliers back in 1883, stopped up here to look back in anger:

> In that red-roofed village, the centre of all that was fashionable and select, there was not a bed to be had for love or money; all home comforts, all convenience to which well-bred people were accustomed were deliberately sacrificed for the sake of a lodging amongst a little society that loved its band, its pier, its shingle and its sea.

What on earth would Scott have made of the Cromer Country Club which now fills the high ground by the lighthouse with nearly a hundred time-share holiday homes, all staring red brick and Alpine roofs; or the pre-fab chalets spilling down a tree-lined cleft just below, known to generations of Cromer children as Happy Valley? He would probably have fired off another verbal salvo and turned his back on the whole affair, to strike out east into Poppyland.

In those days the cornfields stretched out and up to a ridge on the cliff edge, thick with the poppies that so enraptured Clement Scott. He was enchanted by the courtesy of the locals ('a chat about the weather or the crops, a bow from the lads or a curtsey from the lasses') and fell head over heels in love with the quietness, rich colours and heady scents of a corner of the country very far removed from the London where he earned his bread as a drama critic:

> A blue sky without a cloud across it; a sea sparkling under a haze of heat; wild flowers in profusion around me, poppies predominantly everywhere, the hedgerows full of blackberry-blossom and fringed with meadow-sweet; the bees busy at their work, the air filled with insect life, the song-birds startled from the standing corn as I pursued my solitary way.

How could the Victorian gentry resist such seductive description? They couldn't – and responded by creating the Royal Cromer Golf Club right across Scott's clifftop ramble. The path runs between the devil of the flying golf balls and the deep blue sea itself, with fine views inland down

*The cliffs of Poppyland, fast
crumbling into the sea.*

over the greens and fairways towards the village of Overstrand among its trees. As you reach the seaward outskirts of the village, the warning notices begin to appear: 'Footpath ahead dangerous'. A glance over the edge of the cliffs shows how quickly they are slipping into the sea; they slope downwards and outwards from the rim in a gentle curve to the beach, the yellow scars of recent falls soon covered in a tangle of scrub. In some places the cliffs' edges are 20 or 30 yards inland from their feet. This section of the north Norfolk coastline is one of the most unstable in Britain, and local people are accustomed to waking up to find that familiar roads, paths, fields and even houses have gone over the edge during the night. The path that Clement Scott trod through the cornfields might have been several hundred yards further out than the present brink. For many years it was thought that pesticides had killed off the famous poppies for good; but when recent financial cutbacks saw the spraying machines replaced by men with scythes, the poppies re-emerged, their seeds having lain dormant but not dead for decades.

228

Overstrand was a tiny farming and fishing village when Scott first walked by; but his articles soon changed it beyond recognition. It became a millionaires' refuge as the great men and women of the time came to Poppyland and built their enormous residences on the clifftop. Some of these splendiferous buildings are still in private hands; others have been converted into rest homes (Overstrand Hall) or Christian holiday centres (Lord Battersea's 'The Pleasaunce'). There are glimpses of black-and-white half-timbering and red-brick and flint elaborations behind Overstrand's boundary walls as you continue along the cliff-path to a spot where the roadway has subsided dramatically for a stretch of 200 yards (252406). Beyond this slip, the path is eroded to extinction and the land is all private, but Coast Road takes you inland to turn left on the B1159 road into Overstrand's adjoining hamlet of Sidestrand. The old Mill House on your left (253403), a square red-brick building with a red tiled roof shaded by trees, became for Clement Scott the heart of his Poppyland, and for his fashionable friends an object of pilgrimage.

Alfred Jermy was Sidestrand's miller, and it was his 19-year-old daughter Louie who gave the London journalist his supper that night in 1883: ' "Could I eat eggs and bacon," was the modest request, as the miller's daughter uncovered a smoking dish, and pointed to the farmhouse bread and fresh butter.' No modern advertising agency could have thought up a simpler or more appealing image than that.

But Sidestrand's attractions for a jaded city-dweller's palate didn't stop short at an apple-cheeked country girl and her wholesome fare and lavender-scented sheets. There was also a Romantic Ruin in the shape of the hamlet's church-tower, perched on the very edge of the cliffs a few hundred yards to the east. To reach the site, continue from the Mill House along the B1159's pavement to turn left down Tower Lane (256401). Flanked by alexanders, and thorn bushes that arch overhead to make a green tunnel, the lane turns into a rough track and then a grassy path which ends abruptly on the cliff edge at a quiet spot full of the sounds of birdsong and waves (260401). Cliff falls have eaten inland nearly a quarter of a mile since Clement Scott first stood here at what was then a bend in the main coast road and saw, 300 yards to the north, the cylindrical flint tower standing on its own in an abandoned graveyard. St Michael's church had also stood here until two years before Scott's visit, the round tower a replacement for an earlier one that had fallen over the edge in 1841. By 1881 the body of the church had been removed from its precarious position and rebuilt next to Sidestrand Hall, and the tower was left to bear up as long as it could. The pathos of the abandoned tower and graveyard among the poppies struck straight to Scott's heart, and gave rise to the second verse of his *Poppyland Papers* poem:

> In my garden of sleep, where red poppies are spread,
> I wait for the living, alone with the dead!
> For a tower in ruins stands guard o'er the deep,
> At whose feet are green graves of dear women asleep!
> Did they love as I love, when they lived by the sea?
> Did they wait as I wait, for the days that may be?
> Was it hope or fulfilling that entered each breast,
> Ere death gave release, and the poppies gave rest?
> O! life of my life! on the cliffs by the sea,
> By the graves in the grass, I am waiting for thee!
> > Sleep! Sleep!
> > > In the Dews by the Deep!
> > > > Sleep, my Poppy-land,
> > > > > Sleep!

Was it Louie Jermy for whom Scott waited in his Garden of Sleep? It would be nice to think so, but all the evidence points to a friendly but fairly formal relationship between the two.

In any case, the Jermys soon had other fish to fry. The Mill House, once publicized by Scott in his articles, became a touchstone of rural tranquillity for fashionable and famous Londoners. Actors, politicians, poets and socialites, among them Beerbohm Tree, Henry Irving, Ellen Terry, Wilson Barrett and Algernon Charles Swinburne, came flocking to Sidestrand to flirt with Louie Jermy, scandalize the locals with their rowdy behaviour and apostrophize the moon by the tower in the Garden of Sleep. Visitors to Overstrand's 'millionaires' row' considered their stay in Poppyland incomplete without at least a sight of the miller's daughter, her charming house and the nearby tower.

Scott himself, at first amused by the interest he had stirred up, quickly sickened of the commercialization of Poppyland. Hard on the heels of his articles came poppies on railway posters, poppies on cups and saucers, Poppyland Bouquet perfume, Poppyland postcards, books and pictures. He didn't care, either, for the patronizing attitude of many of the visitors towards the Jermys and other local people. Within a few years Scott was setting his face against what had for him become 'Bungalowland' as vehemently as he had set it against Cromer on the first day of that first ecstatic visit in 1883.

It's hard to estimate the effect of all this publicity on Louie Jermy. Many people thought her one of the most remarkable women they had met, full of curiosity and personality. She certainly fell in love with the romantic image of herself, and made many trips to London to go to the theatre and meet more famous folk, sometimes with Clement Scott as chaperon. She was even, briefly, in service with his family there. But it was in Poppyland itself that she could truly bloom as a celebrity, and she came back to reign at the Mill House. Scott died in 1904; the Garden of Sleep, tower and all, went over the cliff in 1916; but Louie lived on, unmarried, until 1934. In the last years of her life she occupied a cottage in Tower Lane (now also slipped away), selling flowers around the local houses and reliving her great days with anyone who would listen. Her grave is in Sidestrand's churchyard just up the hill.

If you feel like a rest before descending to the beach at Overstrand (at low tide) or strolling back along the clifftop path to Cromer, there's a conveniently sited bench beside the B1159 road halfway between Tower Lane and the Mill House. Dilapidated and overgrown with brambles as it is, you can still decipher the inscription carved into the back-rest:

In memory of Louie Jermy of Poppyland.   1934.

43   Walberswick to Dunwich

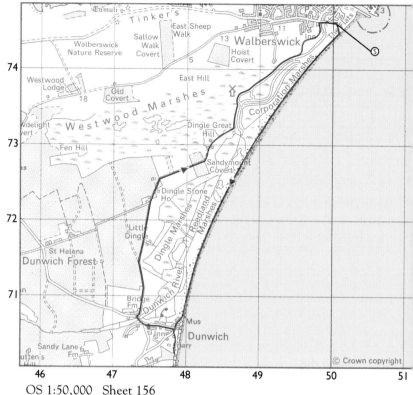

OS 1:50,000   Sheet 156
7½ miles, the round trip

This walk by shingle bank and salt-marsh is punctuated by two towns, once rivals in trade, which both suffered a drastic sea change in medieval times: in the case of Walberswick, a decline from which it recovered, after a fashion; for Dunwich, a gradual but complete catastrophe.

It was the Victorian taste for pleasantly sited seaside towns capable of becoming genteel that rescued Walberswick from three long centuries of slump. When the doctors, the schoolteachers and the parsons arrived with their families in this low-lying landscape of marsh, small woods and huge, light skies, they found a little fishing village, flint-built and hugging the muddy bank of the River Blyth. 'Walserwig', the locals called it; wet salt-marsh surrounded it, kept from inundation by the sea by means of a brick wind-pump and a bank of shingle. Wilson Steer captured that little huddle of houses and the wide, level land under the great skies in his oil paintings and water-colours; and other artists arrived to find lodgings in fishermen's cottages or build themselves wooden shacks on the beach or by the river.

In the fifteenth century Walberswick had been a well-to-do little town, rich enough from fishing to build itself a superb church, dedicated to St Andrew, with an 85-foot tower and fine local craftsmanship in its interior. Boat-building in the yards on the river contributed to the town's prosperity, and pirates and smugglers based there added their contributions. Then the old East Coast story repeated itself: the port silted up and the fishing trade declined – largely due, it was said, to the Reformation and its relaxing of religious laws which meant that poor people no longer looked to fish for their staple diet. St Andrew's began to fall to pieces, and there was no more money to repair it. Cromwell's 'fanatical visitors' paid a visit in 1644, smashed 40 windows and went away, a step nearer Heaven.

In 1695 most of the remaining structure was pulled down, but the tower was left as a landmark for sailors and a slice of the south aisle for the few hundred worshippers who remained in the town. A disastrous fire in 1749 reduced the number of their houses by a third. Poverty hit Walberswick, and poor it remained until the seaside resort boom of the nineteenth century gave it a new lease of life. The rickety little Southwold Railway reached it by way of a swing bridge across the mouth of the Blyth in 1879, and there was a chain ferry to Southwold which 'had a nasty habit of sinking on occasions'. Walberswick smartened itself up and put out a few brick tentacles; but not too fast, and not too far. Nowadays it is Southwold across the river that gets most of the tourists; Walberswick stays content with its artists, its long-time faithful visitors, bird-watchers and walkers.

From the grassy car park by the sea-bank (500746) you turn your back on Southwold's flint church-tower and white finger of lighthouse and head south along the top of the shingle bank. Walking through shingle is usually the kiss of death to enjoyment, but this crunchy surface is surprisingly firm under foot. You can also go by rough paths under the bank along the edge of the marsh that stretches all the way to Dunwich, but it's a dirty and slippery alternative. A line of blistered, peeling old wooden beach-huts, a sprinkling of caravans, beyond them a scatter of handsome houses on a low rise of ground . . . and Walberswick is behind you. In front, the curve of shingle sweeps round the bay towards the dark-green stretch of woods running inland from Dunwich, and on beyond that to the incongruous square grey block of Sizewell nuclear power station looking grimly out to sea. To your left, the level sea rolls out to the horizon; below on the right, the salt-marsh runs in dun browns and drab greens back to the gentle ridge swell behind it, cut with brackish watercourses, silent, windswept and apparently lifeless. The long narrow bar of shingle that separates these two worlds is a rich ground for bushes of leathery sea-kale and the spindly tendrils of yellow horned poppy whose four large, delicate petals fall away at a slight touch.

As you walk the three miles down the shore to Dunwich, the few upstanding features of the salt marsh (the ruins of the old wind-pump, a couple of slightly humped, gorse- and broom-smothered 'islands' and the cattle that are turned loose to graze the marsh) seem magnified by the complete flatness of their surroundings. Dunwich itself appears from the shingle bank as a few houses under a low, wooded cliff, eaten by the sea into a bite-shaped curve. The state of this cliff is the key to the riddle of the whereabouts of the ancient capital of East Anglia and seat of the first bishop of that realm. It lies to your left under the cold waves, the bells of its nine great churches reputedly still heard tolling on stormy nights and the ghosts of its citizens walking the cliffs.

The Romans called it 'Sitomagus', the Anglo-Saxons 'town with the deep-water harbour' – strange irony nowadays! St Felix founded a church here, the first of many to be taken by the sea, and it became the base for his Christianization of the eastern part of England. Danish raids in the ninth century halted its progress, but by the time of the Norman invasion Dunwich was on its feet again. A great forest, Eastwood, stretched for several miles east of the town where the sea now lies, and a number of privileged gentlemen were given the Conqueror's permission to hunt and hawk there. Even then, King William was receiving disturbing reports of how the sea was ravaging the eastern edges of the forest, but for a few centuries more Dunwich continued to prosper. By the twelfth century its population was more than 4000; it had a large fishing and trading fleet, dealing in stone, tin, steel, timber and salt as well as luxuries like wine, spices and silk. The town seal reflected the basis of Dunwich's wealth: a merchant ship (though equipped for defence with fighting castles fore and aft), riding under bare poles with a king amidships steering it to prosperity. At the height of its glory the town boasted nine splendid churches, a Knights Templars' station, a large leper hospital, two monasteries (one Franciscan and one Dominican), a bustling market place, extensive lands and its own mint.

But the town of the deep-water harbour was founded on shifting tides. A sixteenth-century chronicler of 'antient' Dunwich recalled 'a City surrounded with a Stone-wall and brazen Gates', but even by his time the waves had advanced to batter down the seaward side of that wall. They brought the sand, mud and shingle with them to silt up the harbour that stood a few hundred yards north of the town where the Dunwich River met the Blyth, which then flowed through the marshes between Walberswick and Dunwich. The sea came relentlessly on, sucking away the churches and houses one by one, tearing gaps in their ranks during storms and, by 1677, licking at the eastern edge of the market place itself.

The Black Friars of the Dominican monastery south of the town had long since lost their home and church to the sea, and the Franciscan Grey Friars had been dispossessed of theirs at the Reformation. Now the market place slid into the waves, the last churches fell (all but one), and the good folk of Dunwich went away, too. There were only 100 or so of them to watch De Ruyter's fleet of Dutch adventurers trying conclusions with the English at the Battle of Sole Bay in 1672, and 200 years later the tower and gaping shell of All Saints' church on the cliff edge were all that remained of those nine proud medieval churches. The tower stood, a landmark for passing ships, until 1919 when it, too, took the plunge. The sea, which had given to old-time Dunwich in full measure, had claimed virtually all, leaving only a handful of houses, a few fragments of the Grey Friars' building, a tumbledown remnant of the leper hospital well inland, and a solitary gravestone on the edge of the cliff to mark the site of All Saints.

You can reach this lonely resting place by way of the beach car park with its tearoom (best fish and chips for miles around) and the fresh fish shack. Walk up the road beyond the car park and past the Ship Inn. Where the road bends to the right, take a narrow track up to the left which runs among trees along the clifftop. After about a quarter of a mile, and before the flint wall on your right comes to an end, turn left through the trees to the edge of the cliff (479703). Take care: it's an unguarded drop to the shingle. The plain, grey stone tablet stands with its back to the sea, inscribed:

Sacred
to the memory of
JOHN BRINKLEY
EASEY
who died September 2nd
1826
AGED 23 YEARS

Soon, as the waves continue to bite away at the land, John Easey's bones will lie under the sea with those of his fellow townsmen.

Retrace your steps to the road and turn left for a few hundred yards. The road bends to the left, and there in the flint wall are two arched gateways (477704), the smaller one decorated above with carefully knapped flints in columns, topped with leaf-head shapes. Through them you can see an angle of flint and brick wall, pierced with round-headed windows and covered in ivy and elder – the last standing remains of the Franciscans' power and pride.

The Ship Inn (478706), outside which lies a large, salt-rusted anchor, is a friendly pub which serves food and Adnam's celebrated ale, brewed nearby at Southwold. A few yards down the street is the small but beautifully kept museum (for opening times, see the end of this chapter) which contains a chronological account of the rise and fall of Dunwich and a splendid relief model of the medieval city. Upstairs is a display of the area's natural history and a collection of pictures, including a sequence of 22 that show the progressive disappearance over the cliff of All Saints' church.

Continue down the road from the museum to reach the church of St James (475706), built in 1830 and rich in wood-carvings of flowers and fruit in its roof. In the churchyard stands a jagged needle of flint – a buttress from All Saints' that somehow remained standing on the cliff edge when its parent body fell in 1919, after which it was painstakingly dismantled and moved to this site. Just to the east is all that remains of

On the Brink and taking it Easey . . . a snooze in the sunshine in the company of the last occupant of All Saints' churchyard, Dunwich.

the great leper hospital of medieval Dunwich: a truncated oval of yellow limestone and flint with a row of small Norman arches in its east wall. The large, low, grey vault of the Barne family fills the interior; they owned most of the land north of Dunwich, built many of the houses in and around the village and paid handsomely for the new church and its later additions.

At the junction of roads above the church, bear right to cross the Dunwich River (shrunken from its former splendour to a stagnant, reedy ditch) and turn right (473707) to follow the bridle-path around the red-brick barns of Bridge Farm. The path runs along the eastern edge of Dunwich Forest, a Forestry Commission conifer battalion screened by oak trees. This sandy, boggy heath has its character well defined by place-names on the OS map: Fen Hill, Sandy Mount, Sandy Lane, Broom Hill. You pass above Little Dingle and then Dingle Stone House, Barne Estate buildings with ornate pinnacles on their roofs, whose curly tiles were made at Dunwich.

The path continues between bracken banks and twisted old thorn trees between which you can glimpse the cows grazing on the marsh. At

Dingle Great Hill (483730) you come to a curious, isolated community of a few houses which stand, well separated, among the trees, looking out over the salty wastes and thick pink clumps of rosebay willowherb. Past these, the path runs into the marsh where you push your way between head-high reeds along a firm strip between the muddy blocks of sea couch grass and steel-grey channels of water. The track skirts the lower of the two flat hillocks which were constructed, some stories say, to give the Anglo-Saxon settlers here a dry and raised place to gather for discussion and decision-making. Beyond this 'hill' the path meets a watercourse (487732), where you turn left to reach the brick cone of the pumping tower (486737). During the First World War this pump was closed down to allow the meadows that lay here to flood as an anti-invasion precaution – and they have remained marshland ever since. A few charred wooden struts poke out of the top of the tower, remains of a fire in 1960 which destroyed the interior works.

Turn right over a narrow plank footbridge by the tower to thread your way over the marsh towards the caravans and shacks and the car park on the southern outskirts of Walberswick. Herons and bird-watchers tiptoe around the glinting creeks in their ritual of flight and pursuit. This area is a National Nature Reserve, popular with ornithologists and amateur bird-spotters who bring their binoculars for the terns, black-headed gulls, oystercatchers and redshanks that live here. Montagu's harriers and avocet are visitors, and in winter hen harriers, merlins and waxwings may be seen. Marsh harriers breed here, as does the bittern, shy boomer among the reeds. Guarded from the tides by the shingle bank, and safe from disturbance among the tangled blocks of marsh and intricate watercourses, these and other species thrive in this bleak environment – not so lifeless after all.

Dunwich Museum: Opening times (2.00 P.M.–4.30 P.M.)
August – every day
May, June, July, September – Tuesday, Thursday, Saturday, Sunday, public holidays
March, April, October – Saturday, Sunday, public holidays
January, February, November, December – by appointment
Curator – Tel. Westleton (072 873) 358

44 Mersea Island

OS 1:50,000   Sheet 168
12 miles, the round trip

Mersea Island, the most easterly of all the inhabited islands of Britain, is only 4½ miles long and 2 miles wide; but the ins and outs taken by the sea-wall in skirting the creeks and marshes that surround it make this a long, though absorbing, walk. There is a very special atmosphere to Mersea, composed of the flatness of its landscape (around 50 feet above sea level at its highest point), the mud and marsh that completely encircle it, the single narrow causeway that is its only link with the mainland, its history of seafaring and smuggling, the constant wind and the salty smell of the sea that reach every corner of the island. True sons of Mersea have little to say to outsiders, and preserve that air of remoteness and indifference to the outside world that characterizes their territory. Separated from the mainland by the glistening mud-banks of the Pyefleet and Strood Channels, Mersea Island turns its back on outside affairs and looks out over its encircling fringe of mud and marsh to the open sea.

Down at the south-western tip of the oval-shaped island is West Mersea, the starting place for this walk around the perimeter of Mersea, and the only substantial settlement here. The Romans, Saxons and Danes all came, saw, conquered and passed on, though the Saxons left a legacy in Mersea's name: 'Meres-ig' or 'Island of the mere'. They panned salt, dredged up oysters and worked the salt-laden fertile ground, built houses and subjected the dour inhabitants to their various religions and disciplines. St Peter's Well, the only constant source of fresh water on the island right up until the 1920s, flows from the foot of the low cliff at West Mersea, which was a good reason for the settlement to fix itself at this end of the island. It stayed small, fishing and smuggling, until the seaside boom of the late nineteenth century. Shops and houses began to sprout along the shore, multiplying as the new-fangled motor car made it a pleasant possibility to live by the sea here and commute to work in Colchester. There were big plans for hotels, piers, promenades and even a railway – but the First World War put paid to them. Nowadays West Mersea relies on yachtsmen great and small for its prosperity, and has a fine rash of chalets, beach huts and caravans to accommodate them.

Looking seaward from the Dab-chicks Sailing Club at the end of Coast Road (001129), the view bristles with masts. The sailing dinghies and yachts lie drawn up in droves on the foreshore, or ride at anchor in the narrow gut of murky water between Mersea and Cob-marsh Island. The air is full of the musical chinking of halyards tapping against metal masts in the ever-blowing breeze. You walk south down the road, through a specialized world for the sailor: sailing clubhouse, chandleries, sail shops, boat builders' yards. Sailing men and women stand chatting in twos and threes, leaning comfortably across the gunwales of their brightly painted craft, or bend over greasy chunks of machinery, ropes and paint-pots. Smocks, spattered with oil and paint, are

great gear here, as are nautical blue caps, the filthier the better. Coast Road curves from south to east past the brown sails of restored sailing barges and the retired cruisers wedged into the creeks, festooned with TV aerials and power lines, which make cheaply run, unrateable homes – though the occupants must spend all that saved money on paint, judging by the number of owners hanging over the sides, brush in hand. Oysters are still business here, though the trade is declining as pollution, disease and cold winters make inroads into the stocks; there are roadside shacks where you can buy a handful of the glutinous shellfish fresh from the water, and a tiny market where the oysters are weighed out on old-fashioned balances from concrete tanks in long, netted wooden trays. It's a busy and contented scene, even to a non-sailor.

In under a mile the road bends inland (008124), and a concrete footpath sign points down to a wide, firm path along the foreshore which

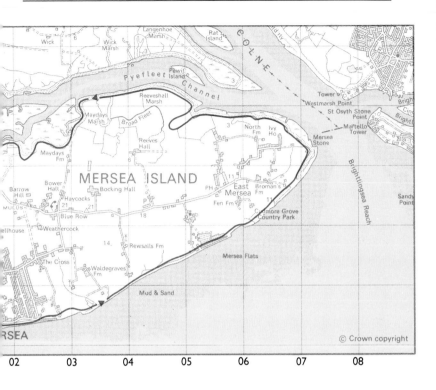

runs across the marsh through sheets of purple sea lavender. It emerges on to pebbly sand, hard enough to walk on, and continues along the shore past rotting stakes, half on the beach and half sticking up out of the water, which mark the sites of long-vanished jetties. Some handsome Edwardian villas look out from their cedars, pines and cypresses across the water to the northern shore of the Bradwell Marshes a couple of miles away. A long double row of beach huts and a caravan site mark the eastern end of West Mersea; dark green is the preferred colour for the huts, which are in fact, like the caravans, far more homely, spacious and carefully furnished than many more orthodox dwellings. Deep armchairs, well-filled bookshelves, double beds and expensive cookers soften the days and nights of the beach-dwellers – their fishing rods poke out from the sea-wall which guards this less sheltered part of the island, and the brightly striped sails of their windsurfing craft slide up and down

241

between the two shorelines. Many Essex families spend all their summer leisure-time here, water-sporting and lazing on the narrow strip of sand that favours the south side of the island.

The sloping sea-wall, reinforced after the disastrous sea-surge and floods of 1953 that devastated huge areas of this coastline, runs on below trees in the field-hedges whose foliage has been forced by the sea-breeze to grow in clotted lumps angled away from the wind. The well-marked path passes a Youth Camp (040132) in a field above the shore which in summer is full of tiny green ridge-tents and large white marquees. Behind the camp, the cornfields rise in a gentle yellow slope towards the red roofs of Rewsalls Farm, with the tower of St Edmund's church at East Mersea peeping over the treetops ahead. Turnstones skim away over the waves on their crescent-shaped wings, and oystercatchers stalk along the tide-line. The seaward view swings eastward from an empty horizon to the houses of Brightlingsea across the estuary of the River Colne, up which large cargo ships move towards the port of Wivenhoe further north.

East Mersea was home for one eminent Victorian parson and writer, the Reverend Sabine Baring-Gould, who was Rector here from 1870 to 1881. A West Countryman in exile and writer of poetry, church history, hymns (including 'Onward, Christian Soldiers') and novels, he hated his time among the uncommunicative, suspicious farmers and peasants in this flat, dull landscape, which in cold, rainy winter weather can present a very different face from the smiling one of summer. The village he lived in had never expanded like its neighbouring West Mersea, due to its isolated position away from the causeway and the freshwater spring. Between 1801 and 1971, West Mersea's population grew from 660 to 4148; East Mersea during the same period added only 29 inhabitants to its roll: from 246 to 275. It still remains a tiny, straggling collection of individual houses – though there is a pub, the Dog and Pheasant.

Beyond East Mersea is a low cliff of orange sand, from which oak trees have toppled to line the shingly beach below with their carcasses. At low tide the black, slimy mud stretches out for a good mile to the edge of the sea, picked over by shelduck, brent geese and plovers. The path climbs a concrete slope and runs on the sea-wall into the Colne Estuary Nature Reserve, whose other inhabitants include curlew and redshank – also sanderling, those plump, speckled little winter visitors which dash about on short legs following the waves as they ebb from the shore. The Mersea

*Spring breeze flutters the flags of a barge
in much-visited retirement at West Mersea.*

Stone (072153), a spit of gravelly scrub once used by the Romans as a harbour, can be reached from the wall, and there is a good view across the estuary to Brightlingsea from its tip.

Now the path moves into the essential Mersea landscape: salt-marsh, mud, water and sky. Sheep graze on the low-lying fields inland, whose long acres are relieved by few roofs or trees. Over the water, flat islands and peninsulas of marsh stand a few feet out of the waves, archaic dredging engines and the bright orange blobs of moored dinghies breaking up their long parallel lines. The plants of the marsh and sea-wall are stout, succulent, water-retaining things: prickly hawkweed oxtongue, covered in painful-looking white blisters; fat-leaved sea purslane, sea lavender and pink clumps of thrift. The sea-wall curves around the marshes – Reeveshall Marsh, Maydays Marsh – in a general silence full of particular sounds that impinge on the ear the further you walk: screech and piping of birds, whistle of wind across the saltings, slap of water against the knobs and islets of mud and occasional rattle of small-arms fire from Fingringhoe Ranges across the channel.

Soon you pass the tall, wooden-slatted buildings of an oyster and lobster farm. Oysters are delicate creatures and won't breed if it's too cold. The old-time oyster fishers, wise in the ways of their prey, dug oyster pits or beds to provide a source when natural supplies failed; these craters are dotted all over Mersea Island's muddy skirt. The Romans loved oysters and left enormous piles of shells to prove it; so did Colchester cloth-manufacturers in the Middle Ages, whose greed for oysters turned them from a cheap peasant food into a luxury. By the mid-nineteenth century there were 300 oyster smacks working out of Mersea – but decimation of the shellfish through pollution and hard winters, and a decline in demand, has cut their number to almost nothing. The local newspapers regularly carry interviews with oystermen predicting the end of the trade; meanwhile mass-producing farms like this one keep the oyster's hat in the ring.

The sea-wall path winds on, turning inland and then outward again, until ahead a long, low barrier blocks off the channel. This is The Strood (pronounced 'Strode'), a causeway first built by the Romans and maintained ever since as Mersea Island's one link with the mainland (013151). Until it was strengthened and its height raised in the mid-eighteenth century, The Strood was only passable for eight hours a day during low tides; water covered it the rest of the time, cutting off the island completely and provoking either the curses or benedictions of excisemen and smugglers, depending on which side they were on at the time! Even in its modern state it is not invulnerable – the 1953 surge covered it to a depth of seven feet.

The sea-wall path meets the East Mersea road below The Strood, where you turn left, then right down the West Mersea road for a few hundred yards, before bearing right on to the sea-wall again (015144) for the final stretch into West Mersea. The long island across the channel is the Ray, shaped like a curving dagger-blade or bird's bill – appropriately, as it is now a nature reserve. A farmhouse stood on the Ray in the nineteenth century, and here lived the beautiful, wild and strong-minded heroine of Sabine Baring-Gould's novel *Mehalah*. Those 11 years of observing rather bitterly the primitive, inward-looking, often savage natures of his parishioners bore fruit in this now neglected story of the resolute Mehalah (known as 'Glory'), her weak-willed and pliable mother and their implacable, bloody-tempered landlord, Elijah Rebow. Murder, religious fanaticism, doom, gloom, madness, obstinacy and sexual passion writhe together in a Technicolor plot which grinds merci-lessly to a thunderous conclusion – strong meat for strong stomachs. Over all and influencing all broods the dour, isolated Mersea landscape where boats pass stealthily from creek to creek, madmen run babbling to their deaths in the dark waters, bullets whistle out of the night and Elijah Rebow stands over the mother and daughter repeating his dirge: 'I have bought the Ray for eight hundred pounds. All here is mine, the Ray, the marshes, and the saltings, the creeks, the fleets, the farm. You are mine, and Glory is mine!'

45   Secret Sheppey: Shell Ness and Harty Marshes

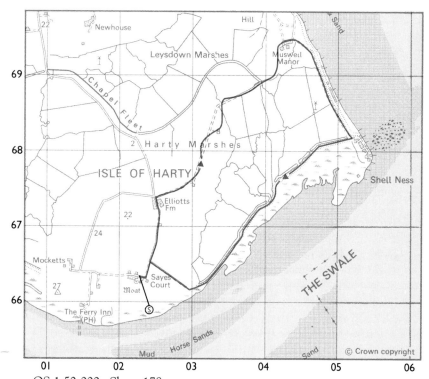

OS 1:50,000   Sheet 178
6 miles, the round trip

CONDITIONS:

Sited in superb bird-watching territory, this walk is probably best done in winter when the great flocks of ducks, geese and waders are, around – and so are bitterly cold winds blowing across Sheppey from the North Sea. Once committed to the six-mile circuit, there are no short cuts over the marsh. Between November and April, therefore, this is really a walk for well-wrapped adults, though in summer the sea-wall path between Shell Ness and Sayes Court makes a good stamping ground for young members of the family.

'Mostly flat and drab and without much to recommend it' is the rather dismissive summing-up of the Isle of Sheppey by the *Visitor's Guide to*

Kent. Perhaps the writer had forgotten his scarf and gloves. Mostly flat it may be – though there are tremendous views from the ridge where the abbey settlement of Minster perches – but there are plenty of delights for the walker in this large and largely unvisited slab of island lying off the northern coast of Kent in the throat of the Thames.

Leaving the A250, Sheppey's main arterial east–west road, you drop downhill on to a great apron of flat green marshland, cut across with brackish watercourses, which stretches some four miles southwards to the muddy shore of the Swale Channel separating Sheppey from the mainland. Until Kingsferry Bridge was opened in 1860, the only way to get on to the island was by ferry, an uncomfortable journey when those sharp North Sea winds piled up the narrow waters of the Swale into lumpy waves. In its isolation Sheppey made an excellent stronghold for anyone up to no good, from eighteenth-century smugglers back to the ninth-century Danes who based themselves here for their raids into south-east England. Even today, there are many islanders who don't cross Kingsferry Bridge from one year's end to the next.

This feeling of isolation becomes more strongly marked the further south you go. Before agricultural trends switched from cattle and sheep grazing to arable farming, the southern portion of Sheppey was divided by winding fleets of water into two separate islands: Elmley Island to the west, and the Isle of Harty (round whose shoreline this walk runs) to the east. Here the farmhouses, well separated from each other, stand squarely against the wind looking over the saltings and the grey waters of the Swale to the neat towns spread out along the Kent coast: Whitstable, Herne Bay and Reculver. A few wind-flattened trees give shelter to the farms, but only the thickest of thorn hedges really thrive in the brisk, salty air. This is prime bird-watching territory, with vast squadrons of ducks, geese and waders swirling like smoke against enormous cloud-scapes.

The church of St Thomas beside Sayes Court Farm (023662) is Kent's remotest church, a title whose accuracy you appreciate as you stand in its quiet graveyard with glimpses of the Swale's waters sweeping by below. Sir John Betjeman, connoisseur of curious churches in curious places, loved St Thomas's with its dark interior where the noise of the wind dies to a faint whisper. It must be one of the county's oldest churches, too, dating back almost to the Conquest. A tiny bell-cote stands on the roof, braced inside the building by a criss-cross frame of crooked and seamed timbers 500 years old. The interior is simple: a curving roof to the short nave, a heavy north aisle, and a Lady Chapel on the south side brightened by clear light through the window from which you can look up and down the Swale. In this chapel is St Thomas's most prized treasure, a solid oak chest of the early fifteenth century with a splendid jousting scene carved on the front. An unfortunate knight, his own lance splintered in his hand, is rocking back in the saddle as his opponent's lance crashes into his shield, watched mournfully by his squire holding his redundant sword. The chest was probably built by a Flemish or German craftsman, but its appearance in the remote little church at the tip of Sheppey is a mystery. According to the church notes, some lucky beachcomber found it floating down the Swale.

From St Thomas's the saltings and their shifting populations of wildfowl are a few minutes' stroll away; but by starting your walk in the opposite direction – through the farmyards and fields of the Isle of Harty – you can catch the character of the area before arriving at its outer limits. From the yellow-brick block of Sayes Court Farm, follow the long, rutted lane north-east to Elliotts Farm (025674), where you bear right on to a track weaving past Brewers Hill Farm (030675) across the reclaimed fields of Harty Marshes. Between them, the sea-wall and drainage channels have kept this rich grazing land captive from the sea for centuries, but recently there have been changes. More and more is going under the plough as the thick, fertile, yellow-grey earth is won from these wetlands. The fields each side of the path are scored by deep ploughing, which throws up ridges like medieval strip farming. Ahead and to the left, the ground gently slopes up to the ridge where Eastchurch village stands, while away to the right the dun-brown skirt of the saltings leads out to glistening slabs of mud-flats where oystercatchers, redshanks, knot and curlew compete for the buried worms and shellfish.

In front of you, the isolated hulk of Muswell Manor (042695) comes steadily nearer over the salt meadows and their wriggling fleets and ditches. Romantically isolated, it's a prosaic shock seen close-to, its bare grounds full of mobile homes and little jerry-built holiday hutches. There is a stiff dash of romance in its history, however; for a heady year in 1910, the house was the headquarters of the infant Royal Flying Club. The previous year Lord Brabazon had made Britain's first officially acknowledged powered flight from a nearby field, and for a short time Sheppey was the centre of operations for those dashing young men (the Hon. C. S. Rolls and Winston Churchill among them) who staggered around above these marshes in their canvas-and-piano-wire contraptions.

The track turns right above Muswell Manor to reach the sea-wall, where the wind does its best to push you back down to marsh level. Now an enormous seaward view is suddenly revealed, stretching out across the Thames Estuary to the coastal towns of Kent along their low bank of hills and away north to a sea horizon. A grassy path on the top of the sea-wall runs south past a semi-derelict settlement of holiday huts (049688) with shuttered windows, festooned with chicken wire and overgrown shrubs, their gardens full of tatty bushes and decrepit rowing boats. Beyond this sad ghost village, the path passes above wooden groynes sloping down into the muddy estuary waves, to reach the sheltered little world of Shellness Hamlet (053681).

Until the early years of this century there were just a couple of coastguard cottages here on the hooked spit of shells and pebbles at the eastern tip of Sheppey. Then the isolation of their position began to attract city dwellers in search of peace and quiet. Their conversion to holiday cottages was the first stage in a gradual growth of small houses along a single narrow street, rented out to friends of the original incomer. Nowadays the hamlet is owned co-operatively by its dwellers, but it remains a private world apart. These lovingly maintained, neat little houses – Cockle Cottage, The Fairy House, The Haven – are passed down the family generations, and snapped up within hours when they very occasionally come up for sale. Their bow-windows, diamond panes and glazed pottery name-plates breathe pride of ownership. There's a miniature tennis court and open-air swimming pool, but this is a place for those who take their pleasure in bird-watching, sailing, walking and painting. On clear nights the lucky cottagers of Shellness look out on a superb ten-mile scatter of lights from the Kentish towns across the water.

Our path leaves the gate of the hamlet – strictly private property – to go over a stile into the 'internationally important marshlands' of the Swale Nature Reserve. Their importance stems from their remoteness, which until recently has preserved them from destructive development. On the seaward side of the sea-wall as you walk south-west into the mouth of the Swale are the salt-marshes, and beyond them at low tide

The North Kentish hills lie low across the waters of the Swale from the shell-carpeted shore of Shell Ness at the eastern tip of the Isle of Sheppey.

the wide, gleaming mud-flats. Only the presence of the sea-wall prevents the salt-marshes and muds continuing the creep inland that nature intended for them. The muds are literally crammed with invertebrates (over 350 species) which keep the long-legged wading birds riveted beak to mud, and on them flourishes the zostera (eel-grass) which attracts and holds a winter population of up to 600 brent geese. Waders such as turnstones, oystercatchers and plovers also enjoy stalking along the margin of Shell Ness spit, looking for recent full additions to the millions of empty cockle, oyster and mussel shells dumped here by the tide. On catching sight of a violently hued anorak, whole aerial towers of birds build above the marshes with great clamour, circle a couple of times and then settle again for the long lenses of bird-photography enthusiasts who lie flat out below the sea-wall.

Water-borne pollution is the main threat to the salt-marshes and mud-flats, but over the sea-wall on the landward meadows the danger to the area's wildlife comes from the yellow dredging and mounding machines, already champing away at the grazing fields to get at the rich soil underneath. This grassland is a favourite feeding-ground of shelduck, and most species of geese and ducks fly over the sea-wall to roost in this sheltered environment during winter storms. The grazing marsh and its intersecting ditches and channels of semi-salt water support many types of plants and insects which feed and shelter mice and small birds, such as yellow wagtail and reed bunting, which in their turn attract black-backed gulls and short-eared owls, and hunting hawks, including hen harriers and kestrels. The whole intricately balanced mechanism of natural life in these remote marshes would be fatally upset if much more of them went under the plough. The Reserve managers and their hard-working warden struggle day by day to maintain the balance, refilling drained ditches and flashes by building sluices, negotiating with local farmers, signposting ramblers along the sea-wall path, producing leaflets and signboards explaining the importance of the marshes – and trying not to look over their shoulders at similar areas now vanishing beneath crops or concrete in other parts of the country.

As you look down from the sea-wall on to the landward grazing meadows, you'll notice rounded humps lying in twos and threes on the marsh. Until recently they were thought to be burial barrows of the Danish invaders, but research has unmasked a more commonplace origin as spoil heaps from medieval salt workings. The salt-impregnated mud of the marsh was boiled in cauldrons, the resultant crust of salt skimmed off and the waste mud tipped aside to form these now grassed-over hummocks.

The pointed bell-cote of St Thomas's church is a landmark ahead as you round the last of the bends in the sea-wall and turn your back on the open water to climb a rough track to Sayes Court Farm. A mile down the road at the southernmost point of Sheppey is the Ferry House Inn (015660), a hospitable house dating back 500 years in part, where you can drink good locally brewed beer and eat either in the bar or in the restaurant. The smoke-oranged, low-ceilinged bar gets very crowded in summer, but there's a terrace outside overlooking the site of the ferry crossing, where travellers once risked their breakfasts, if not their lives, to sample the secrets of Sheppey.

Index

Index

Numerals in *italics* refer to captions

Abbotsbury, Dorset 33–4, 39
    Abbey of St Peter's: remains 34, 35, *37*
    St Catherine's chapel 35, *37*
    St Nicholas's church 34, 35
    strip lynchets 35, 36, *37*
    Swannery 36, 39
    Tithe Barn 35
Aberdaron, Gwynedd 151
Aberystwyth 139–40, *142*
Ames, John 43
Anglesey 150, 154, 155, 157
Arthur's Quoit, Dyfed 137
Austen, Jane 45
    Persuasion 43
Axe, River, Devon 44

Bangor, Gwynedd 154, 158
Bardsey Island, Gwynedd 81, 140, 150–1, *152*,
    152
Bardsey Sound, Gwynedd 150
Baring-Gould, Rev. Sabine 242
    Mehalah 245
Barmouth, Gwynedd 144, 148
    Bridge 145–6, *147*
    harbour 145
Barrowmouth, Cumbria 181, 182
    Marchon Chemical Works 177, 179, 180–1
    pollution at 181
Beaumaris Castle, Anglesey 154
Beeching, Dr 199
Bethesda, Gwynedd 154, 158
Betjeman, Sir John 19, 89, 90, 92–3, 247
Bishop and Clerks archipelago, Dyfed 136
Black Stone, The, S. Devon: loss of *Marana*,
    1891 56
Blackchurch Rock, Devon 99
Blackmore, R. D. 103
Blackpool 166–8, 170–1
    boarding-houses 171
    Central Beach 168
    Central Pier 166, 168, 171
    Golden Mile 166, 168, 170, 171, 172
    Illuminations 167
    North Pier 166, 170–1
    Promenade 166, 167, *169*, 171
    South Pier 166, 171
    South Shore 166–7
    Tower 166, 167, 168, 170, 171, 172, 176
    trams 166, 171
Blériot, Louis 12
Borth, Dyfed 140, 141, 143
Bosherston, Dyfed 130, 134
    Broad Haven beach 130, 132
    Church Rock offshore 131, 132
    lily ponds 131, *133*
Bray Hill, Cornwall 89, 90, 93, 94
    lost village under 91

Brean Down, Somerset 107–9, *109*, 110–11
    flora and fauna 109–10
    fort 110, 111
    Iron Age settlement 107, 108
    Roman temple 107, 108
    test of Expendable Noisemaker weapon 111
Brighton 1, 13–19
    Aquarium 16
    Black Rock 19
    Brighton Pavilion 16
    Chain Pier 19
    Electric Railway 19
    Grand Hotel bombing, 1984 13
    Kemp Town 14, 15, 18, 19
    Marina 14, 19
    Marlborough House 15, 16
    Mods and Rockers riot, 1964 16
    New Steine 17
    nudist beach 18
    Old Steine 15, 16
    Palace Pier 13, 14, 16, *17*, 19
    Royal Albion Hotel 15, 16
    Royal Crescent 18
    Steine House 15, 16
    West Pier 13
Broadstairs 2, 5
    Archway House 5
    Bleak House 5
    Dickens' connection 5

Cantref-y-Gwaelod, mythical city of 88, 141
Carn Llidi, Dyfed 136, 137, 138
Carne Beacon, Cornwall 65
    legends concerning 65
Cartmel Priory, Lancs 174
Castle Ditches fort, S. Glamorgan 121
Chapel Jane, Cornwall 81
Chesil Bank, Dorset 34, 35, 36, 38
    bird life 38
Cheviot Hills 186, *187*
Chichester Harbour 20–3, *23*, 24–6
    bird life 23
    channels in 20–1, 22
    East Head 21–3 *passim*, *23*, 26
Clarach Bay Holiday Village, Dyfed 140–1
Cleadon Windmill, Tyne and Wear 193
Cleethorpes, Humberside 214, 215, 216
Cleveland Way 196
Clovelly, Devon 95–6, *97*, 98, 100
    All Saints' Church 98, 100
    'Angels' Wings' summerhouse 98
    Clovelly Court 96, 98, 99, 100
    Gallantry Bower 98
    harbour 98
    restoration work 96
Cobbett, William
    on Brighton Pavilion 16
    on Dover 11
Col-huw Beach, S. Glamorgan 117, 118, *119*, 121

Cornwall, Cape 74
  The Brisons off 74
Cosmeston Lakes Country Park, S. Glamorgan
  115–16
Cosmeston medieval village, S. Glamorgan 116
Craster family 184
Craster, Northumberland 184, 188
  Craster Tower 184, 185
  fishing at 184
Cromer, Norfolk 225, 226
  Happy Valley 227
  lighthouse 227
  museum 226
  ⸱Royal Cromer Golf Club 227
Cumbrian Coastal Way 177

Dart, River 50
  estuary 51, 53, 55
Dartmouth, Devon 50, 52
  Castle 51–2
  RN College 51, 52
  St Petrox Church 52, 53
Dawkins-Pennant, George (Lord Penrhyn) 154,
  157, 158
Dawsmere village, Lincs 224
Daymer Bay, Cornwall 90
Dee, River, Merseyside 159
Dickens, Charles
  connection with Broadstairs 5
  on Clovelly 95
  stays at Blackpool 170
Dinas Oleu, Gwynedd 146, 147
Dingerein Castle, Cornwall 66
Dover 11
  Castle 9, 11
  Citadel 10, 11, 12
  harbour 9, 11
  White Cliffs 10, 10
  World War II scene 11–12
Droskyn Point, Cornwall 84
  rock bridge 87
Dunscombe Cliff, Devon 46, 47
Dunstanburgh Castle, Northumberland 185, 186
  gatehouse 186, 187
  legend of Sir Guy the Seeker 186–8
  view from 187
Dunwich, River, Suffolk 235, 237
Dunwich, Suffolk 232, 234
  engulfed by the sea 234, 235
  history 234–5
  museum 236, 238
  solitary gravestone 235–6, 237

East Fleet, Dorset 34, 38
East Prawle, S. Devon 59
  Pig's Nose pub 59, 60
East Wittering, Sussex 20, 21
Exmoor 105, 108
Exmouth, Devon 46

Fairbourne, Dyfed 144, 145
  Railway 145, 146
Farne Islands, Northumberland 186
Faulkner, J. Meade: Moonfleet 38
Fishbourne, Sussex 22
  Roman palace 21
Flamborough Head, Humberside 201–5, 207
  Dane's Dyke 203–4
  lifeboat and shed 202, 204
  lighthouses 202, 205
  North Landing 202, 204, 205
  South Landing 205
Flamborough Village 201, 202
  castle ruins 203
  monument to men of Two Brothers 203
  St Oswald's church 203
Flat Holm Island, Bristol Channel 108, 113, 114
Fleet, River, Dorset 37, 38
  eighteenth c. smuggling 38
Fleswick Bay, Cumbria 180, 181, 182
Folkestone 7, 9
  harbour 8, 10
  relics of defences 8–9
Foreland Point, Devon 102
Fowles, John 43
  The French Lieutenant's Woman 43

Gedney Drove End, Lincs 220–4
  air bombing ranges 223, 223, 224
  Dutch seventeenth c. reclamation 221
  'marsh ague' 221
  New Inn 222, 224
  saltings 222–3, 224
  sea-wall 220, 221, 224
Gerrans Bay, Cornwall 65, 66
Glamorgan Heritage Project 121
Glan-y-môr, Dyfed 140
Gower Peninsula, W. Glamorgan 122, 127
Grange-over-Sands, Cumbria 172, 174
Grimsby, Humberside 214, 215, 217
Gurnard's Head, Cornwall 81, 82
  Hotel 82

Hallsands, S. Devon 54, 57, 59, 60
  inundated, 1917 55–6
Hamlyn, Christine 100
  work to restore Clovelly 96, 100
Heath, Edward
  connection with Broadstairs 5
Hoylake, Merseyside 159, 160, 162
  Hoyle Lake 160
  Royal Liverpool Golf Club 160, 164
Humber, River 211, 212, 215
  RSPB reserve 218
  ships 217
Humberston Fitties, Humberside 216–17
  Haile Sand Fort 217–18

Immingham, Humberside 214, 218

Jermy, Alfred 229
Jermy, Louie 229
  connection with Poppyland 230–1
  grave and inscription 231
Jesty, Benjamin 28–9
Jones, John Paul: raids Whitehaven, 1778 179

Kemp, Thomas Read 19
  plan for Kemp Town, Brighton 18
Kent, River, Lancs 172, *174*, 174, 176
Kents Bank, Lancs 172, *174*
Kilvert, Francis
  on Gurnard's Head 82–3
  on Land's End 77
  on Zennor *82*, 83
Kingsgate Castle, Kent 4
Kingsley, Charles 100
  Westward Ho! 100
Kingswear, Devon 52, *53*
  Castle 51, 52
Kynance Cove, Cornwall 68–9, 69, 70

Landewednack, Cornwall 71
Land's End 73, 75
  commercial ownership 76
  Hotel 77
  Longships lighthouse off 75, 76
  loss of *Khyber*, 1905 74
Langarrow, fall of city of 88
Langton Herring, Dorset 34, 37, 38–9
  Church 39
  Elm Tree Inn 39
Lavernock, S. Glamorgan 114
  Point 112, 114, *114*, 115
Ligger Point, Cornwall 84, 85
Little Dartmouth Farm, S. Devon 50, 53
Liverpool Bay, Merseyside 159, 160
Liverpool dockland 165
Lizard Point lighthouse, Northumberland 186
Lizard, the, Cornwall
  hidden rocks off 67–8
  Killigrew's coal-burning light 67
  lifeboat rescues from *Suevic* 70
  lighthouse 68, 70–1
  Lizard–Cadgwith lifeboat station 70, 71
  Lizard Town 68, 69, 70, 72
  St Wynwallow church 71–2
  serpentine cliffs 69–70
Llanfairfechan, Gwynedd 154, 155, *157*, 158
Llantwit Major, S. Glamorgan 120, 121
  St Illtud's church 120–1
Lleyn Peninsula, Gwynedd 140, 149, 153
  Ffynnon Fair (St Mary's Well) 152
  St Mary's Church 81, 151–2
Louth Canal, Humberside 218
  See also Tetney Lock
Lyme Regis, Dorset 43, 44
  Cobb, the 42, 43
Lynmouth, Devon 101, 106

cliff railway 101–2, 103
  disastrous flood of 1952 102–3
Lynton, Devon 101, 105
  Exmoor Museum 105
  North Cliff Walk from 101
Lyonesse 75–6, 88, 141

Margate 1–3
Marsden, Tyne and Wear 189
  Bay 189
  'Grotto, The' 189–90, 193
  Marsden Rock 190, *192*, 193
  Quarry 189, 190
Mawddach, River 144, 145, 146, *147*
Menai Strait 154, 156
  Lavan Sands 154–5
  Menai Bridge 155
Mersea Island, Essex 239–45
  East Mersea 242
  floods of 1953 242, 245
  oysters 240, 244
  West Mersea 239, 241, 242, *243*
Morecambe Bay sands, Lancs 172–6
  crossing *174*, 175–6
  guides 172, 174–5
  Hest Bank 172
Mother Meldrum's Cave, Devon 103

Nanjizal Bay, Cornwall 77
Nare Head, Cornwall 63, 65, 66
  Gull Rock off 63, 64, 65
  Middle and Outer Stones off 64, 65
  Whelps reef off 65
  wreck of *Hera*, 1914 65
National Trust 21, 50, 65, 66, 76, 100, 149
New Brighton, Merseyside 162, 164
  lighthouse 164
  Perch Rock 164, 165
  promenade 164
  Tower 164
North Foreland 1
  lighthouse 4, 5

Overstrand, Norfolk 228, 229
Oxwich, W. Glamorgan 122
  Castle 125
  Oxwich Burrows 122, 123, *124*

Padstow, Cornwall 90, 93
Pen y Cil, Lleyn Peninsula 149
Penarth, S. Glamorgan 112–13, 115, 116
  docks 113
Penhale Point, Cornwall 85
Penhale Sands, Cornwall 86, 88
  St Piran's Oratory and cell 86–7, 88
Penlee, Cornwall: lifeboat disaster 71
Penrhyn, Gwynedd 154
  Castle 154, 156, 157–8
Pentire Point, Cornwall 93

Perran Beach, Cornwall 84, 85, 86
Perranporth, Cornwall 84, 88
Polzeath, Cornwall 93
   surfing 93–4
Poppyland, Norfolk 225, 226, 227–9
   cliffs 228
   commercialization 227, 229, 230–1
   publicized by Clement Scott 225–6, 230
Port-Eynon, W. Glamorgan 122, 123
   Culver Hole 125
   Salt House 124, 125
Portloe, Cornwall 61–3, 64, 66
   beached whale 63
   fishing 61–2, 63
   Lugger Hotel 61, 62
   Ship Inn 62, 66
Prawle Point, S. Devon 54, 56, 58, 59
   loss of Lallah Rhookh, 1973 58
Purbeck, Isle of, Dorset
   Ancient Order of Purbeck Marblers and
      Stonecutters 30
   Dancing Ledge 30
   Dorset Coast Path 30, 36, 38
   Priest's Way 29
   Purbeck stone quarries 29–30, 31
   Spyway Barn 30
   West Man 31
   wreck of Halsewell, 1786 31

Ramsey Island, Dyfed 135, 136
Ramsgate 1
Ravenscar, N. Yorks 199
Ray Island, Essex 245
Rhosili, W. Glamorgan 126, 127
   beach 127, 129
   remains of Helvetia 127, 129
   Rhosili Down 127, 129
Robin Hood's Bay, N. Yorks 195–6, 197, 199,
   200
Robinson, Cedric 172, 174, 175
Rock, Cornwall 89–90, 94
Ruskin, John 148
   his Guild of St George 147–8
Russell, Dr Richard 1, 15
   'The Use of Sea-Water in Affections of the
      Glands', 1754 15

St Alban's Head, Dorset 31
   chapel of St Aldhelm 31–2
St Bees, Cumbria 182
   church of St Bees Priory 182–3
St Davids Head, Dyfed 135–6, 137
   Warrior's Dyke 136
St Donat's Head, S. Glamorgan 118
   Atlantic College 118
St Enodoc, Cornwall 89, 90
   Betjeman's grave 89, 92
   church 90–1, 92
St Govan, Dyfed 130–1

   chapel 131, 132, 133–4
St Govan's Head, Dyfed 130
St Illtud 118
   'university monastery', S. Glamorgan 117, 120
St Piran 85–6
   Oratory, Cornwall 86, 87, 88
Salcombe Regis, Devon 48
   church of St Mary and St Peter 48
Sarn Cynfelyn, Dyfed 141
Scott, Clement 227, 228, 231
   pleasure at Poppyland 227, 229
   Poppyland Papers 226, 230
   sees Poppyland become 'Bungalowland' 230–1
   verses on Poppyland, Norfolk 225, 230
Sellafield nuclear processing plant, Cumbria 177,
   182
Sennen, Cornwall 74–5, 77, 78
   Church 74, 77
   lifeboat 74–5
Shakespeare Cliff, Kent 9, 11
   appearance in King Lear 10–11
Sheppey, Isle of, Kent 246–51
   danger to wildlife in 251
   Harty, Isle of 247, 248
   Harty Marshes 248
   mud-flats 250
   Muswell Manor 248, 249
   St Thomas's church 247–8, 251
   salt-marshes 249, 250, 251
   Sayes Court Farm 246, 247, 248, 251
   sea-wall 249, 250, 251
   Shell Ness 246, 250, 250
   Shellness Hamlet 249
   Swale Channel 247, 248, 249, 250
   Swale Nature Reserve 249, 251
Sidestrand, Norfolk 229, 231
   church tower 229–30, 231
   Mill House 229, 230, 231
Sidmouth 45
Skipsea, Humberside 206
   crumbling cliffs near 206, 208, 209
Sole Bay, Battle of, 1672 235
South Cheek, N. Yorks 196
   Raven Hall Hotel 196, 198, 199
Southwold, Suffolk 233, 236
Spurn Head, Humberside 210–14
   birds 211
   Bull Sand Fort 212, 217
   children's playground mural 213, 214
   coastguard and pilot centre 213
   community at 211–12
   flora 210, 212
   lighthouses 212, 217
   mentioned by Shakespeare 211
   Yorkshire Wildlife Trust Information Centre
      212
Start Point, S. Devon 54, 55
   lighthouse 56
Steep Holm Island, Bristol Channel 110, 113

Sully Island, S. Glamorgan 112, 114, 115, 116

Tetney Lock, Louth Canal, Humberside 216, 217, 218
　Crown and Anchor 216, 218
Thanet, Isle of, Kent 1
Trebetherick, Cornwall 93
Tresilian Bay, S. Glamorgan 118
　Reynard's Cave 118
　Tresilian House 118
Trwynhwrddyn (Cape of the Ram), Dyfed 136, 137

Undercliff, Dorset-Devon 40, 41, 42, 42, 43–4, 123
　cliff composition 40
　flora and fauna 40–1
　Goat Island 44
　landslips 40, 44

Valley of Rocks, Devon 101, 103, 104, 104, 105

Walberswick, Suffolk 232–3, 234, 235, 238
　decline from sixteenth c. 233
　recovery in nineteenth c. 232, 233
　St Andrew's Church 233
Wash, the: plans for barrage 223
West Itchenor, Sussex 25
　Ship Inn 25–6
West Lyn River, Devon 101, 105
　flood of 1952 102
West Wittering, Sussex 21
Weston Mouth, Devon 48

Watch House 48
Whitburn, Tyne and Wear 191–2
　Colliery 190, 191
Whitby and Scarborough Line 199
　used as footpath 199–200
Whitehaven, Cumbria 177, 179
　Candlestick Chimney 179
　decline of coal mining 177, 179–80
　docks 177
　fine seventeenth c. buildings 177
　industry 177
　Wellington Pit disaster, 1910 179
Wirral, the, Merseyside 159, 160, 161
　Leasowe Castle 163
　Mockbeggar Wharf 163
　sea-wall 162, 162–3, 164
Wordsworth, Dorothy 101
Wordsworth, William 101, 146, 175
Worms Head, W. Glamorgan 127–8, 128, 129
　accessibility 126
　Devil's Bridge 128
　Inner Head 127, 128
　Low Neck 127, 128
　Nature Reserve 128
　Outer Head 127, 128, 129
　sea-birds 128, 129
Worth Matravers, Isle of Purbeck 27, 28, 28–9, 32
　St Nicholas of Myra church 27–8, 31

Zennor, Cornwall 79–80, 82, 83
　St Senara's church 80, 83
　Wayside Museum 80